Reproducible

Ages 5–10

The SUPER-SIZED Book of Bible Craft Gifts

Rebecca White &
Karen Whiting

ROSEKiDZ®

The Super-Sized Book of Bible Craft Gifts

Published by RoseKidz®
a division of Tyndale House Ministries
P.O. Box 3473
Peabody, Massachusetts 01961-3473 USA
www.hendricksonpublishinggroup.com

Managing Editor: Karen McGraw
Assistant Editor: Talia Messina
Contributing Editors: Lisa Larson, Nicole Viera

Front Cover Design: Drew McCall
Back Cover Design: Karen McGraw
Interior Design & Layout: Cristalle Kishi, Karen McGraw
Photographs and Illustrations: Lisa Larson, Karen McGraw

R50030
ISBN: 978-1-64938-038-8
RELIGION/Christian Ministry/Children

Printed in the United States of America
Printed September 2021

Dedication

This book is dedicated to our children:

Michael Whiting · James Whiting · Darlene Pena · Daniel Whiting · Brittany White · Ashley White

and our grandchildren:

Joseph Pena · Ethan Whiting · Elizabeth Pena · Lily Whiting · Lydia Pena · Thomas Pena · Jessie Whiting · Julia Pena · Jacob Whiting · Ezra Whiting · Layla White · and Lily Sims

All of whom we enjoyed crafting with as they've grown up.

It is also dedicated to Juliette Walsh and Kyleigh Kelly who helped us with trying out crafts ahead of time.

—Rebecca White & Karen Whiting

Table of Contents

Supplies & Tools

Having a good supply of the materials listed below will meet a great deal of your needs. A few of the crafts call for specialty items, so be sure to check the materials list for each craft.

In addition, some tools have been suggested. Some, like the scoring board, may not be necessary to complete the crafts, but can give a more polished look to the finished craft.

- ✯ **Adhesives**: Double-sided tape, liquid glue (both white and tacky), tear tape (double-sided tape that can be torn—available at craft stores), foam mounting tape, glue dots, or pop dots (glue dots that are thick to add dimension), occasionally a low-temperature glue gun (with adult supervision) or clear packing tape
- ✯ **Brads:** (a.k.a. paper fasteners) Available in a wide variety of colors and styles.
- ✯ **Cardboard**
- ✯ **Coloring & Writing Instruments**: crayons, colored pencils, gel pens, markers, etc.
- ✯ **Decorating Materials**: Beads, wiggle eyes, glitter, adhesive-backed jewels, craft-foam shapes, paper flowers, stickers, stamps and stamp pads, or anything that can be added as decoration (See Decorate It Up! on p. 13.)
- ✯ **Envelopes**: Normally A6 (regular card size) or letter size envelopes
- ✯ **Foam Core**
- ✯ **Hole Punches**
- ✯ **Index Cards**
- ✯ **Needles**: Used to punch smaller holes—a piece of cardboard under the item will help punch the holes more easily
- ✯ **Newspapers or Plastic Tablecloths**: For all the crafts, we recommend covering tables with newspapers or plastic tablecloths. This is especially important any time you are using paint with children. If you have carpet, you may want to cover the floors as well.
- ✯ **Paint**: Water-based for easy cleanup
- ✯ **Paper**: Many of the crafts work best with lightweight papers like construction paper and copy paper. Other papers include:
  - **Acetate**: Found in office-supply stores for making transparencies, report covers, or in packaging
  - **Cardstock**: A variety of colors and patterns as well as weights; when specifically call for, heavy cardstock should be 100 lb. or heavier to work properly
  - **Patterned Paper**: Decorative paper, available in craft stores in letter and 12x12-inch sizes
  - **Tissue Paper**
  - **Wrapping Paper**
- ✯ **Paper Bowls, Cups, Plates**
- ✯ **Paper Cutting Tools**: For many crafts, scissors and rulers are required. If an adult leader or helper is doing a lot of the prep, a paper cutter will make this easier. (See Paper Crafting Techniques, p. 9.)
  In addition, keep a supply of scissors on hand for children to use with all the crafts.
- ✯ **Paper Straws**
- ✯ **Paperclips**
- ✯ **Pipe Cleaners**
- ✯ **Poster Board**
- ✯ **Ribbon**
- ✯ **Rulers** Keep a supply on hand for all the crafts.
- ✯ **Scoring Board**: Available at craft stores (See Paper Crafting Techniques, p. 9.)
- ✯ **Skewers** or **Toothpicks**: Length can matter in many of the crafts
- ✯ **Stapler** and lots of staples, available in lots of colors
- ✯ **Thread**: Basic white sewing thread is best, but you can use monofilament (fishing line) instead.
- ✯ **Velcro®** or adhesive hook-and-loop dots and squares
- ✯ **Yarn** or **String**

Paper Crafting Techniques

Knowing some of the basic techniques of working with paper will result in sharper looking projects. Practice the techniques below so that you can instruct children in how to do them when the technique is called for in a craft.

Paper Grain

Paper grain is the direction in which its fibers align. All paper has a grain, although it makes a bigger difference in cardstock. Hold a paper on one edge and see if it naturally curves down. Then turn the paper ninety degrees and hold it on the edge. See if it naturally curves down. Whichever way it curves more naturally is the grain of the paper. If you trim and score a paper with the grain it will fold more easily.

Folding and Scoring Paper

Everyone knows how to fold a piece of paper. But scoring the paper first creates a crease that allows the paper to fold more easily and results in a better looking line.

To score a fold, use a stylus and a ruler. Press the ruler down firmly on the paper at the place you want a fold. Then take the stylus and draw a line along the ruler's edge. Press down firmly enough to create a valley in the paper to allow the paper to fold easily, but not so firmly you make a hole!

Here are some items you can use instead of a stylus

- Flat side of a knife
- Pen or pencil
- Toothpick or skewer
- Back of scissors
- Ruler
- Bone folder
- Paperclip
- Scoring board (pictured above)

Note: Crafts which require scoring will indicate "Scoring materials" in the **What You Need** list. If you have a scoring board, use that. If not, follow the directions above, using the suggested tools.

Quick Tip

When cutting out shapes with scissors, you will have more control if you hold the scissors in position and move the paper.

Cutting Slits or Shapes in the Center of a Paper

To use a paper trimmer to cut a slit into a sheet of paper, place the paper under the trimmer where you need the slit and move the blade to the beginning of the slit. Then put it down and push the blade to the end of the slit.

If you need a shape other than a straight line, poke a hole into the center of the shape with the point of your scissors, and then cut the shape out from the inside (see image at right).

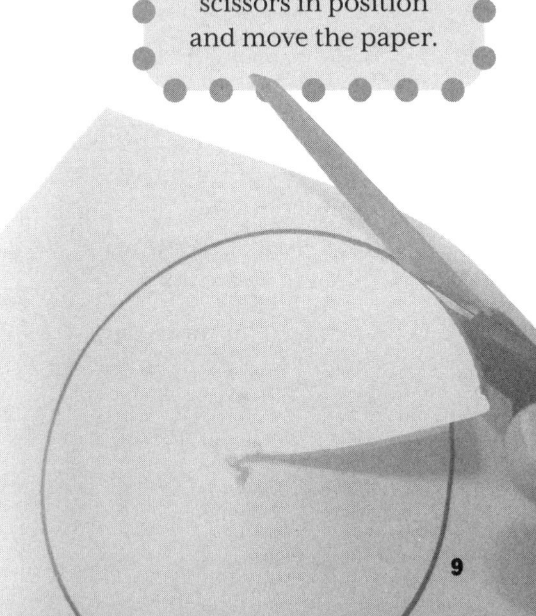

How to Use This Book

This book is packed with crafts that make wonderful gifts. This article will tell you how to understand the layout of the instructions for the crafts.

Teaching Tip

It's a good idea to complete each craft yourself ahead of time, before leading the children to make the craft. That way, not only will you be better able to give instructions and help, but you will have a sample of the craft for children to use as a reference as they work.

Outreach Ideas

Each section begins with a description of the craft as well as Outreach Ideas to put the crafts to practical use.

Age Level

This indicates for which age level the craft is most appropriate:

☆ means the craft is appropriate for younger elementary age levels.

★ means the craft is appropriate for older elementary age levels.

☆★ means the craft is appropriate for ALL elementary age levels.

Scripture

There are Bible verses connected to each craft. It's important to talk about the Scripture with children. Begin by reading the passage aloud.

What It's All About

This section has guided conversations you can use with children to connect the activity to the craft. Throughout the book, text set in **bold** type is to be spoken aloud.

What You Need and Preparation

Before class, gather the items from the "What You Need" list and follow the instructions under "Preparation." Your gathering of materials will be easier or in many cases unnecessary if you have already collected the "Supplies & Tools" listed on page 8.

Unless otherwise indicated, all directions for photocopying patterns assumes they will be photocopied onto regular white copy paper.

What Children Do

Instruct children in the easy step-by-step instructions to complete the activity.

Laminate It!

Some of the patterns and diagrams are designed to be photocopied and shared between children. Others may be used in more than one craft. In either case, laminating the cards can make them more durable.

Instead of laminating, you could cover patterns and diagrams with clear Con-Tact paper or clear packing tape.

Optional and Alternate Ideas

Occasionally, there will be optional techniques or supplies, or alternate ideas for the crafts. Choose what will work best for the children making the crafts.

S.T.E.A.M. Lesson Extensions

At the back of the book are several pages of Lesson Extensions. These are ideas to further the learning of crafts in the areas of Science Technology Engineering Art and Mathematics. Use the suggested ideas as part of the classroom learning, or send them home with kids to do at home with their families.

Greeting Cards

Opening the mailbox and finding a card is exciting! It can light up our day and give us a warm fuzzy feeling if the words are kind or silly. It's also a rare treasure to get such joyful mail. Most people use the speed of phone calls, text messages, and emails. Handwritten messages show someone cares. Making a card is an expression of caring, a gift of kindness.

The Apostle Paul took the time to write and send letters.

HERE IS MY GREETING IN MY OWN HANDWRITING—PAUL. 1 CORINTHIANS 16:21

The letters Paul wrote are called *epistles*. These epistles form many of the books in the New Testament. In writing his epistles, Paul dictated to scribes, called *amanuenses* (uh-MAN-yoo-ehn-sees), who would write down his words. Then, at the end of the letter, Paul would take the pen in hand to write a few closing thoughts in his own handwriting. It was a way to validate that the words written by scribe were correct, and also to give extra meaning to those last few, handwritten thoughts.

Paul wrote words to praise people, spoke of praying for them, and expressed love for the people who would read the letters. Paul shared his faith in Jesus when he wrote to people—both by hand or by scribe.

Make cards and think about what to write in them. Give cards to friends who are sick, feel sad or bad, to celebrate a special day, or just to say hello. You don't need a holiday to spread cheer. You can do it every day with handmade cards. Learn new skills in how you cut, fold, and decorate cards to make them special.

Outreach Ideas

Cards are great for sharing words of encouragement, love, the good news about Jesus, or other positive messages.

Here are a few outreach ideas for the crafts in this section:

- Make cards for groups like a military base or nursing home. Be sure to include an encouraging message inside.
- Send a special hand-written greeting to someone with a card created especially for them.
- Make a card as a gift that someone else can send. Leave the inside of the card blank. Consider gifting the card to a women's shelter or other place where people do not have money. If you do, be sure to include a stamped envelope in case they wish to mail the card.
- Make a card as a group to send expressions of love and care to someone from your class or church who is ill or struggling.

Basic Cards & Embellishments

Age Level: ☆★

In the beginning the Word already existed. The Word was with God, and the Word was God. He existed in the beginning with God. God created everything through him, and nothing was created except through him. The Word gave life to everything that was created, and his life brought light to everyone. JOHN 1:1–4

What It's All About

The Word of God is powerful. Our words also have power, so be careful using words in writing and speaking.

Make different cards to match the giver and the reason for the card. They might be funny or pretty; filled with hope to perk up someone's day, filled with silliness to bring laughter, or filled with words that show you care about a tough time the person is going through. You want to encourage them so take time to write thoughtful words.

To make a basic card, simply score and fold a piece of cardstock in half. Then, decorate it and add a message.

Alternate Ideas

- You can also fold the card off center, so that the top of the card is not as wide as the inside and decorate the edge that shows.
- Simple decorations can be a small photo or short handwritten message on the cover, such as Happy Birthday or Get Well Soon. Adding little sparkles like glitter and sequins are called embellishments or decorations.
- Also, you can cut your card to fit inside an envelope. See pages 14–15 for ideas on decorating envelopes.

Note: Mailing a card with anything that is not flat (like a glued-on jewel) will add cost to mail.

Follow the directions below to make the birthday card pictured above right.

What You Need

- Happy Birthday Card Patterns (p. 13)
- Paper Cutting Tools (see p. 8)
- Coloring & Writing Instruments (see p. 8)
- Cardstock in white, yellow, and at least five other colors
- 10 wiggle eyes for each child

Preparation

On white cardstock, photocopy Happy Birthday Card Patterns, making one for each child.

What Children Do

1. Fold a piece of cardstock in half.
2. From other colors of cardstock, use a pencil and ruler to measure and draw lines for five candles. You can use all the same color or make one candle in each of five different colors. Cut out five strips of paper approximately 1-inch wide and at least 3 inches shorter than the height of your card. Cut out (image a.).
3. Glue candles onto the front of your card. They don't have to be straight up and down.

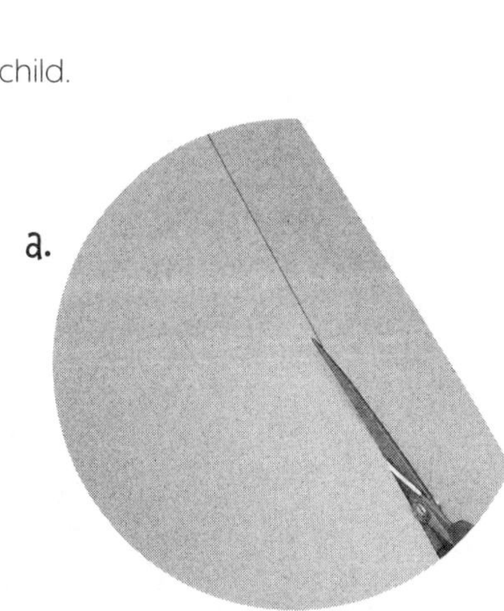

a.

4. Color flame patterns, cut out, and glue to the tops of the candles.
5. Cut out and draw decorations on the "Happy Birthday!" message paper. Glue on top of candles.
6. Glue two wiggle eyes to each candle, under the flame.

Decorate It Up!

Walk through a craft store and you'll see lots of sparkle to add a little something extra to cards. Keep a good supply of these decorating materials for children to use as they make cards.

- Add buttons to make eyes or a nose on an animal you've drawn. Group buttons to form a letter. They can become wheels of a vehicle or just be a colorful decoration. They also make great centers for flowers.
- Add sparkle with glitter.
- Brads (paper fasteners) are sold in many colors, shapes, and sizes. Use them to add a bow or piece of ribbon or just to add color to a card.
- Shapes cut from scrap paper or magazine cutouts add a new depth and more color.
- Ribbons can be added for a special touch. Tie a bow or just add a strip of ribbon across the card to add a splash of color.
- Rhinestones are another fun way to add sparkle and shine. You can buy them in different shapes, use them to make a flower, and even add them as a period for a sentence.

Happy Birthday Card Patterns

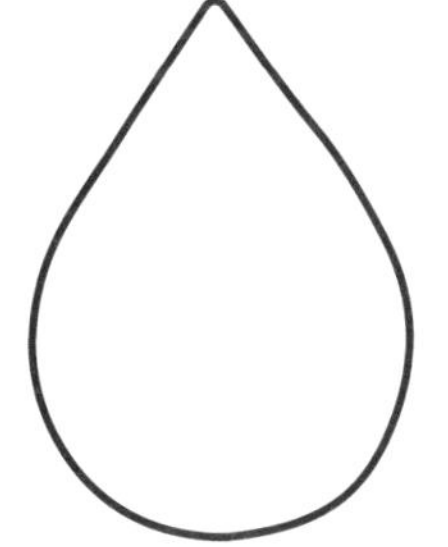
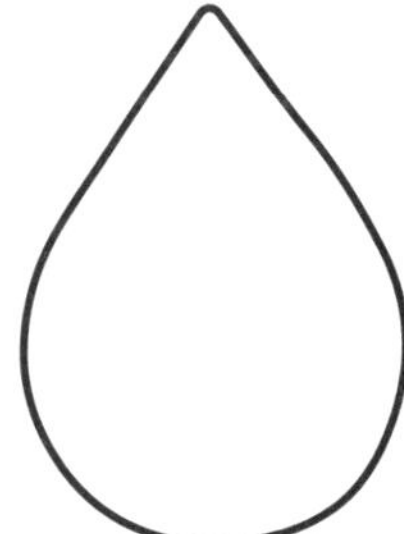
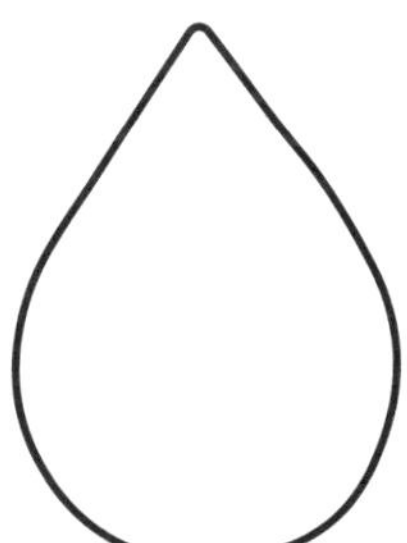
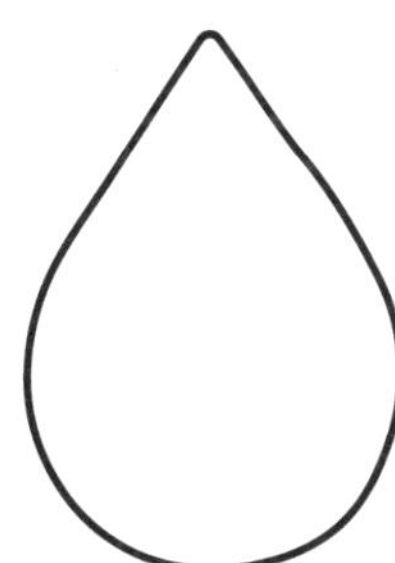
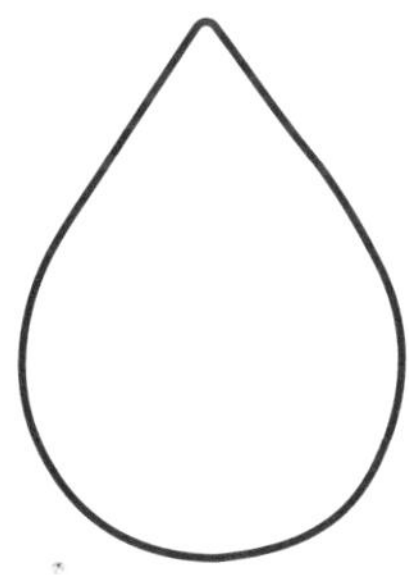

HAPPY BIRTHDAY!

The Envelope Please

Age Level: ☆★

This letter is from Paul and Timothy, slaves of Christ Jesus. I am writing to all of God's holy people in Philippi who belong to Christ Jesus, including the church leaders and deacons. May God our Father and the Lord Jesus Christ give you grace and peace. Every time I think of you, I give thanks to my God. PHILIPPIANS 1:1–3

What It's All About

At the beginning of the book of Philippians, Paul shared to whom he was sending this letter. For us, when we mail a letter, the envelope does that. The envelope is the first thing someone sees when you send a card so make it show that you care. Little touches such as decorating an envelope give a welcome before the card is opened.

What You Need

- Addressing an Envelope (p. 15)
- Coloring & Writing Instruments (see p. 8)
- Envelope, one for each child

Preparation

Photocopy the Addressing an Envelope, making one copy for each child.

What Children Do

1. Referring to Addressing an Envelope as needed, write your return address in the top left corner of the flat side (not the side you close and seal).
2. Print the address of the person who will receive the card (the recipient) in the middle of the envelope.
   - On the top line write the title (see What's in a Title above) and name of the person.
   - On the second and third lines write out the street address or post-office box number.
   - On the next line write the city and state two-letter abbreviation and then the zip code.

What's in a Title?

A title, like *Mr.*, *Miss*, *Ms.* or *Mrs.*, shows respect. Other titles include *Dr.* for doctor, *Pastor* or *Reverend*, and military ranks such as *Admiral* or *Captain*. Many titles such as doctor are earned by years of study and hard work. Using titles shows your good manners. When you write to a good friend, you can simply write their name.

Optional: Draw on both sides of the envelope, attach stickers, or decorate the flap, such as turning it into an animal face.

Follow the directions on page 15 to make this cute Bear Envelope.

Bear Envelope

What You Need

- Bear Envelope Pattern (below)
- Paper Cutting Tools (see p. 8)
- Beige, white, or light gray paper (any type of paper will work, but if it's textured, that's even better!)
- Glue
- Brown, gray, or white envelope, one for each child
- Markers

Optional

- 2 wiggle eyes or black circle stickers for each child

Preparation

On beige, white, or light gray paper, photocopy Bear Envelope Pattern, making one for each child. **Note:** Depending on the size of your envelopes, you may have to enlarge or shrink the pattern to fit. Test the size before you make your copies.

What Children Do

1. Cut out Bear Envelope Pattern and glue to envelope under the flap.
2. On envelope flap, use markers to draw two eyes.

Optional: Instead of drawing eyes, glue two wiggle eyes or black circle stickers to the envelope flap.

Bear Envelope Pattern

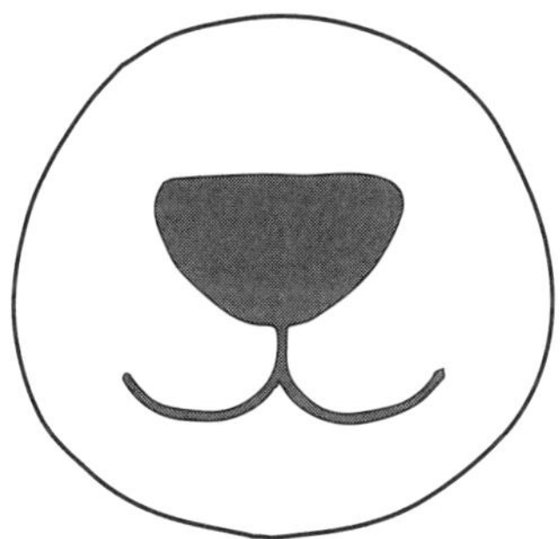
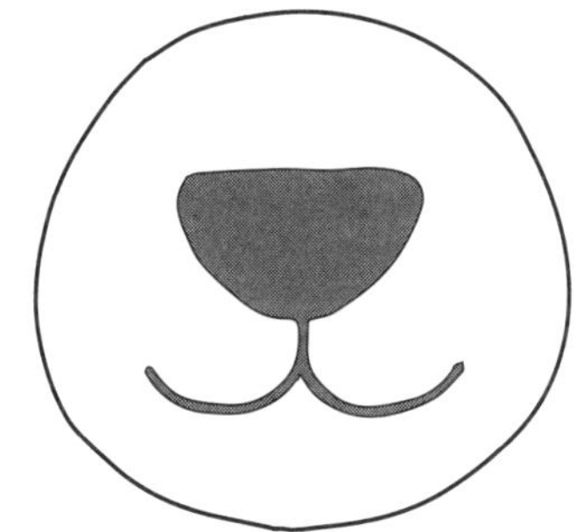
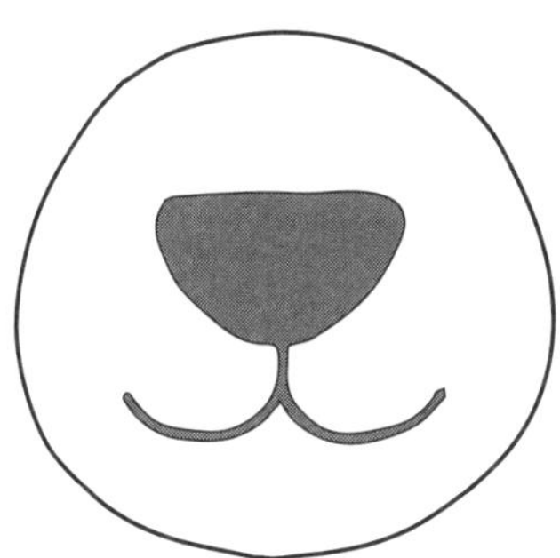

Addressing an Envelope

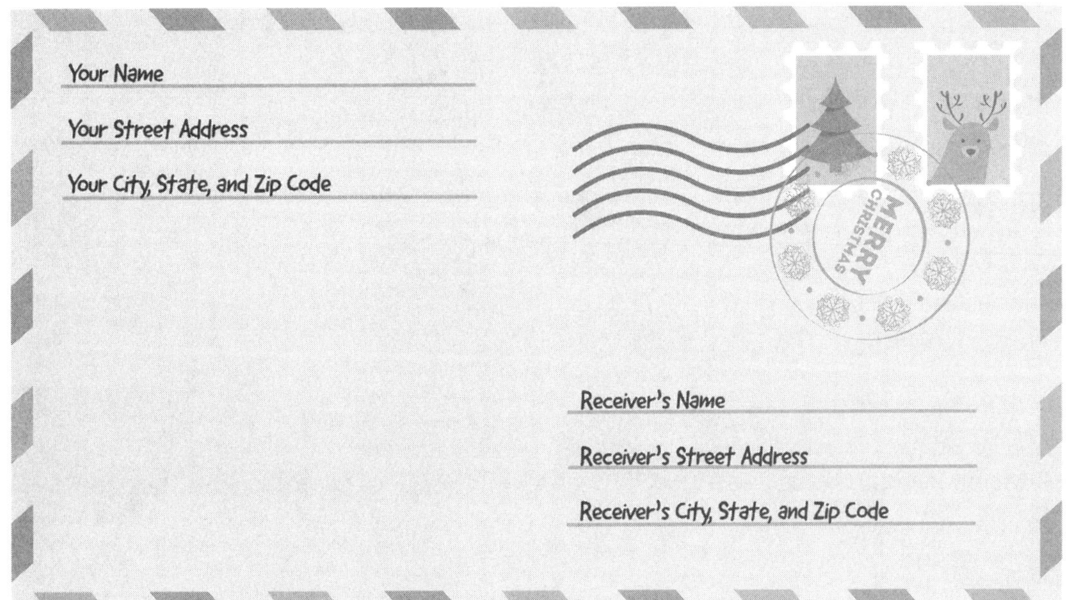

Tunnel Greeting Cards

Age Level: ★

What It's All About

The secret is in the fold. These tunnel greeting cards have three folds and a cutout which make a fun pop-up window. A message or artwork can be seen through the window.

These are the basic materials and instructions you will need to make all of the tunnel greeting cards described on pages 16–20. If a specific card needs additional materials, those will be listed with the directions for that card.

On the following pages are materials and instructions for building off the basic card to make a variety of different tunnel greeting cards.

Basic Tunnel Card Instructions

What You Need

- Folding Pattern (p. 17)
- Paper Cutting Tools (see p. 8)
- Scoring materials (see p. 9)
- Cardstock
- Pencils
- Markers
- Double-sided tape or glue

Optional

- Die-cut for tunnel opening
- Decorating materials (glitter, stamps and stamp pads, stickers, adhesive gems, wiggle eyes, etc.)

This is an example of the Heart Tunnel Card. Instructions for making this card begin on page 18.

Preparation

Photocopy Folding Pattern, making one copy for every two or three children to refer to.

Note: You may want to laminate the patterns if you will be making several tunnel greeting cards. Laminating the pattern will make it last longer (see Laminate It on p. 10).

Cut the following, making one for each child, or children choose cardstock and use scissors and rulers to cut for themselves:

Note: For simplification, in this example, the cover will be referred to as white cardstock and the inside of the card as red cardstock. You can use whatever colors you wish.

- One 5½x8½-inch piece of white cardstock for the outside cover
- One 5½x8½-inch piece of red cardstock for the inside of card

What Children Do

Make the Card Cover

1. Score and fold the white cardstock (for the outside cover) in half, making a 5½x4¼-inch card (image a). The right side is the front of the card.

a.

Make the Inside of the Card

2. Follow the measurements on the Folding Pattern (p. 17) and use the scoring materials you have to score three lines on the red cardstock (the inside of the card).
3. Fold red cardstock in half, along line B.

4. Fold lines A and C in the opposite direction from the first fold (image b).

Note: If you look from the top or bottom edge, the red cardstock piece should look like an *M* (Or a *W*, depending on which way it's sitting!) (image c).

b.

Make the Tunnel Opening

5. On red cardstock, center a pattern on line B (the center fold). Trace pattern and use scissors to cut out.
6. Place the red cardstock on top of the *inside* of the white cardstock piece (the card cover). (You don't want to trace on the outside of the card!)
7. Use a pencil to lightly trace the shape on the inside of the card cover.

c.

Add the Message or Decoration

8. Remove the red cardstock and add a message or decorate the inside of the shape you traced on the white cardstock. This will be seen through the card's tunnel when the card is opened. See Meaningful Messages and Message Center on pages 21–22.

d.

Assemble the Card

9. Once again, place the red cardstock on top of the white cardstock. You should see your message inside the cut opening. Use double-sided tape or glue to attach the outside flaps of the red cardstock to the white cardstock (image d)

Optional: Children use decorating materials to decorate cards.

Folding Pattern

for Tunnel Greeting Cards

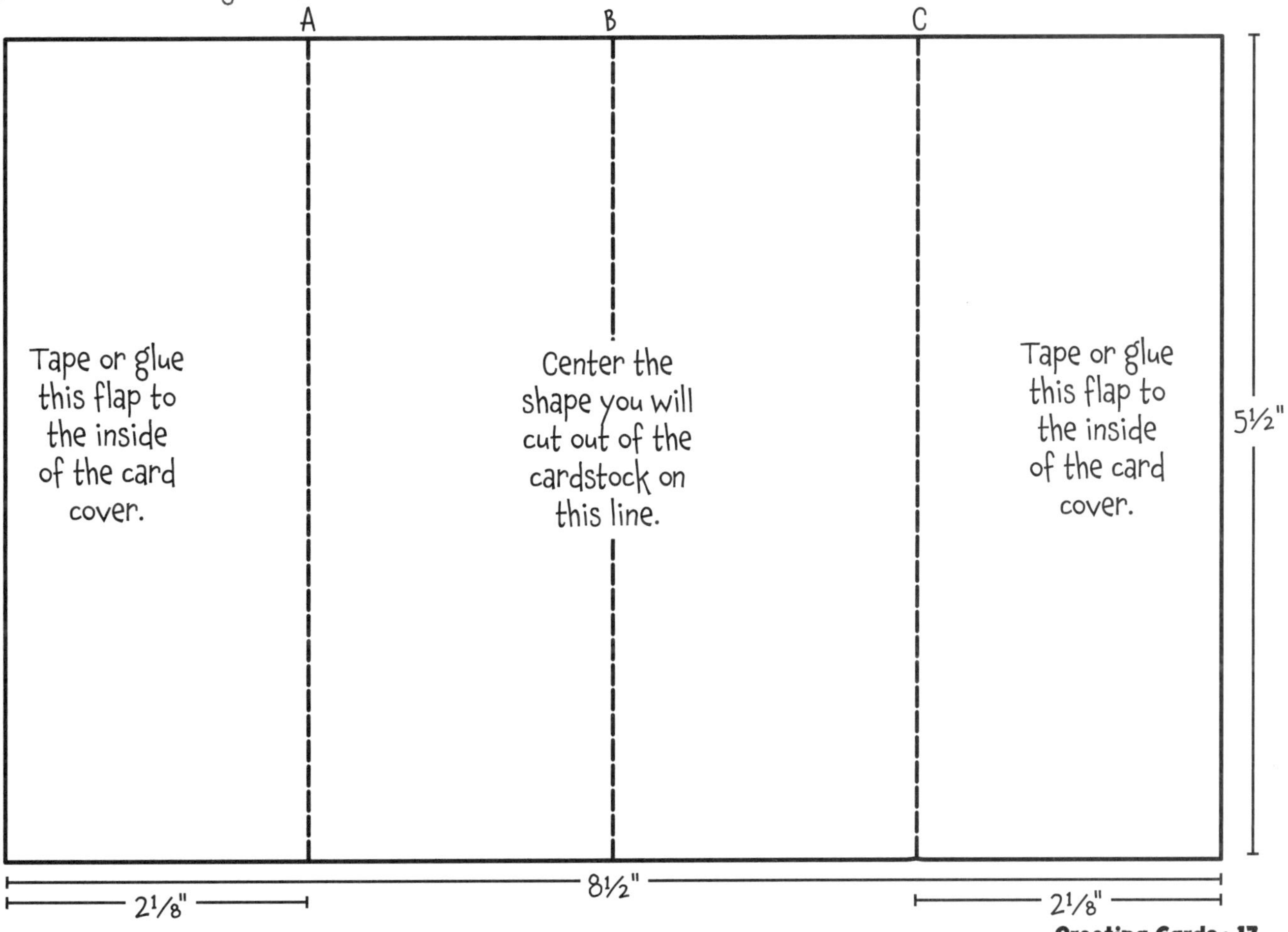

A B C

Tape or glue this flap to the inside of the card cover.

Center the shape you will cut out of the cardstock on this line.

Tape or glue this flap to the inside of the card cover.

5½"

8½"

2⅛" 2⅛"

Heart Tunnel Card

That very night the believers sent Paul and Silas to Berea. When they arrived there, they went to the Jewish synagogue. And the people of Berea were more open-minded than those in Thessalonica, and they listened eagerly to Paul's message. They searched the Scriptures day after day to see if Paul and Silas were teaching the truth. ACTS 17:10–11

What It's All About

We should rejoice like the Bereans did when we receive messages and read them carefully. We're going to make cards that send a message of love and give the recipient a reason to rejoice.

What You Need

- Folding Pattern (p. 17)
- Heart Tunnel Card Patterns (p. 19)
- Paper Cutting Tools (see p. 8)
- Scoring materials (see p. 9)
- Coloring & Writing Instruments (see p. 8)
- Cardstock in white, red, and pink
- Double-sided tape or glue, acid-free

Optional

- Decorating materials (glitter, stamps and stamp pads, stickers, adhesive gems, etc.)

Preparation

Photocopy Heart Tunnel Card Patterns, making one set for every two or three children. There are six sets of Heart Tunnel Card Patterns, enough for twelve to eighteen children. You may want to laminate the patterns for durability (see Laminate It on p. 10).

Cut the following, making one for each child, or children choose cardstock and use scissors and rulers to cut for themselves:

- One 5½x8½-inch piece of white cardstock for the outside cover
- One 5½x8½-inch piece of red cardstock for the inside of card

What Children Do

Make the Basic Card

1. Follow instructions on pages 16–17 to Make the Card Cover, using the prepared white cardstock and to Make the Inside of the Card using the prepared red cardstock.

Make the Tunnel Opening

2. On the middle fold of the red cardstock, center the smaller heart from Heart Frame Pattern, use a pencil to trace it (image a), and cut out to make the tunnel opening (image b).

a.

b.

Add the Message or Decoration

c.

3. Lay the white cardstock open on the table, inside up, and place the red tunnel cardstock over it.
4. Trace the heart opening on the cover, remove the red cardstock, and write a message or decorate the heart. You could write, "I love you," "My heart always has room for you!" or whatever message you wish.

Frame for Heart Opening

5. Use larger heart from Heart Frame Pattern to cut a frame for heart opening from the pink cardstock. Don't forget to cut out the center of the frame (image c).
6. Fold frame in half (so it will bend when the card opens) and glue over the heart opening on red cardstock.

Assemble the Card

7. On the inside of the white folded card, tape or glue only the side flaps of the red cardstock to the sides of the white card, as shown on the Folding Pattern paper.

Optional: Children use decorating materials to decorate cards.

Heart Tunnel Card Patterns

Wreath Tunnel Card

Age Level: ★

All athletes are disciplined in their training. They do it to win a prize that will fade away, but we do it for an eternal prize. 1 CORINTHIANS 9:25

What It's All About

Our Bible verse talks about a prize athletes would win. Greeks used wreaths made from branches (usually from the laural tree) as crowns to honor someone such as the winner of a race or a leader. We use wreaths at Christmas time to remember God's eternal love that has no beginning or end.

What You Need

- Folding Pattern (p. 17)
- Wreath Tunnel Card Patterns (p. 21)
- Paper Cutting Tools (see p. 8)
- Scoring materials (see p. 9)
- Cardstock in green and two other colors
- Pencils
- Markers

Optional

- Provide additional colors of cardstock to allow children to customize the color of their cards.

Preparation

Photocopy Wreath Tunnel Card Patterns, making one copy for each child. There are two sets of Wreath Tunnel Card Patterns.

Cut the following, making one for each child, or children choose their cardstock and use scissors to cut for themselves:

- One 5½x8½-inch piece of cardstock for the outside cover
- One 5½x8½-inch piece of a different color of cardstock for the inside of card

What Children Do

Make the Basic Card

1. Follow instructions on pages 16–17 to Make the Card Cover, using the prepared cardstock cover and to Make the Inside of the Card using the prepared cardstock for the inside of the card.

Make the Tunnel Opening

2. On the middle fold of the cardstock you prepared for the inside of your card center the circle from Wreath Frame Patterns, use a pencil to trace it, and cut out to make the tunnel opening.

   Hint: It will help you cut out and center the circle if you first fold it in half.

a.

3. Using green cardstock, trace the leaf pattern from Wreath Frame Patterns, and cut out enough leaves to encircle the tunnel opening you cut (image a). Glue leaves around the opening.
4. Lay the cover cardstock open on the table and place the tunnel cardstock over it.
5. Trace tunnel opening on the inside of the cover. Decorate inside opening.
   - Draw a picture of baby Jesus.
   - Write "John 3:16," "Congrats on your win!" or other text of your choosing.

Wreath Tunnel Card Patterns

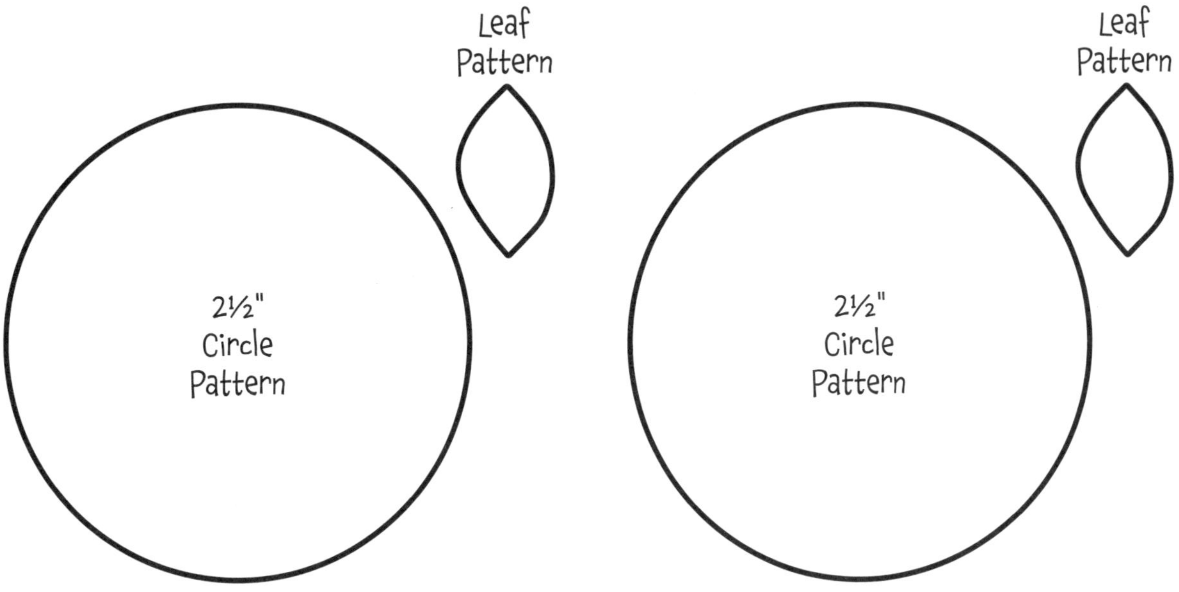

Meaningful Messages

Age Level: ☆★

Be happy with those who are happy, and weep with those who weep. ROMANS 12:15

What It's All About

Words have the power to hurt or heal. They can show people that we care and want to be happy with them over good news and sad with them over bad news. That's called empathy. Our verse, Romans 12:15 is all about having empathy for others.

It can be hard to choose the words to say to someone, especially when someone you care about is hurting. When you want to send a card to someone, think of what to say before you write the message.

- **To become more empathetic think of the times you have felt different emotions. Then consider how your friend feels.**
- **Sometimes a problem is more than you can imagine. That's okay. Those are times to admit the truth with, "I cannot imagine how you feel but I care about you."**

Preparation

Photocopy Message Center on page 22, making one copy for each child.

Message Center

In the table below are several occasions for which you might want to send a card to show someone you care. For each occasion, there are suggested messages and ways to decorate a card.

Occasion	Suggestions
Get Well	✮ Use a pun to make them laugh. For example, use a picture of a whale and write "Get Whale Soon" (see image above). ✮ "I hope you FEEL better soon." Glue a piece of soft fabric around the words.
Missing You	✮ "A piece of me is missing. It's you!" Decorate card with a puzzle piece. ✮ Write out the alphabet without the letter *U* and add: "Missing You!"
Congratulations and Happy Days	✮ "You are so deserving, princess!" Decorate card with a crown. ✮ "You're a winner!" Draw or glue a picture of a trophy. ✮ "ConGRADulations!" Decorate with a graduation cap. ✮ "You Shine!" Add stars or a sun. ✮ "I'm Dancing with Joy over Your Good News!" Include dancing shoes, feet, or musical notes. ✮ "High 5!" Trace your hand.
Sympathy or Loss **Note:** For all the sympathy cards, keep decorations simple and the colors soft and soothing. Perhaps pictures of flowers or a photo of the person who has passed away.	✮ "I'm sorry for your loss." ✮ "I can't imagine your pain. I'm ready with hugs whenever you need them." ✮ "Death is so sad. I'm sure you miss that person so much." ✮ "I am praying for you."
Friendship and Just Because I Care	✮ "Letting you know that I care about you!" Add a drawing or photo of you and your friend together. ✮ "God loves you and I do too!" Add lots of hearts. ✮ "Thumbs up! Let's get together." Trace your thumb or draw a hand giving a thumbs-up sign. ✮ "Your friendship warms me up!" Draw a face and glue around the face fabric to look like a blanket. Or draw a cup of steaming hot chocolate. ✮ "Your smile makes my day!" Add a smiling mouth or face.
Cancer or Other Serious Illness	✮ "I'm praying for you!" Draw praying hands. ✮ "The world is a better place because of you!" Add a drawing or glue on a picture of a globe. ✮ "I admire your courage. Keep smiling!" Add a smiling mouth or face.

Twirling Turtle Card

Age Level: ★

Praise the Lord from the earth, you creatures of the ocean depths. . . . wild animals and all livestock, small scurrying animals and birds, kings of the earth and all people, rulers and judges of the earth. PSALM 148:7,10–11

What It's All About

Praise God and celebrate the wonderful creatures he made! Let a twirling card remind others that you care about them. The instructions below are for making a twirling turtle card. *(Show sample card you made.)* **Using your own pictures, you could make additional twirling cards featuring any image you want.**

What You Need

- Twirling Turtle Patterns (p. 24)
- Paper Cutting Tools (see p. 8)
- Scoring materials (see p. 9)
- Colored cardstock, letter-sized (8½x11 inches)
- Pencils
- Thread, thin yarn, or monofilament fiber (fishing line)
- Transparent tape
- Glue

Preparation

On colored cardstock, photocopy Twirling Turtle Patterns, making one for each child. Use a variety of colors.

What Children Do

Make the Card

1. Score a sheet of cardstock down the middle and fold in half, making a card that is 5½x8½ inches in size.

Make a Circle Window

2. Choose a color of cardstock that is a different from your card. Cut out 3½-inch Circle Pattern.
3. Use pencil to trace the circle in the middle front of the card, about ½ inch from the top edge.
4. Cut out the traced circle to make a window opening on the front of the card. **Tip:** Poke a hole into the center of the shape with the point of your scissors, and then cut the shape out from the inside (see p. 9).

Assemble the Twirling Shape

5. Cut out the two Turtle Patterns.
   Optional: Trade a Turtle Pattern with someone else so you both have two differently colored Turtle Patterns.
6. Cut a piece of thread, thin yarn, or monofilament a few inches larger than the circle opening in your card.
7. Lay one Turtle Pattern facedown on table. Make sure the head is at the top. Place the thread in the center of the circle, running from top to bottom of the circle. Tape in place (image a).
8. Place the second Turtle Pattern faceup over the first circle. Make sure the head is at the top. Pinching the pieces together, pick up and check to make sure both sides have the head facing the same direction. Then, glue circles together, sandwiching thread in the middle (image b). This is your Twirling Turtle!

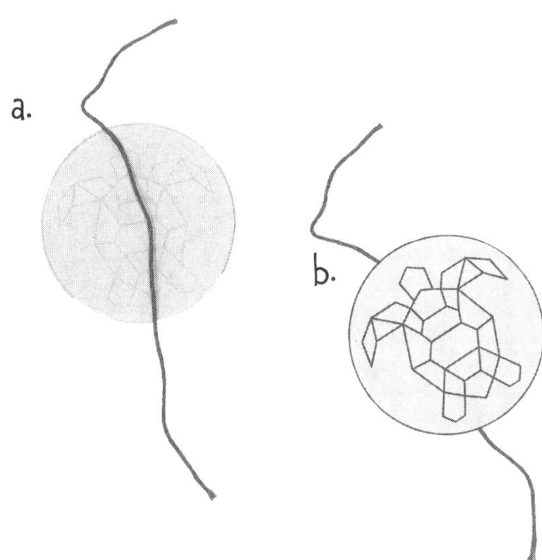

Assemble the Twirling Creature Card

9. Open the card, and place the Twirling Turtle in the center of the circular window. Make sure the turtle's head is up (or down if you want).
10. Tape the thread so that it is going up and down through the center of the circular window in your card (image c). Trim off any excess thread.
11. Cut a piece of cardstock to fit under the twirling turtle on the front of your card. On it, write a message. It could be something like, "Little creatures make the world spin with joy! Help care for them."
12. Glue message to front of card under twirling turtle (image d).

Optional: Cut a slightly larger piece of a contrasting color of cardstock and glue it under the message (image d).

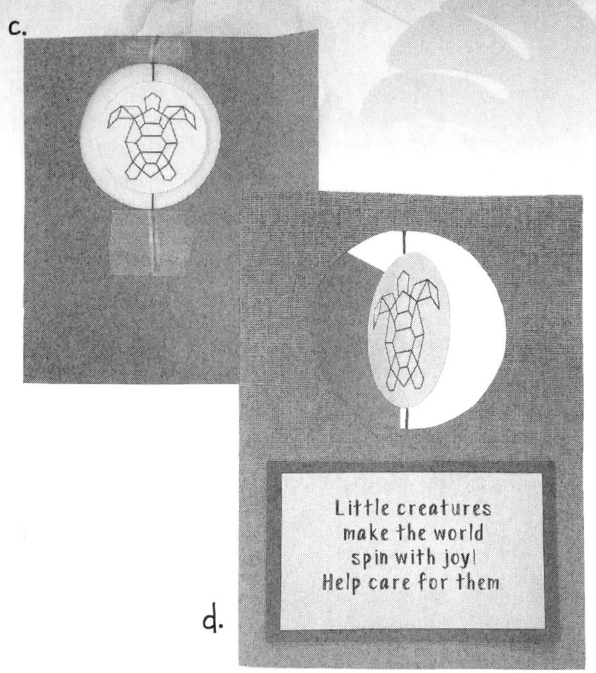

Twirling Turtle Patterns

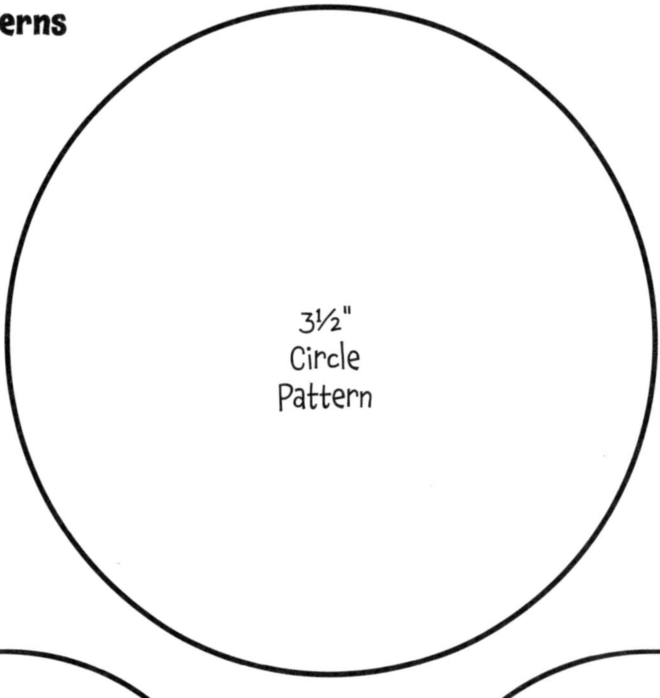

3½"
Circle
Pattern

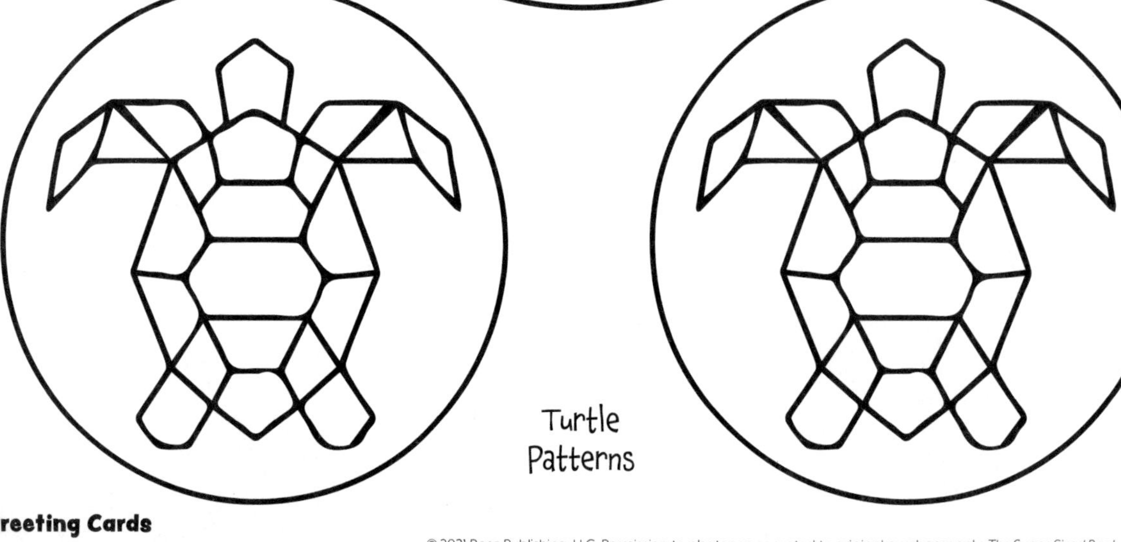

Turtle
Patterns

Easel Friendship Card

Age Level: ★

A friend is always loyal, and a brother is born to help in time of need. PROVERBS 17:17

What It's All About

Friends can always be kind, loving to one another, and stand up for each other. An easel stands up so people can see the artwork. Add a photo with your friend and give it as a gift to say thanks for being your friend.

What You Need

- Easel Card Patterns (p. 26)
- Paper Cutting Tools (see p. 8)
- Scoring materials (see p. 9)
- Coloring & Writing Instruments (see p. 8)
- Colored cardstock
- Pencils
- Glue
- Pop dots or foam dots

Preparation

Photocopy Easel Card Patterns, making one for every two or three children. You may want to laminate the patterns for durability (see Laminate It on p. 10).

Cut the following, making one for each child, or children choose their cardstock and use scissors and rulers to cut for themselves:

- One 4½x9-inch piece of cardstock

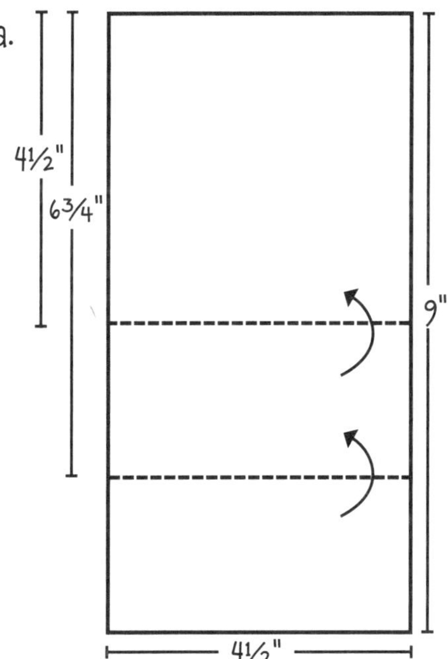

What Children Do

Making the Base and Stand

1. Score a fold line across the cardstock at 4½ inches and 6¾ inches (image a).
2. Fold both scores in the same direction (see arrows on image a).
3. The long, unfolded part of the card is the bottom of the card. Check that the folded sections form a triangle that stands up above the base (see image of finished card, at top right). This triangle is the easel or stand. It is also the front cover of your card.

Adding a Shape to the Stand

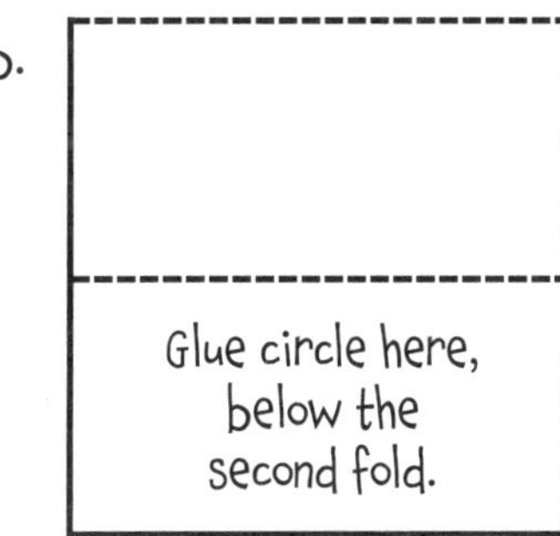

4. Use Circle Pattern to trace and cut out a 4-inch circle from cardstock.
5. Decorate the circle with a message; or alternatively, stickers, photo, or drawing.
6. Lay card flat on table with the folded edge at the top (image b).
7. *It's important that you do not glue the entire back of the card down to the front!* If you do glue the entire circle, the card will not be able to form an easel.
8. Put double-stick tape or glue on the bottom half of the circle. Center circle on front of card so that only the portion of the cover beneath the second fold (image b).

Decorate the Easel's Base

9. Choose either an Oval Message Pattern or Rectangle Message Pattern. On a piece of cardstock, trace the pattern and cut a piece of cardstock.
10. Add a message to this cutout. Write something like "You are an outstanding friend" or "Thanks for such an outstanding gift." **Optional:** Write your message on a separate sheet of paper, or type it on a computer and print out (image c). Trim the message to fit and glue to the message cutout you made from cardstock.
11. Use pop dots or foam dots to attach the cutout to the base of the card, in front of the triangle stand. Tucking the bottom edge of the triangle behind this piece helps the triangle stand upright.
12. You can write an additional message on the inside of the card, above the message cutout you attached in Step 11.
13. Untuck the bottom edge of the easel to close card. Now you can hand the card to your friend or place it in an envelope for mailing.

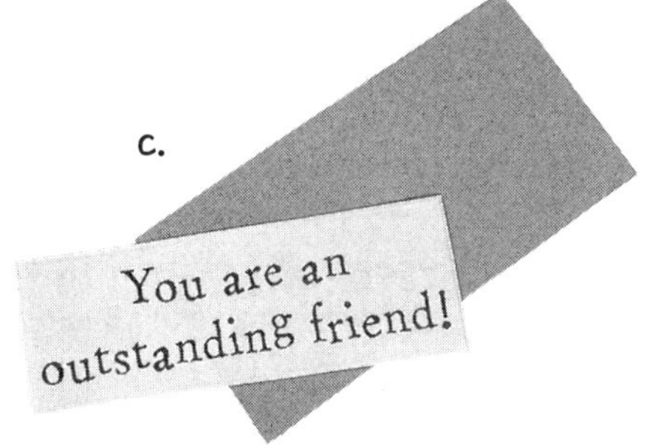

Easel Card Patterns

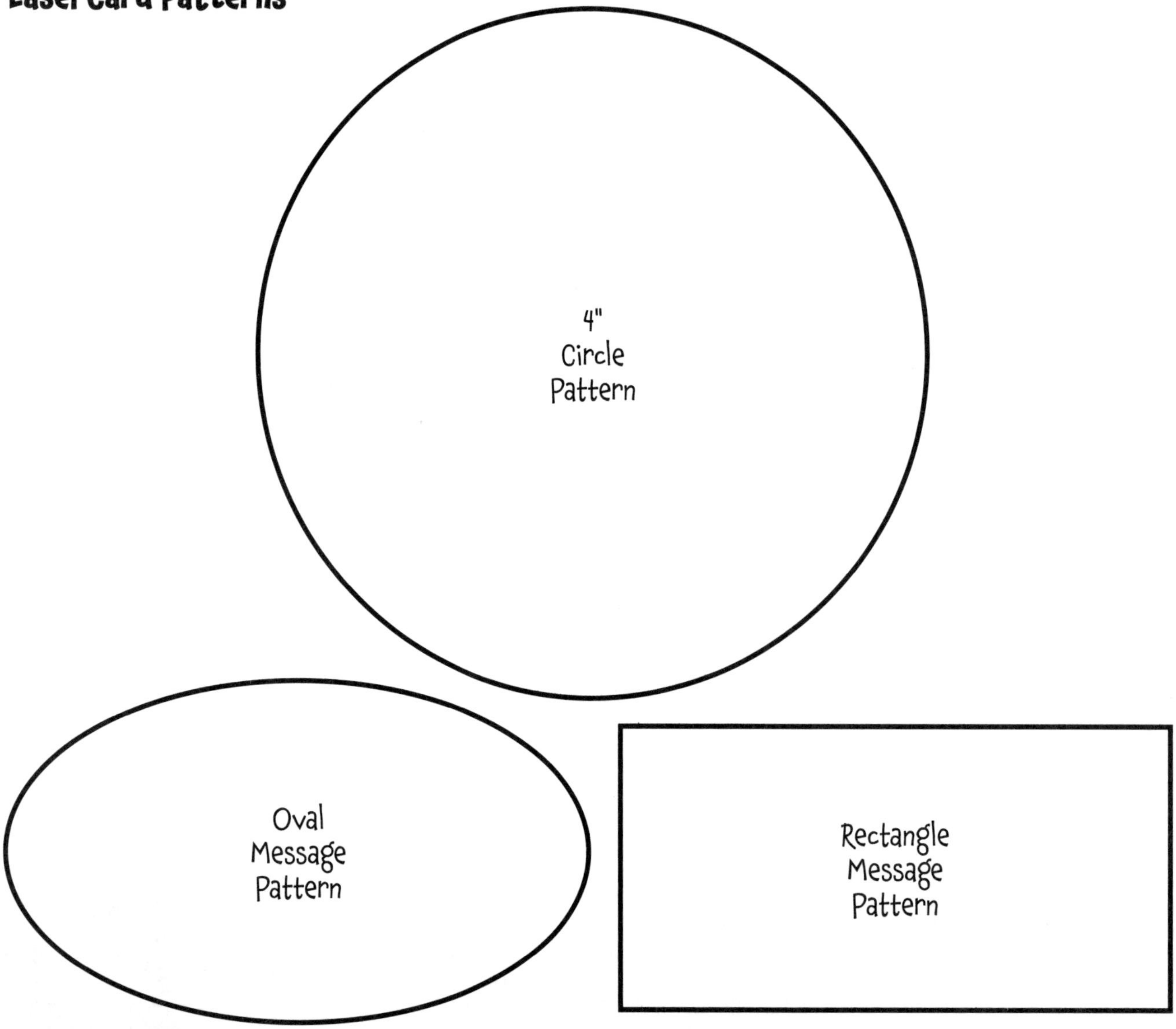

4"
Circle
Pattern

Oval
Message
Pattern

Rectangle
Message
Pattern

Trifold Card

Age Level: ★★

On the day of Pentecost all the believers were meeting together in one place. Suddenly, there was a sound from heaven like the roaring of a mighty windstorm, and it filled the house where they were sitting. Then, what looked like flames or tongues of fire appeared and settled on each of them. And everyone present was filled with the Holy Spirit and began speaking in other languages, as the Holy Spirit gave them this ability. At that time there were devout Jews from every nation living in Jerusalem. When they heard the loud noise, everyone came running, and they were bewildered to hear their own languages being spoken by the believers. They were completely amazed. "How can this be?" they exclaimed. "These people are all from Galilee, and yet we hear them speaking in our own native languages!" ACTS 2:1–8

What It's All About

The Bible passage for today talks about when the Holy Spirit came to the disciples on the day of Pentecost. God has three persons: the Father; the Son, Jesus; and the Holy Spirit.

Let's make a trifold card to remember the Father, the Son, and the Holy Spirit. *Tri* means *three*. That means a trifold card has three folds.

Can you think of three ways to show love to others?

What You Need

- Paper Cutting Tools (see p. 8)
- Scoring materials (see p. 9)
- Coloring & Writing Instruments (see p. 8)
- Colored cardstock
- Double-sided tape or glue, acid-free
- Decorating materials (glitter, stamps and stamp pads, stickers, adhesive gems, etc.)

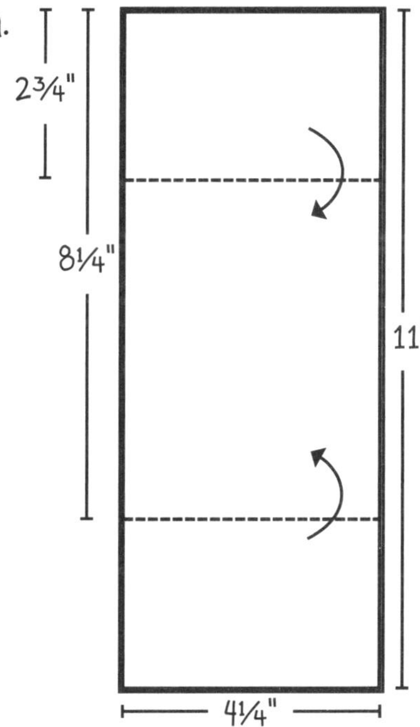

Preparation

Photocopy this page, making one for each child.

Cut the following, making one for each child, or children choose their cardstock and use scissors and rulers to cut for themselves:

- One 4¼x11-inch piece of cardstock
- One 3½-inch square of cardstock

What Children Do

1. Score the cardstock on the long side at 2¾ inches, and 8¼ inches (image a).
2. Fold each of the flaps toward the middle of the card to look like doors that meet in the center (see arrows, image a). This is the basic card.
3. Tape or glue a 3½-inch square of cardstock to the left side of the front of the card about 1 inch from the side fold. The square will overlap the other side of the card. Do not tape or glue the square to the right side of the card! You won't be able to open the card.
4. Use decorating materials to decorate the front of the card. Consider arranging rhinestones in the shape of a cross.
5. On the inside of the card, write a message such as "God Loves You" (image b) or whatever you want.

Purse or Briefcase Gift Card Holder

Age Level: ★

When the people saw him do this miraculous sign, they exclaimed, "Surely, [Jesus] is the Prophet we have been expecting!" JOHN 6:14

What It's All About

Our verse comes from a Bible story about a boy who shared his lunch with Jesus—and over 5,000 other people!
(Read the whole story at John 6:2–14.)

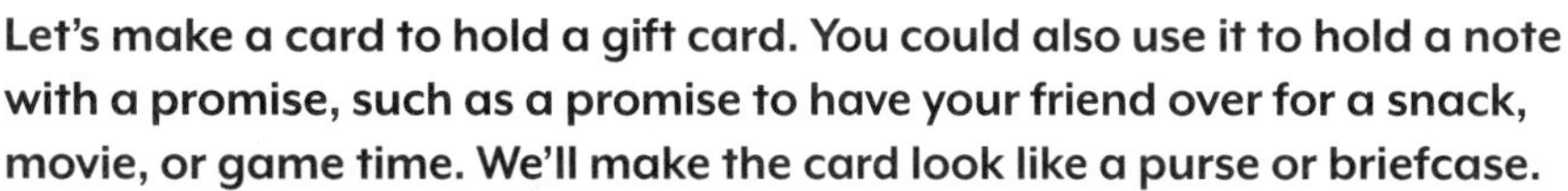

Let's make a card to hold a gift card. You could also use it to hold a note with a promise, such as a promise to have your friend over for a snack, movie, or game time. We'll make the card look like a purse or briefcase.

What You Need

- Purse & Briefcase Patterns (p. 30)
- Paper Cutting Tools (see p. 8)
- Scoring materials (see p. 9)
- Coloring & Writing Instruments (see p. 8)
- Cardstock in colors of your choice
- Pencils
- Double-sided tape or glue
- Adhesive-backed Velcro dot
- Decorating materials (glitter, stamps and stamp pads, stickers, adhesive gems, buttons, etc.)

For Purse

- Hole punch
- 10-inch length of thin ribbon

Preparation

Enlarging patterns to 200%, photocopy Purse & Briefcase Patterns, making one set of patterns for each child.

What Children Do

Make the Body of the Purse or Briefcase

a.

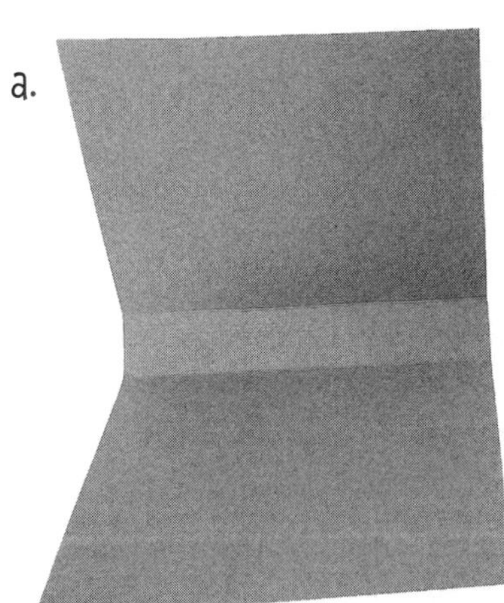

1. Cut out pattern pieces for a purse or briefcase. **Note:** To more easily cut the opening in the briefcase handle, fold paper in half the long way and then cut the oval.
2. On cardstock, trace pattern pieces for the body of the purse or briefcase and cut out.
3. Score and fold paper as indicated for body of purse or briefcase. These lines should be 3½ and 4½ inches from the top of the purse or briefcase.
4. Fold both sides up so that card will stand up on the middle section of the card. (See image a—Only the briefcase is shown, but it's the same for the purse.)

Make the Purse Flap or Briefcase Handle

5. On a second color of cardstock, trace the pattern for the Purse Flap or Briefcase Handle. Cut out.

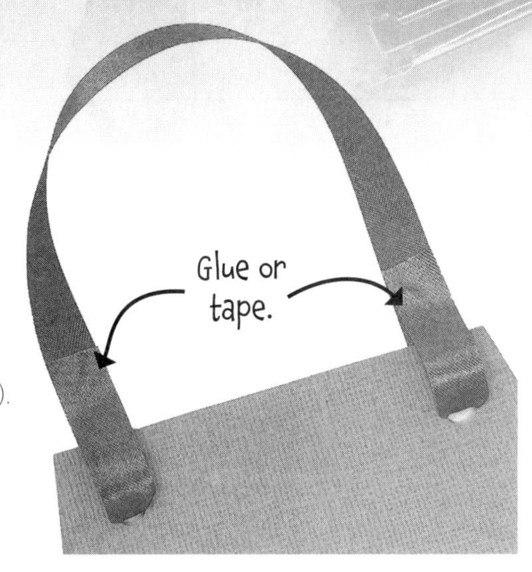

For Purse

6. Use hole punch to make two small holes near the top of the body of the purse as indicated on the pattern. Thread ribbon through holes and loop end back up to the ribbon. Glue or tape to secure (image b).
7. Glue or tape the Purse Handle to the front of the card. Decorate with an adhesive gem, sticker, button, etc. (image c).

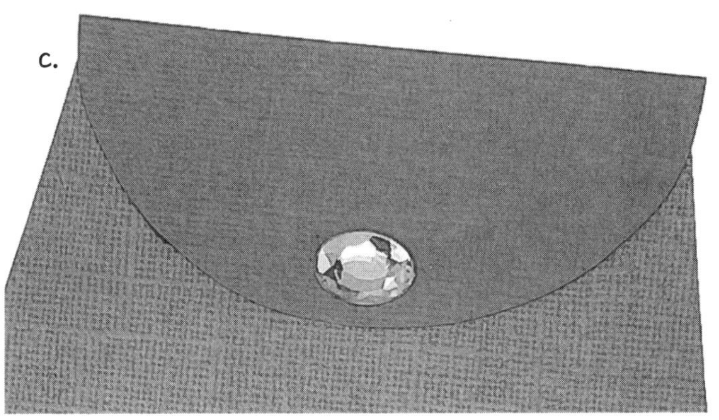

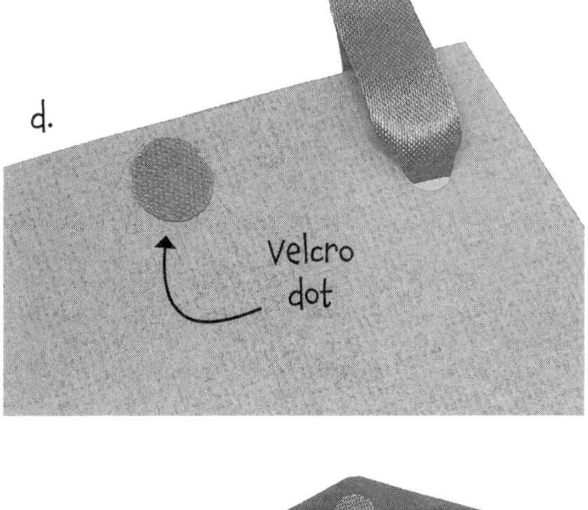

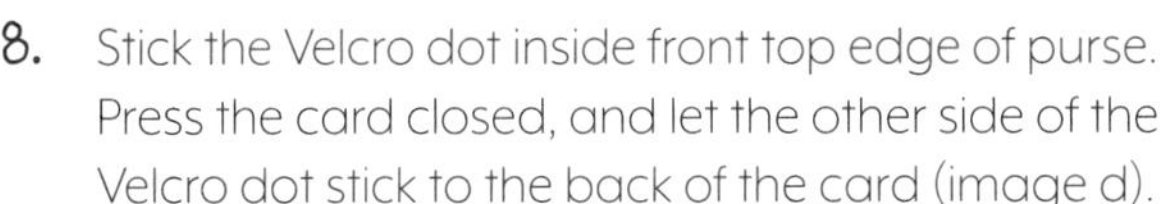

8. Stick the Velcro dot inside front top edge of purse. Press the card closed, and let the other side of the Velcro dot stick to the back of the card (image d).

For Briefcase

9. Score and fold cardstock piece according to the dashed line on the pattern.
10. Glue or tape the back of the handle to the back of the card.
11. Stick the Velcro dot inside front top of handle (near the point), fold down and let the other side stick to the front of the card (image e).

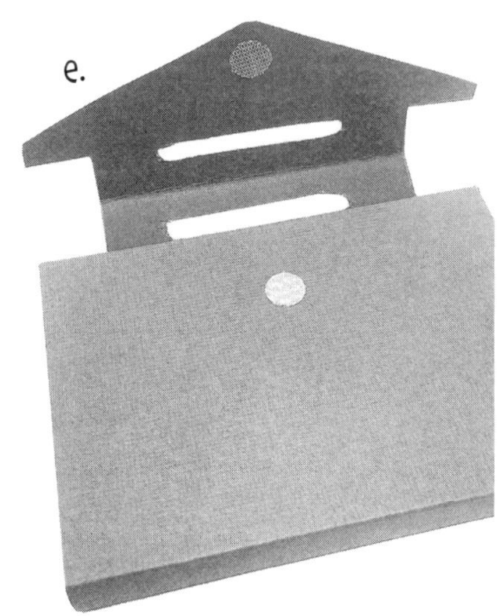

Make the Note or Gift-Card Holder

12. On a piece of cardstock, trace and cut out the Note or Gift-Card Holder Pattern.
13. Cut the two oval slits. **Hint:** Fold paper in half to make cutting slits easier. Glue holder inside the card. Be careful NOT to glue the slits down!
14. Slide note or card inside the slits (image f).

Add the Final Touches

15. Write a message above the gift-card.
16. Use decorating materials to decorate the purse or briefcase.

Purse & Briefcase Patterns

Enlarge these patterns 200%.

Note or Gift-Card Holder Pattern

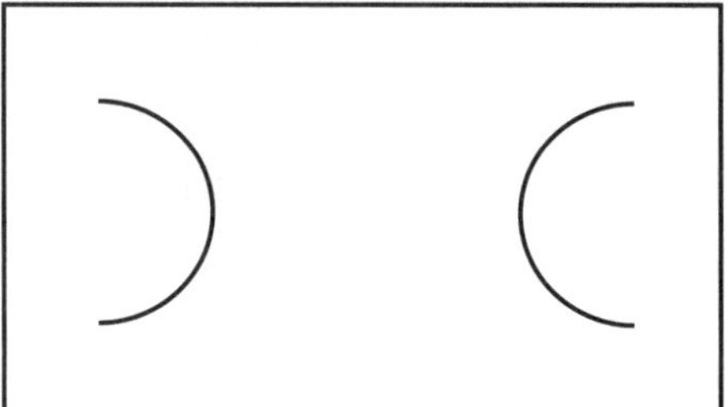

Purse Body Pattern

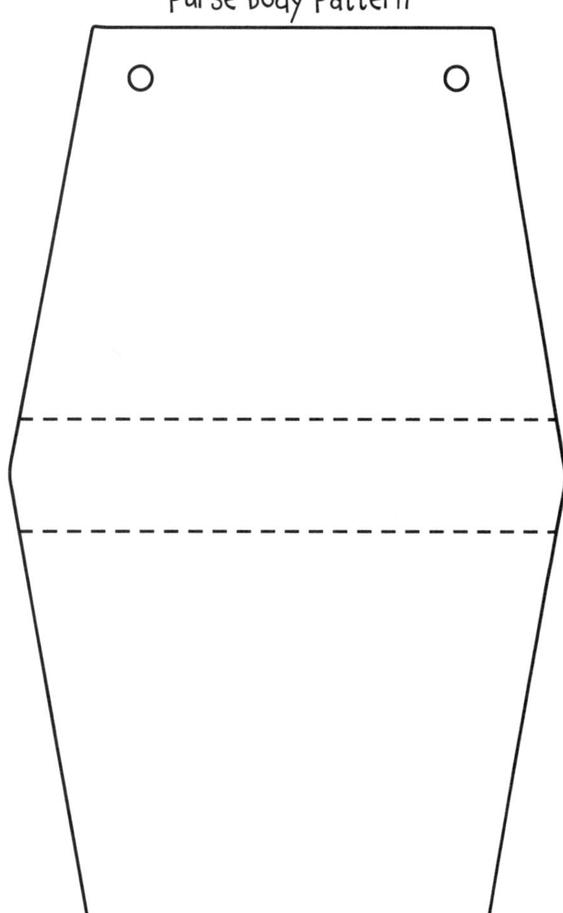

Briefcase Body Pattern

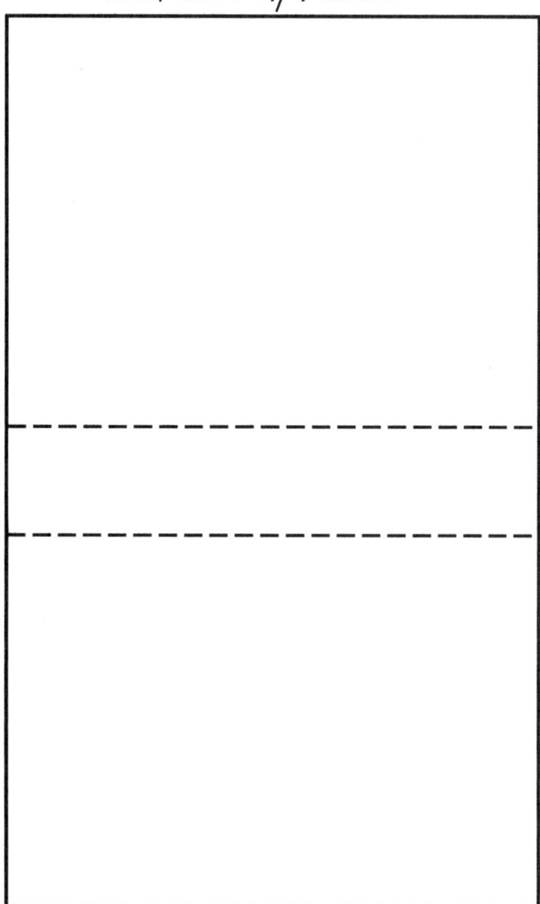

Purse Flap Pattern

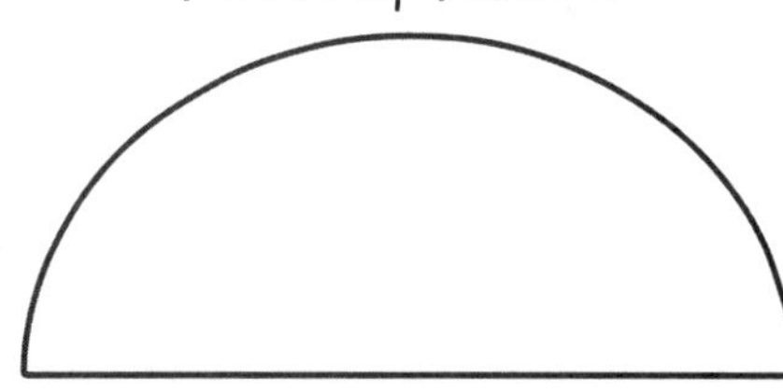

Briefcase Handle Pattern

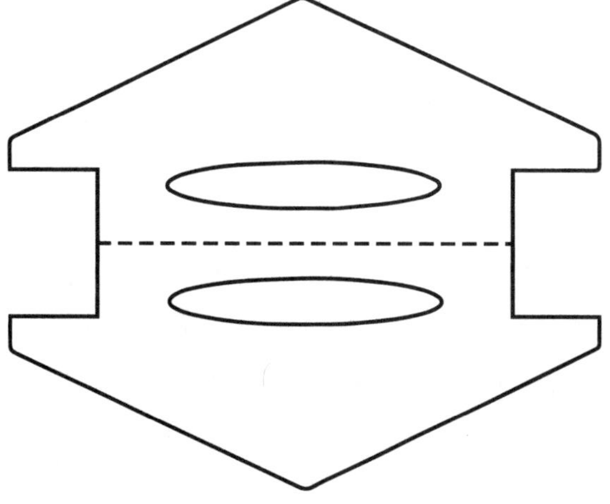

Layered Cloud Card

Age Level: ☆★

Stop and consider the wonderful miracles of God! Do you know how God controls the storm and causes the lightning to flash from his clouds? Do you understand how he moves the clouds with wonderful perfection and skill? JOB 37:14–16

What It's All About

We can take time to appreciate the beautiful environment created by God and praise him for it. Let's make a card to share this joy with others.

What You Need

- Sun & Cloud Patterns (p. 32)
- Paper Cutting Tools (see p. 8)
- Scoring materials (see p. 9)
- Coloring & Writing Instruments (see p. 8)
- Cardstock in yellow, white, light blue, and green
- Double-stick tape or glue

Optional

- Decorating materials, especially with a nature theme (bird and flower stamps and stamp pads, stickers, craft-foam shapes, etc.)

Preparation

Photocopy Sun Pattern on yellow cardstock and Cloud Patterns on white cardstock, making one set of patterns for each child.

Cut the following, making one set for each child, or children choose their cardstock and use scissors and rulers to cut for themselves:

- One 5½x8-inch piece of light blue cardstock
- One 2x8-inch piece of green cardstock

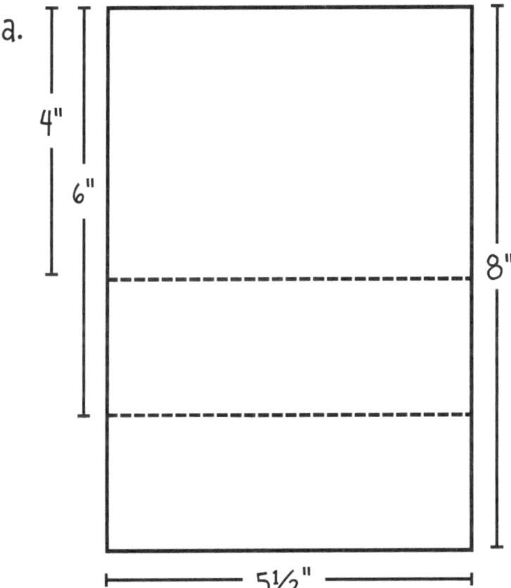

What Children Do

Make the Base Card

1. Score the light blue cardstock twice, at 4 inches and at 6 inches (image a).
2. Fold the cardstock in half at the 4-inch score.
3. Fold the cardstock in the opposite direction at the 6-inch fold—this leaves you with a flap on the front of the card (image b and at top right).

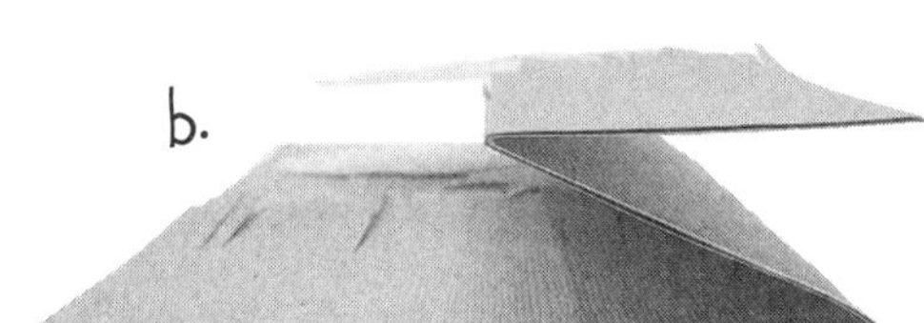

Make the Grass

4. Fringe the top of one long edge of green cardstock piece to make grass. Ruffle the edges of the grass.
5. Score and fold green piece at 4 and 6 inches.
6. Tape or glue green paper at the bottom of the card all the way across.

Add the Sun and Clouds

7. Cut out sun and clouds.
8. Tape or glue the sun to the blue part (the sky) of the cards left panel. Tape or glue the small cloud next to it (image c).
9. Tape or glue only the right half of the large cloud onto the right-hand flap. The left half of the cloud will hang over the fold (image d).

Add the Final Touches

10. Add decorating materials or draw flowers on the grass and birds in the sky.
11. Write a message on the middle panel of the card such as "God allows the sun to shine through the clouds," "Get Well Soon!" or "May the sun shine through the clouds of life."

Sun & Cloud Patterns

Sun Pattern

Small Cloud Pattern

Large Cloud Pattern

Game Crafts

We were filled with laughter, and we sang for joy. And the other nations said, "What amazing things the Lord has done for them." PSALM 126:2

Games are fun to play especially if you are not worried about winning or losing. We play to have fun with our friends and family. It's time to also share jokes, chat, and spend time together.

Be someone who looks at games as fun and not just competition to see who can beat someone else. Playing games provides an opportunity to be kind and joyful.

Try these ideas to show kindness while playing games:

- Let someone else go first.
- Cheer every player on.
- When you are losing, laugh about it.
- Have a rule that the winner cleans up the game, and then offer to help if you lose.
- Enjoy some jokes, talking, or a snack after or while playing games.
- Take photos of friends and family playing games together.
- Learn from playing. You can sometimes develop ways to strategize or understand that other games are just luck and not skill or knowledge.
- Don't be too serious or worry about winning. The idea should be to have ***fun***!

Paper People

Age Level: ✯

For you are all children of God through faith in Christ Jesus. And all who have been united with Christ in baptism have put on Christ, like putting on new clothes. GALATIANS 3:26–27

What It's All About

When our verse talks about how we have "put on Christ," it means that the more we live like Jesus, the more people will see him in us. Our verse tells us that we are all children of God. This means that we are in the same family as people all over the world! Let's make lots of paper people with all colors of hair, skin, and eyes to celebrate that we are all God's children. As we work, think of how God clothes us with something better than pants and tops—Jesus!

What You Need

- Paper People Patterns (p. 35)
- Paper Cutting Tools (see p. 8)
- Coloring & Writing Instruments (see p. 8)
- Cardstock in white (to be hand colored) or in a variety of skin tones
- Pencils

Optional

- Decorating materials (bird and flower stamps and stamp pads, stickers, craft-foam shapes, etc.)

Preparation

Photocopy Paper People Patterns, making one boy or girl for each child.

What Children Do

1. Cut out Paper People Patterns and clothes.
2. Trace the boy or girl pattern onto a sheet of cardstock. Draw on some hair. Cut out.
3. Cut out clothes. Color as desired.
4. Use tabs to attach the clothes to the people.

Alternate Idea: Personalized Paper People

- Cut a child's face from a photo and glue over the head.
- Take a photo of child in swimsuit with arms and legs away from their body. Glue to a sheet of cardstock and cut out. You may need to enlarge or shrink clothes patterns to fit, or have children draw clothes. Remind them to add tabs to attach clothes.

Paper People Patterns

Clean Water Jacks Game

Age Level: ☆★

One day the leaders of the town of Jericho visited Elisha. "We have a problem, my lord," they told him. "This town is located in pleasant surroundings, as you can see. But the water is bad, and the land is unproductive."

Elisha said, "Bring me a new bowl with salt in it." So they brought it to him. Then he went out to the spring that supplied the town with water and threw the salt into it. And he said, "This is what the Lord says: I have purified this water. It will no longer cause death or infertility." And the water has remained pure ever since, just as Elisha said. 2 KINGS 2:19–22

What It's All About

In our story, Elisha purified water with salt. Water is important for people, animals, and plants. We all need it to live, and we need clean water. God uses sunshine and plants to clean water, and he wants us to take care of the earth's water. We can help keep our water clean by removing liter left behind in lakes, creeks, and rivers, and by adding aquatic plants.

What Do the Colors Mean?

- Blue is for water.
- Brown is for pollutants.
- Yellow is for the sun that cleans water through evaporation.
- Green is for aquatic plants that help clean water.
- Black is for coal that can be used to filter water to clean it.

What You Need

- Score Card & Scoring Guide (p. 37)
- Paper Cutting Tools (see p. 8)
- Blue, brown, yellow, green, black cardstock
- Skewer or toothpick, one for each child
- Glue
- Container for jacks (small bowl or box)
- Small bouncing ball

Preparation

Cut the following, making one set for each child, or children choose their cardstock and use scissors to cut for themselves:

- Ten 1x2½-inch pieces of blue cardstock
- Three 1x2½-inch pieces of green cardstock
- One 1x2½-inch piece each of yellow, green, and black cardstock

What Children Do

Make the Jacks

1. Roll each strip by placing the short side of paper strip against the side of a skewer or toothpick and roll it as tight as possible.
2. Glue end closed (image a).
3. Place jacks in the container.

a.

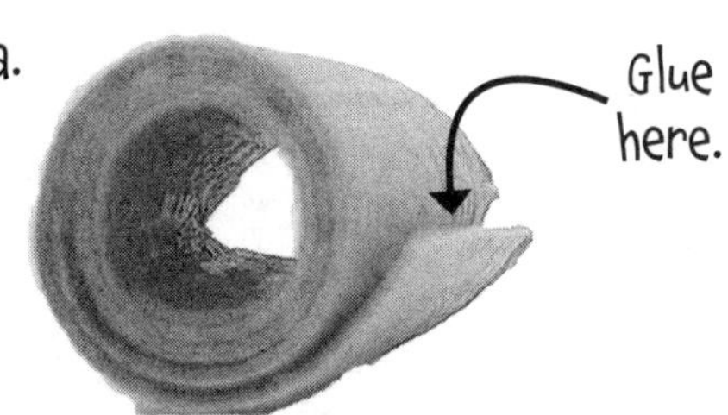

Play Option 1

1. Take container of jacks and dump the jacks on a flat surface.
2. Toss the ball up and pick up as many pieces as possible before catching the ball after it bounces twice.
3. Score according to the point system on page 37.
4. The next player takes a turn.
5. Take turns until someone reaches 20 points. (See Scoring Guide on page 37.)

Play Option 2

1. Leave the pieces in the container and have your friend hold the container above your head.
2. On your friend's signal, reach up and grab as many pieces as you can while friend counts to five.
3. Score with point system below.
4. Take turns until someone reaches 20 points.

Score Card

Round	Player:	Player:

Scoring Guide

Look at the pieces in your hand and sort them between the water (blue), pollution (brown) and water purifying methods (green, yellow, black).

- **Blue:** Add one point for each blue (water) piece.
- **Brown:** Lose one point for each brown (polluted) piece.
- **Green, Yellow, or Black:** Score two points for each green, yellow, or black (purifying method).
- Add points to score the round.
- The first player to score 20 points wins.

SCORING EXAMPLE: Say a player has three blue, two brown, one yellow, and one black. The player would get three points for the blue, lose two points for the brown, and add two points each (total of four) for the yellow and black.

3 – 2 = 1. Then take that one and add four: 1 + 4 = 5.

Kindness Chatterbox

Age Level: ☆★

Don't forget to do good and to share with those in need. These are the sacrifices that please God. HEBREWS 13:16

What It's All About

God always wants us to do good things. Being kind is doing something good. This game is a fun way to remember ways to be kind and to know words that describe kind people.

You may have made a chatterbox (sometimes called a *cooty catcher*) before. You can design your own chatterboxes with other words or pictures on them.

What You Need

- Kindness Chatterbox Pattern (p. 39)
- Paper Cutting Tools (see p. 8)
- Scoring materials (see p. 9)
- Paper Cutting Tools (see p. 8)

a.

Preparation

Photocopy Kindness Chatterbox Pattern, making one for each child.

What Children Do

Make the Chatterbox

1. Cut out chatterbox along thick outside lines.
2. Score and fold in half diagonally (corner to corner). Unfold. Repeat for other diagonal (image a).
3. Open paper and turn it so that the print side faces down.
4. Fold each corner to the center to have corner points meet, but not overlap (image b).
5. Flip paper over and fold each corner into center, without overlapping (image c).
6. Fold the paper in half and then in half the other way.
7. Stick your fingers inside the pockets formed by the folds. Gently push fingers together and then apart to work the chatter box.

b.

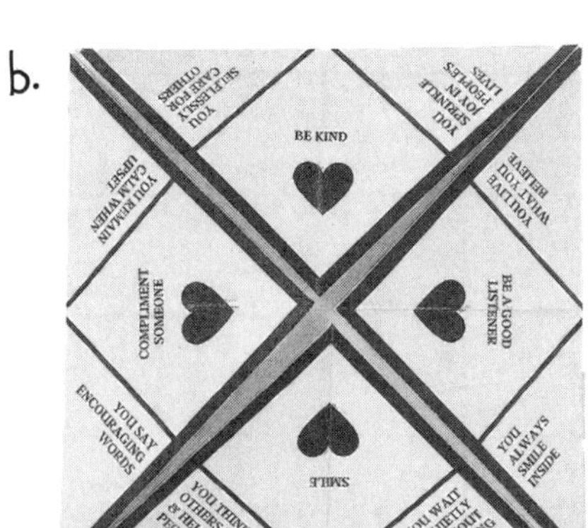

How to Play

8. Ask a friend to choose a number between one and ten. Move your fingers to open and close the chatterbox as you count to that number and stop.
9. Ask friend to choose a corner to lift. Read what's inside.
10. Let your friend take a turn to work the chatterbox as you choose a number.

c.

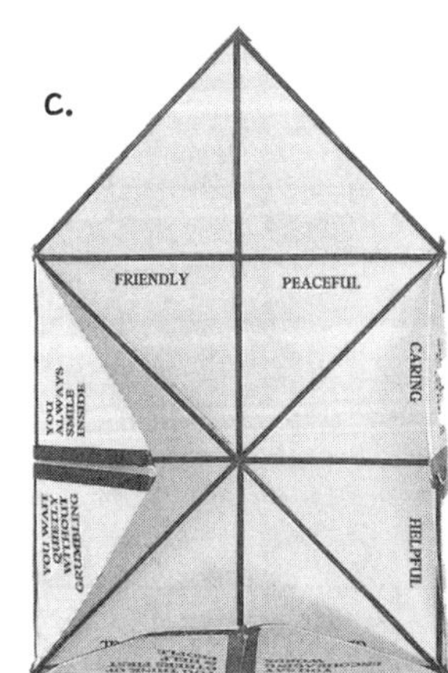

Kindness Chatterbox Pattern

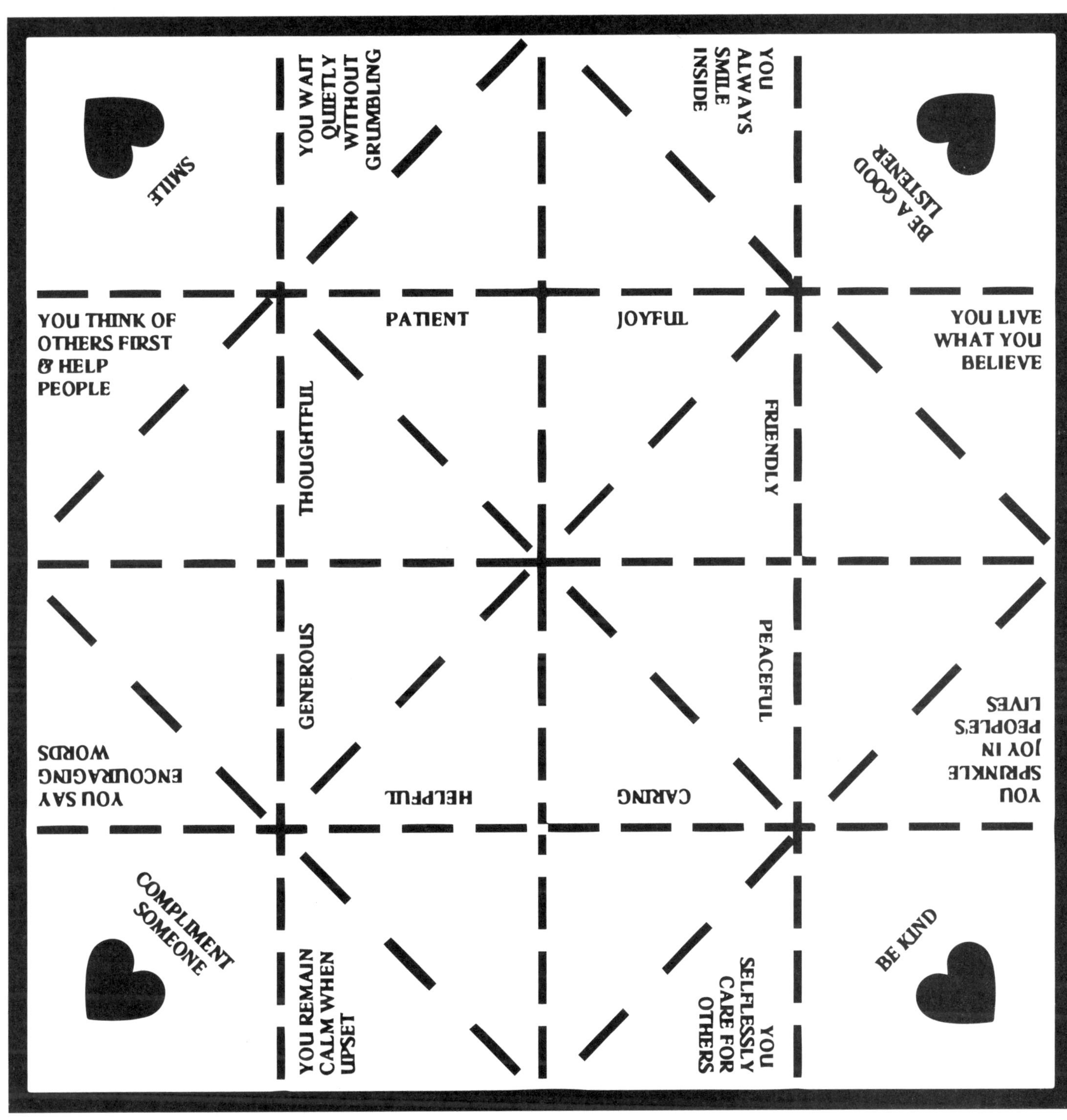

Secret Decoders

Age Level: ★

[Jesus] *replied, "You are permitted to understand the secret of the Kingdom of God. But I use parables for everything I say to outsiders, so that the Scriptures might be fulfilled:*

"When they see what I do, they will learn nothing. When they hear what I say, they will not understand. Otherwise, they will turn to me and be forgiven." MARK 4:11–12

What It's All About

God has given us the key to unlock the mysteries around us as we grow in knowledge of him. Use these decoders to send secret (kind) messages to a friend.

What You Need

- Secret Decoder Pattern (p. 41)
- Paper Cutting Tools (see p. 8)
- Coloring & Writing Instruments (see p. 8)
- Brad, one for each child
- Scrap paper to write messages

Preparation

Photocopy Secret Decoder Pattern, making one for each child.

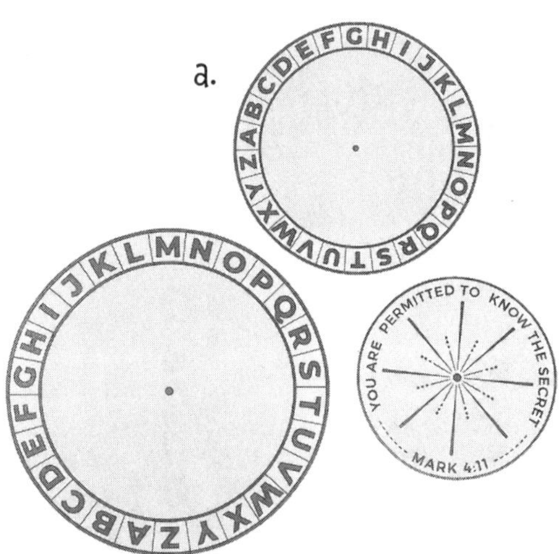

What Children Do

Make the Decoder

1. Cut out each of the three circles (image a).
2. Use the brad to poke a hole in the center of each circle where indicated.
3. Stack the circles with the largest on the bottom, then the medium, and finally the smallest circle on top. Align the holes in the centers.
4. Place brad through the holes from the top to the bottom. Spread prongs apart to secure brad (image b).

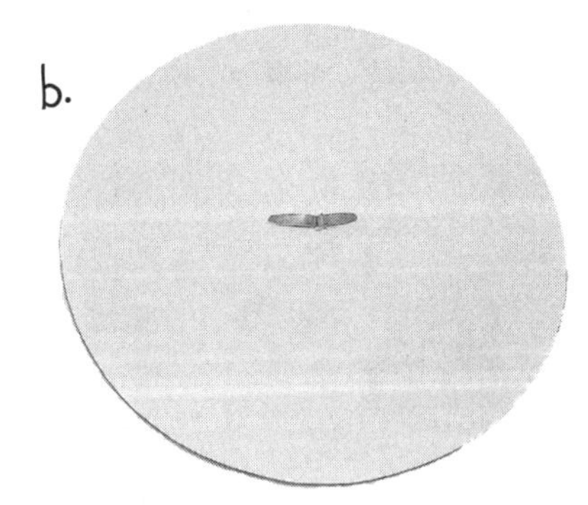

Code the Message

5. Write out a message on a scrap piece of paper.
6. Turn the wheels of the decoder to determine the key. The outside ring indicates the real letter. The inside ring indicates the letter for the code. For example, if you turn the inside wheel so that the letter *B* is under the *A* on the outside wheel, the key to the decoder is "A = B."
7. Then, use the decoder to write the coded message on a piece of scrap paper. Using the outside letter on the decoder, look up each letter in your message. Then, write down the inside letter to write the code. For example, if A= B and the original message is *Jesus loves you*, the coded message would be *KFTVT MPWFT ZPV.*

Decipher the Message

8. Give the coded message to a friend, and tell them what the key is.
9. The friend uses the secret decoder to find and write down the original message.

Secret Decoder Pattern

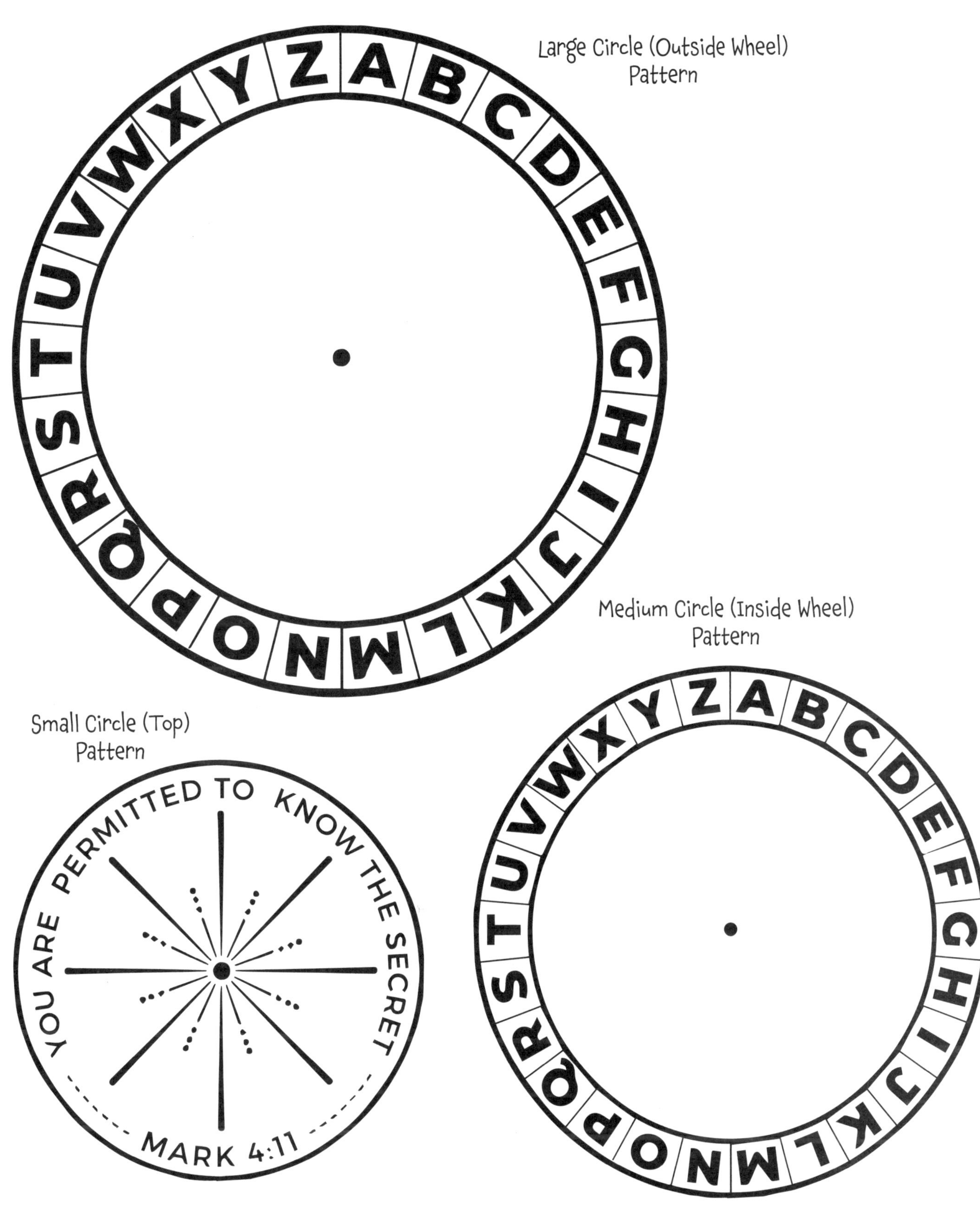

Leaping, Twirling Robot

Age Level: ★

Praise the Lord! Sing to the Lord a new song. PSALM 149:1

This robot is attached to a skewer that slides up and down inside a straw to make the robot go up and down.

What It's All About

People in the Bible praised God with joyful dancing and leaping. Let's remember to be joyful as we make a robot that can leap and twirl. You can use it as you praise God.

Be kind and make one for a friend who needs cheering up. Once you learn to make the basic robot, you can choose to make people or animals instead of a robot.

What You Need

- ★ Coloring & Writing Instruments (see p. 8)
- ★ Paper Cutting Tools (see p. 8)
- ★ Colored paper
- ★ 6- or 7-paper straw, one for each child
- ★ Glue
- ★ Large wooden bead
- ★ 12-inch skewer, one for each child
- ★ Tape

Optional

- ★ Decorating materials, (wiggle eyes, stamps and stamp pads, stickers—especially those that are facial features [eyes, nose, mouth, etc.], craft-foam shapes, etc.)

Preparation

Cut the following, making one set for each child, or children choose their cardstock and use scissors and rulers to cut for themselves:

- ★ Body, 6x4 inch strip
- ★ Inside holder for skewer, 4x½ inch strip
- ★ Arms and legs, four 3x½-inch strips
- ★ Head, 2-inch square (or whatever shape desired)

What Children Do

1. Fold body piece in half lengthwise to make a 4-by-3-inch rectangle. Open paper up, and lay flat on table. The right half of the body will be the front. Draw designs (buttons, knobs, a heart, etc.) on the front.
2. Open body like a card and lay on table. Make sure the front is facedown. Tape or glue the top 1½ inches of skewer to the inside of the front of the body (image a).
3. Glue head onto top of body. If you want, you can cut a short piece of cardstock to glue on as a neck. Color a face. Optional: Add wiggle eyes or stickers that are facial features.
4. Accordion fold the two strips for the arms and the two strips for the legs.
5. Glue the two legs to the bottom edge of the body. Glue each arm to an opposite side of the body. Note: For the arm on the side of the card with the fold, cut a small slit in the fold to slide the arm through.
6. Fold body and glue in place.
7. Slide the skewer into the paper straw (image b).

b.

8. Glue a bead to the bottom of the skewer as a stopper (image b). Or, instead of using a bead, you can wrap and tape a long thin strip of paper around the bottom of the skewer.
9. Hold the straw with one hand and with your other hand, move the skewer up and down or twirl it to make the robot leap and twirl. You can use your robot as a puppet to praise God!

Optional: Draw a second face on back of head.

Fish Pattern (for game on p. 44)

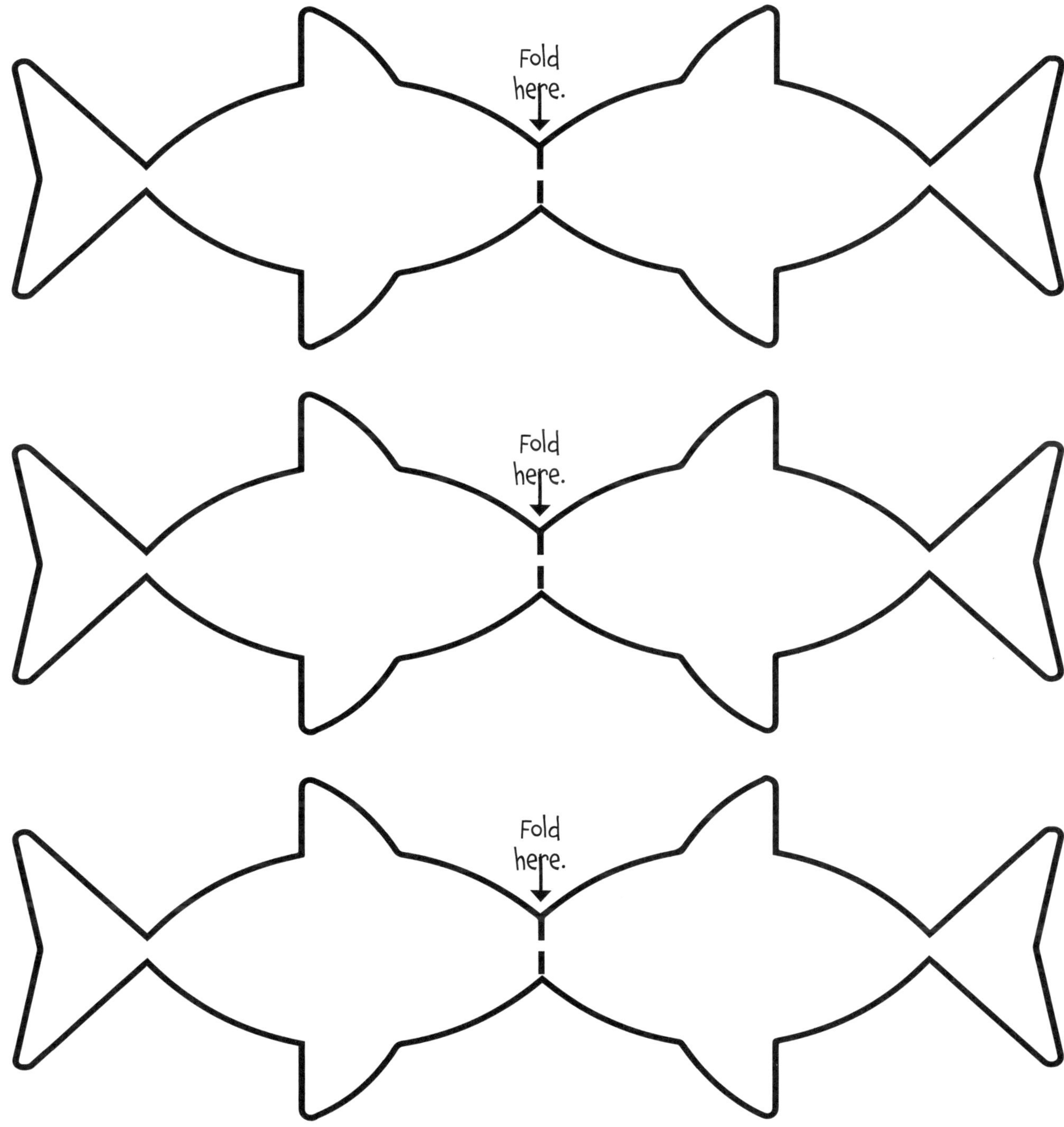

Fishing Game

Age Level: ✯

Jesus called out to them, "Come, follow me, and I will show you how to fish for people!" MATTHEW 4:19

What It's All About

In our verse, what does Jesus mean when he talks about fishing for people? Jesus wanted his disciples to know that it is important to help others, love them, and tell them about Jesus. Let's play a game and read some words that describe people who follow Jesus.

What You Need

- Fish Pattern (p. 43)
- Paper Cutting Tools (see p. 8)
- Coloring & Writing Instruments (see p. 8)
- Yarn or string
- A dowel or straight stick
- Approximately 2-inch magnet
- Colored paper
- Tape
- Paperclips
- Fish pond (inflatable wading pool; blue blanket, tarp, or tablecloth; hula hoop; sheet of blue poster board, etc.)

Preparation

On colored paper, photocopy Fish Pattern, making twelve fish. Cut yarn or string into a 2- to 3-foot length. On strips of paper, print each of the words or phrases found in the Fishy Words box. Alternatively, you can type the words into a computer program, print them out, and cut into strips (image a).

a.

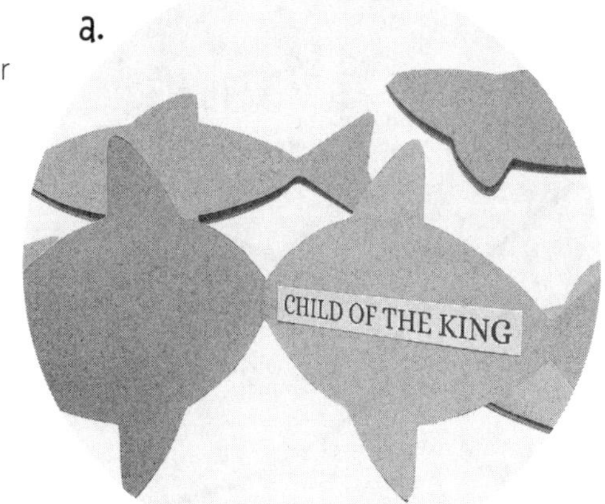

What Children Do

Make the Fishing Pole

1. Tape the magnet to one end of the string.
2. Tie the other end of the yarn to the end of the dowel or straight stick.

Make the Fish

3. Hand each child a word or phrase paper strip you prepared to glue inside a fish (image a).
4. Fold fish closed on dashed line. Place a paperclip over the mouth of each fish.
5. Children repeat until all the fish are ready for the pond.

Play the Game

6. Place the fishpond in the center of the playing area.
7. Children place fish they prepared in the pond.
8. Children take turns using the fishing pole you prepared to catch a fish. When they catch a fish, they open it and read what's written or describe what's drawn inside.

Fishy Words

- Fisher of people
- Jesus follower
- Child of the King
- Loved
- Treasured
- Member of God's family
- Forgiven
- Joyful
- Disciple
- Hopeful
- Blessed
- Friend of Jesus

Flextangle

Age Level: ☆★

Since God chose you to be the holy people he loves, you must clothe yourselves with tenderhearted mercy, kindness, humility, gentleness, and patience. Make allowance for each other's faults, and forgive anyone who offends you. Remember, the Lord forgave you, so you must forgive others. Above all, clothe yourselves with love, which binds us all together in perfect harmony. And let the peace that comes from Christ rule in your hearts. For as members of one body you are called to live in peace. And always be thankful.

Let the message about Christ, in all its richness, fill your lives. Teach and counsel each other with all the wisdom he gives. Sing psalms and hymns and spiritual songs to God with thankful hearts. And whatever you do or say, do it as a representative of the Lord Jesus, giving thanks through him to God the Father. COLOSSIANS 3:12–17

What It's All About

Share kindness by showing love, forgiveness, and peace. You can make a flextangle as a gift for a friend to share kindness and faith with them.

In 1939 British mathematician Arthur H. Stone invented the flextangle. It's a movable toy where the picture changes as you turn it. The one you'll make has pictures and words about faith, hope, love, and kindness.

Teaching Tip

It's good to keep an uncut copy of the Flextangle Pattern on hand to review how to do folds and where to glue end tabs.

What You Need

- Flextangle Pattern (p. 46)
- Paper Cutting Tools (see p. 8)
- Coloring & Writing Instruments (see p. 8)
- White cardstock
- Scoring materials (see p. 9)
- Transparent tape

Preparation

Photocopy Flextangle Pattern, making one for each child.

For Younger Children: Cut out, score, and prefold flextangles beforehand.

What Children Do

1. Color each row of the same images a different color from other rows.
2. Cut out the flextangle. Cut only on outside lines.

Tip: Pay attention to where the patterns says "tabs" and "to glue" and remember these things. See Teaching Tip. Having a reference copy will help.

3. Score and fold the dashed lines toward you (image a). Unfold.
4. Score and fold the solid lines away from you (image b). Unfold.
5. Keep words facing out and gently form a tube using the folds you made. Tape the world shapes to the tabs as indicated (image c).
6. Form flextangle into a circle and tape the end tabs inside the opening.
7. Gently push the flextangle tube inward to rotate the pictures.

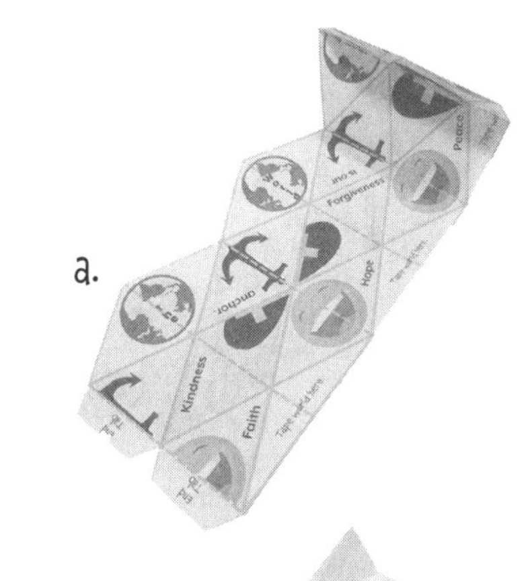

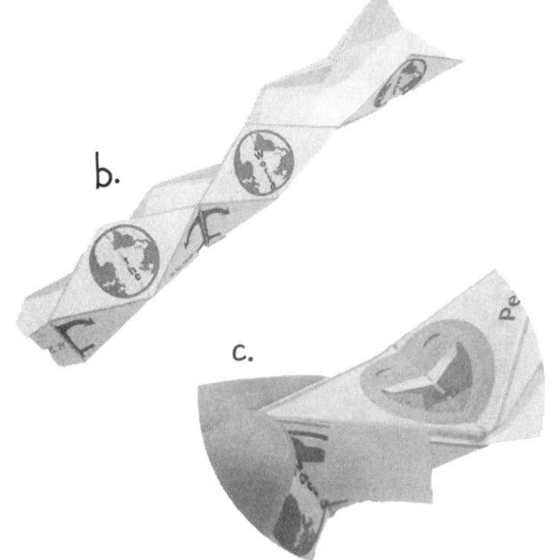

Flextangle Pattern

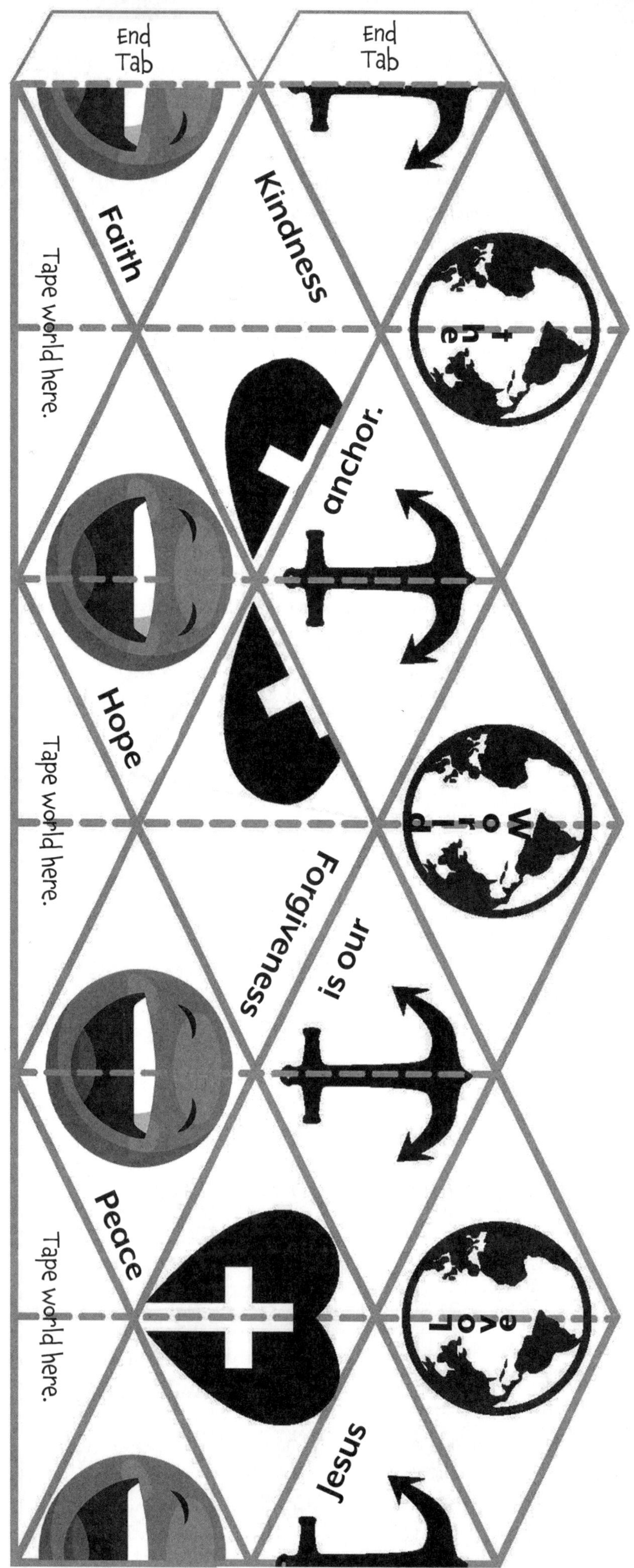

Star Glider

Age Level: ★★

In the same way, let your good deeds shine out for all to see, so that everyone will praise your heavenly Father. MATTHEW 5:16

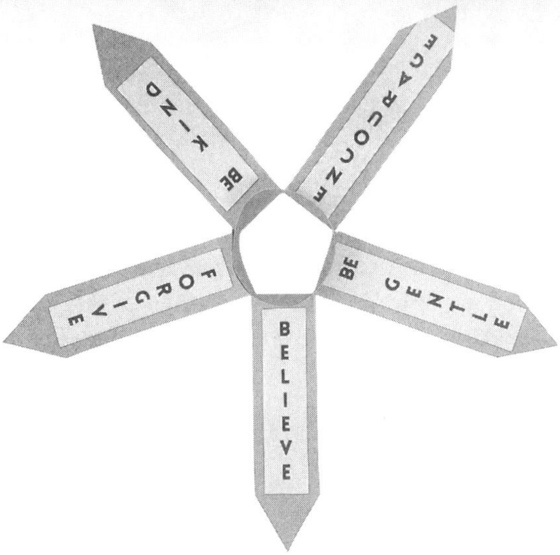

What It's All About

Like a shining star, be a light in the world and share God's love through goodness and kindness.

What You Need

- Star Glider Pattern, below
- Paper Cutting Tools (see p. 8)
- Colored paper
- Glue or tape

Preparation

On colored paper, photocopy Star Glider Pattern, making one for each child.

Optional: Type the words into a computer program, print them out, and cut into strips thin enough to fit on each wing of the star glider.

What Children Do

1. Cut out star glider. Cut the lines between each wing of the glider.
2. To share God's love, write words on each wing of the glider. Consider words such as:
   - Believe
   - God loves you
   - Be kind
   - Be gentle
   - Encouragement
   - God forgives
3. Fold up each wing on the dotted lines.
4. Curve the rectangle into a circle and glue or tape closed with wings facing out of the circle.
5. Hold the Star Glider in one hand, raise it up high, twist it, and let go.
6. Watch it spin as it glides to the ground. Try from different heights by standing on a chair or stairs. Be safe and have a parent help when you stand on a chair.

Star Glider Pattern

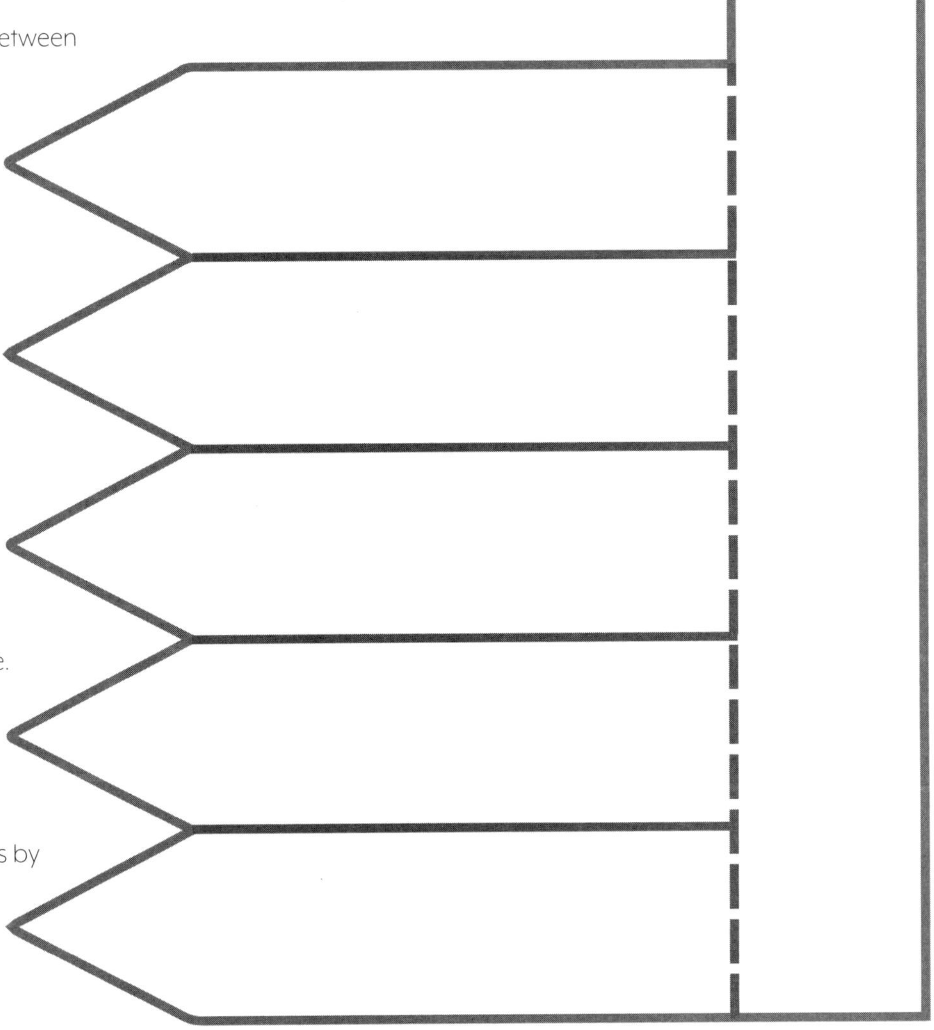

Spinning Sphere

Age Level: ☆★

Encourage each other and build each other up, just as you are already doing. 1 THESSALONIANS 5:11

What It's All About

Words and actions have power. When we encourage someone, smile, or help them, it can lift their spirits. They feel surrounded by love. Make a spinning sphere, adding words about kindness. The kind words will surround a face that can be spun upward.

What You Need

- Colored copy paper
- Paper Cutting Tools (see p. 8)
- Glue or double-sided tape
- Low-temperature glue gun (with adult supervision)
- Drinking straws
- 12-inch wood skewers, one for each child
- Pen or colored pencils
- Tapestry needle (with adult supervision)

Preparation

Cut the following, making one set for each child, or children choose their colored paper and use scissors and rulers to cut for themselves:

- Colored paper: Eight ½x11-inch strips
- Colored paper: Five 1-inch circles (or cut 1-inch squares and round off corners)
- Drinking straws: cut into ¼-inch pieces, one for each child

What Children Do

Make the Spinning Sphere

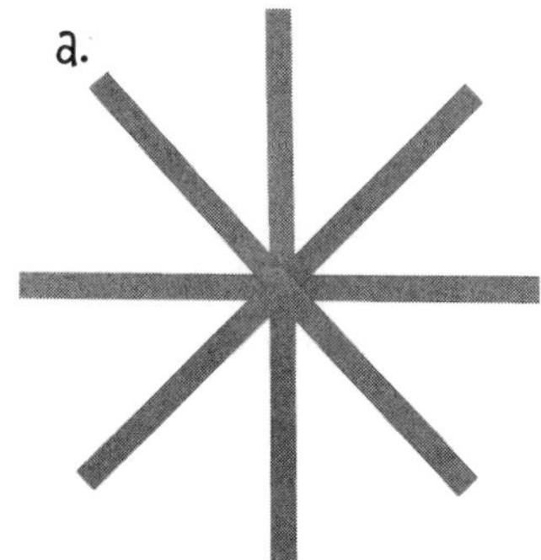

1. On paper strips, write words about kindness.
2. Place one circle on a table. Place dab of glue or double-sided tape on the circle.
3. Place one end of each of the eight strips of paper, evenly spaced on the circle, like rays going out (image a). Add additional glue or tape as needed.
4. Glue or tape a second circle on top in the center.
5. With adult supervision, make a hole in the center of the circle using a tapestry needle.
6. Slide the circle onto a skewer.
7. Use two circles and turn into faces by drawing on facial features and hair.
8. Glue faces to a piece of straw (back to back) and glue side edges of faces together. Slide straw faces onto skewer (image b).
9. With adult supervision, use tapestry needle to poke a hole in the center of another circle. Slide onto top of skewer and use glue gun or other strong glue to secure. Let dry.
10. Place the other ends of all the strips onto the top circle, keeping them straight (do not cross any strips).
11. With adult supervision, use tapestry needle to poke a hole in the center of another circle and slide onto skewer.
12. Use glue gun or other strong glue to secure in place on the skewer. Set aside to dry. The top circles should not be able to move. If they do, apply more glue and set aside to dry.

How to Use the Spinning Sphere

13. Rub bottom of stick between thumb and pointer finger to spin the paper sphere and watch the strips twirl and the face inside go up and down. It's a reminder that we can lift people's spirits when we do something fun with them.

Alternate Ideas

- Type kindness words in a computer program and print off. Children glue word strips to the longer strips used in the sphere.
- Use photographs instead of drawing faces. Take photos of children in your class with an instant camera or have children cut photos from magazines or catalogs.

Playing Piece People

Age Level: ★★

The human body has many parts, but the many parts make up one whole body. So it is with the body of Christ. 1 CORINTHIANS 12:12

What It's All About

Recognizing the uniqueness of people and appreciating them for who they are ways to be kind. We must look for how God has created each person to be special and see the image of God in them.

What You Need

- Playing Piece People Pattern (p. 50)
- Paper Cutting Tools (see p. 8)
- Coloring & Writing Instruments (see p. 8)
- White cardstock
- Glue dots
- Board game that uses playing pieces

Preparation

On cardstock, photocopy Playing Piece People Pattern, making one set for each child.

What Children Do

1. Decorate the playing piece with drawings to look like a friend, yourself, or someone to whom you want to give the piece. Decorate one side to be the front of the person, and the back to be the person's back. Optional: Cut out a small picture of yours or the other person's face and glue on for the face.
2. Cut out the pattern and fold along dashed lines.

For Younger Children: Younger children may have difficulty cutting out complex shapes. Instead, have them cut along the rectangle around the playing piece pattern.

3. Glue the tabs at the bottom onto the bottom support so that the playing piece can stand up.

Kindness Game

To play this game, use the board game you brought, the playing pieces children created, and one die.

Players take turn rolling the dice. If they can say something kind or unique about one person for each number, they roll they can move forward that number of spaces. For example, if they roll a two the player must say something kind about two people also playing to move forward. The game ends when someone reaches the end of the board. To make it harder, you can say that people cannot repeat themselves or others.

Playing Piece People Patterns

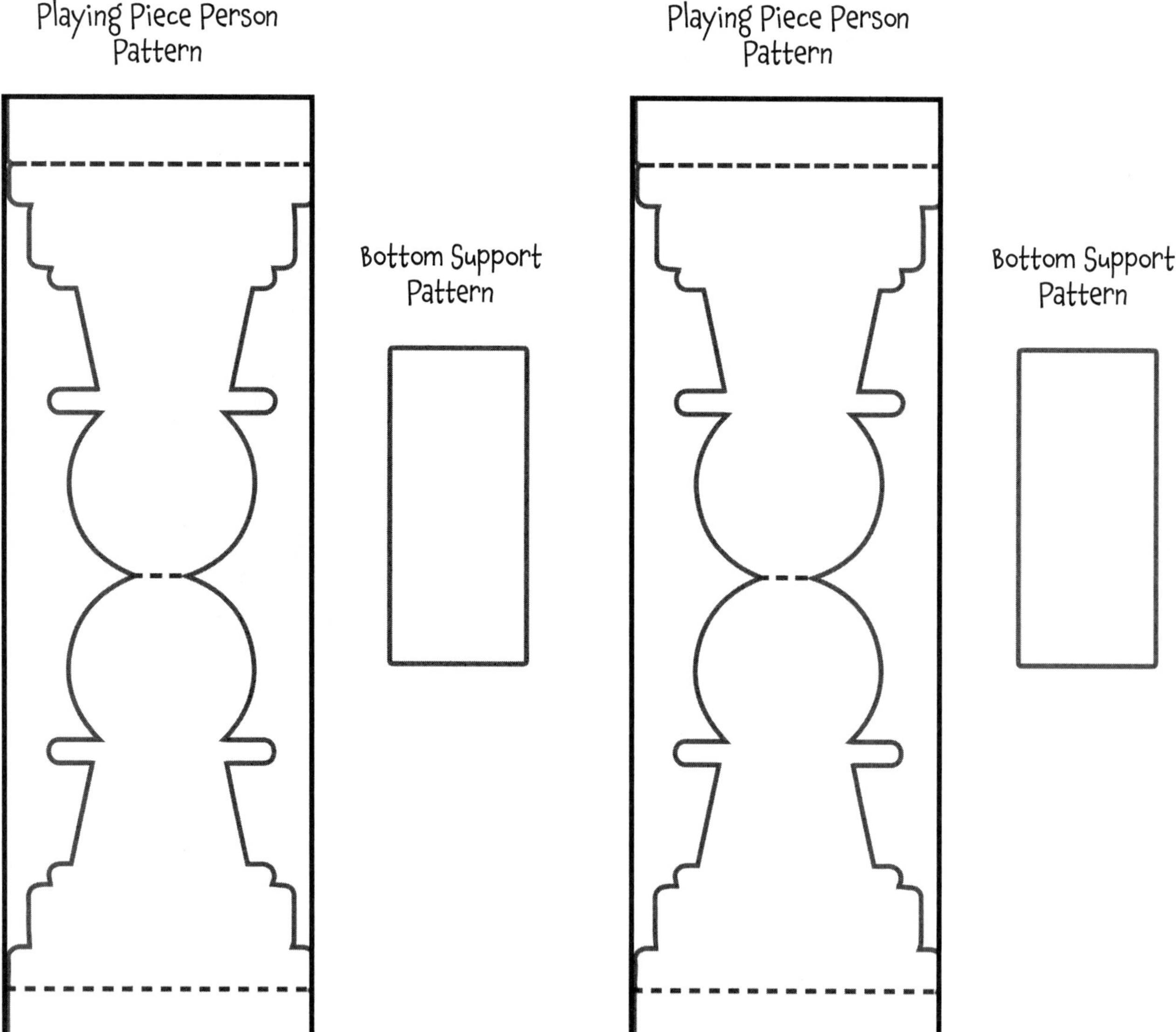

Friendship Projects

Friends are so important. We want to have fun experiences together, share life's joys, and show compassion when a friend has problems.

Part of being a good friend is caring about our friend's feelings. One way we do this by showing empathy and compassion.

- ***Empathy*** means we understand and share the other person's feelings.
- ***Compassion*** means we will care about them and what they are going through even if we don't understand.

Tips to Being a Kind Friend

- Listen.
- Spend time together.
- Try to find out something new about your friend each time you get together.
- Remember times that are special for your friend and celebrate them.
- Keep things they share with you to yourself unless it is dangerous, and then only tell a trusted adult.

Outreach Ideas

Here are a few outreach ideas for the crafts in this section:

- Make an Autograph Wrist Book (p. 52) for a friend getting ready to graduate, so that they can have friends sign it and remember them.
- Make a Friendship Treasure Box (p. 53) to celebrate a friend.
- Send a Hugging Puppet (p. 59) to a friend you cannot visit to give them a hug.
- Make Double Heart Pencil Holders (p. 61) to give to new people as an invitation to be friends.
- Make an A+ Friendship Banner (p. 62) to remind you of how to be a good friend.
- Make a Friendship Treat Holder (p. 65) and fill it with a special treat for a friend.

Autograph Wrist Book

Age Level: ☆★

Rejoice because your names are registered in heaven. LUKE 10:20

What It's All About

Jesus said he will write your name in his book of life. That shows you are important. Asking a friend to add their name to your wrist book shows you value them, and that they are important.

What You Need

- Heart Pattern, below
- Paper Cutting Tools (see p. 8)
- Colored cardstock
- ¼-inch ribbon or pipe cleaners
- Hole punch

Preparation

Photocopy this page, making one for each child.

Cut the following, making one for each child, or children choose their cardstock and use scissors and rulers to cut for themselves:

- One 8½x8½-inch square of colored cardstock
- One 12-inch length of ribbon

What Children Do

1. Fold paper in half twice to form a smaller square (image a).
2. Cut out Heart Pattern.
3. Place Heart Pattern with the point of the heart at the point of the paper folds (image b). Cut curved parts of heart.
4. Punch a hole toward the tip of the point. Be sure not to get too close to an edge!
5. Thread a ribbon, through the hole, or twist on a pipe cleaner.
6. Loosely tie loose ends to form a wrist band that slips over the hand.

Heart Pattern

Friendship Treasure Box

Age Level: ✯★

Nathanael exclaimed, "Rabbi, you are the Son of God—the King of Israel!" JOHN 1:49

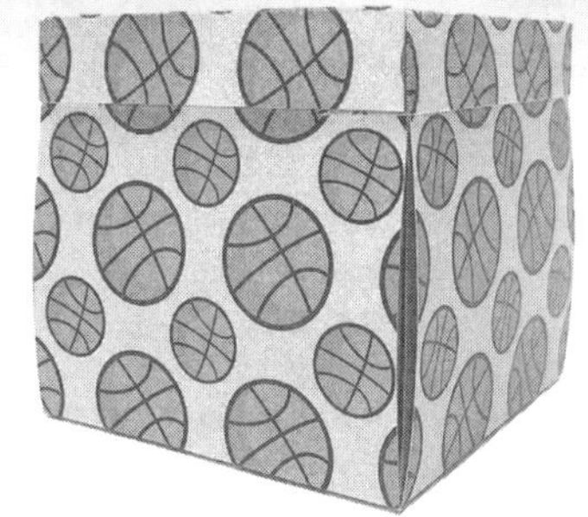

What It's All About

Our memory verse comes from the New Testament. It tells of when Nathaniel met Jesus. (Read the whole story in John 1:45–51.) **Nathaniel sat under the tree in secret, but Jesus saw him. Nathaniel must have been so excited to realize Jesus was the Son of God, and that Jesus wanted to be his friend. We're going to make a box that can hold secret treasures and memories for a friend.**

What You Need

- Friendship Treasure Box Patterns (p. 54)
- Paper Cutting Tools (see p. 8)
- Scoring materials (see p. 9)
- Colored cardstock
- Patterned paper
- Heavy glue

Preparation

Photocopy Friendship Treasure Box Patterns, making one set of patterns for each child.

Cut the following, making one set for each child, or children choose their cardstock and use scissors and rulers to cut for themselves:

- Trace and cut the Small Box Pattern out of colored cardstock.
- Trace and cut the Large Box Pattern out of patterned paper.
- Trace and cut the Box Lid Pattern out of patterned paper.

Make a sample Friendship Treasure Box to show children where they will glue photos after they take boxes home.

What Children Do

Make the Box

1. Trace and cut the small box pattern out of cardstock.
2. Laying the pattern pieces on top of the cut pieces, make a scoring line on each of the dashed lines. Fold upward on each scored line on both of the box pieces.
3. Put glue on the bottom center section of the smaller box and then glue it on top of the center section of the larger box. This will give you two sets of flaps attached to the center.
4. When children take the boxes home, they can decorate each flap with photos, drawings, or other mementos of their friend.

Make the Lid

5. Cut out the pattern including the slits (all solid lines).
6. Score and fold paper along the dashed lines.
7. Put glue on one of the tabs and glue it to the inside of the lid, creating a corner. Repeat this for each of the other three tabs.
8. To put the lid on the box hold the box flaps towards the middle, and then put the lid on. This will hold up the sides in the box. When you lift the lid, the inside explodes outward revealing all the flaps.

Variation: Add small photos of you and friends to both sides of all the flaps on the box.

Friendship Treasure Box Patterns

Large Box Pattern

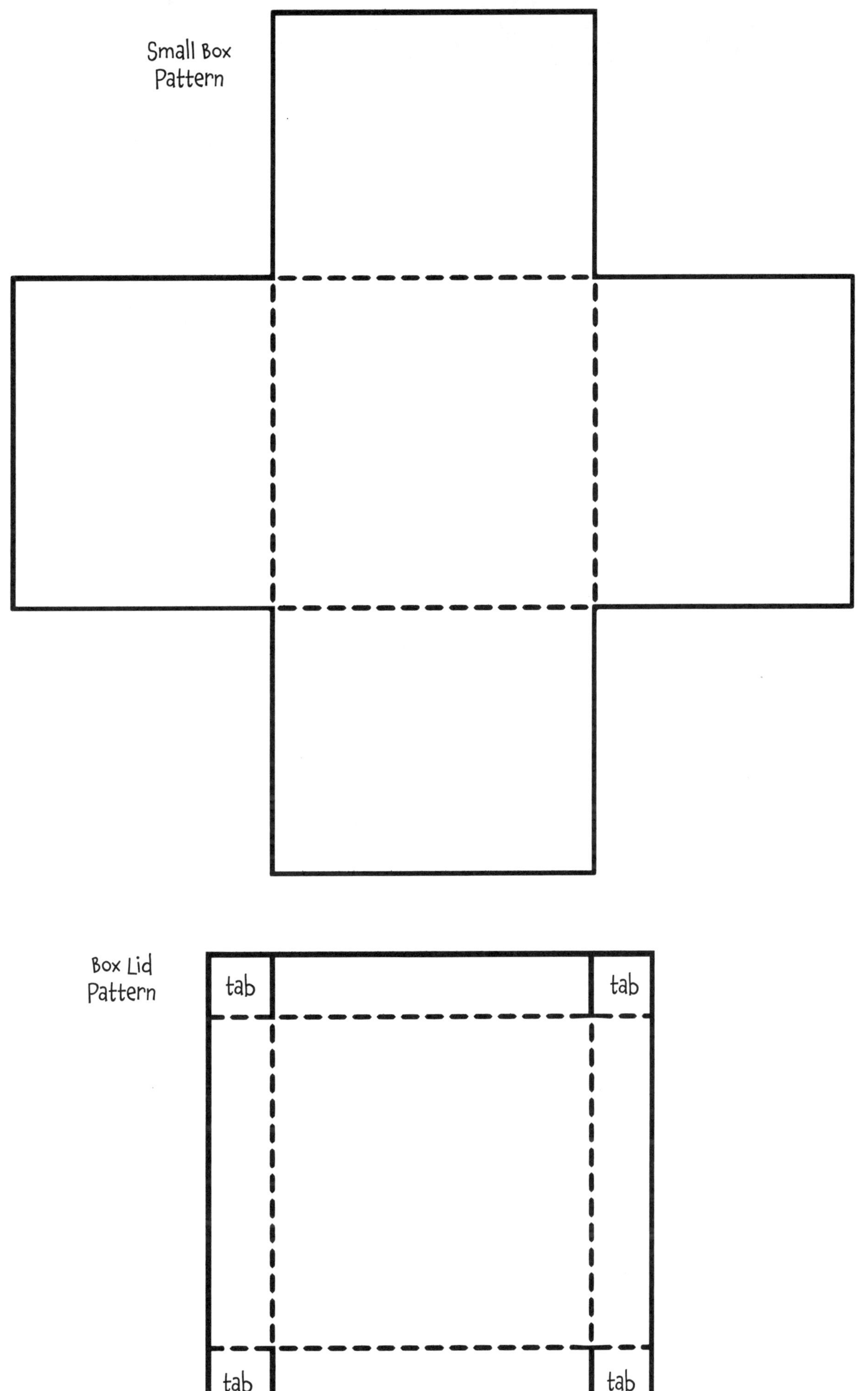
Small Box
Pattern
Box Lid
Pattern
tab
tab
tab
tab

My Kindness Book

Age Level: ★★

Never let loyalty and kindness leave you! Tie them around your neck as a reminder. Write them deep within your heart. PROVERBS 3:3

What It's All About

The Bible says not to ever let loyalty and kindness leave you, so that you will always be sharing God's love. One way to write kindness in our heart, as the Bible verse tells us, is to write about acts of kindness in this mini-book.

What You Need

- Kindness Book Pattern (p. 57)
- Paper Cutting Tools (see p. 8)
- Scoring materials (see p. 9)
- Coloring & Writing Instruments (see p. 8)

Preparation

Photocopy Kindness Book Pattern, making one for each child.

What Children Do

Fold the Paper into a Book

1. Cut out Kindness Book Pattern along the solid outside lines.
2. One at a time, score and fold the paper along each of the solid lines and unfold.
3. Cut along the dashed line. Start by carefully inserting the end of one scissor blade anywhere along the line. Then cut.
4. Fold along the long center line again with the printed side facing out. Hold the two ends of booklet together and gently push them to meet at the center. This will form the kindness book. Turn the pages so your name will be on the cover page.
5. Fill in the kindness book.

More Booklet Fun!

Use blank paper to make your own booklets. You can make a booklet and fill it with encouragement to give to a friend as a kindness gift. Your booklet could include:

- Photos of the two of you
- Compliments
- Thank you note for being a friend
- Drawings you make
- Scripture prayers
- Promises to do something together
- Secret messages

MY KINDNESS BOOK

NAME

DATE

WAYS I PLAN TO BE KIND

HOW I FELT WHEN SOMEONE WAS KIND TO ME

SOMETHING KIND I DID

HOW I FELT

ENCOURAGING WORDS I CAN SAY TO SHOW KINDNESS

KINDNESS ACTIONS I'VE DONE

- ___ LISTENED
- ___ THANKED SOMEONE
- ___ SMILED
- ___ GAVE A COMPLIMENT
- ___ HELPED SOMEONE IN NEED
- ___ LET SOMEONE ELSE GO FIRST
- ___ SHARED MY ___________
- ___ DID EXTRA CHORES TO HELP
- ___ PICKED UP LITTER (SAFELY)
- ___ HELPED WITH A PROJECT
- ___ WROTE A NOTE OF THANKS
- ___ PRAISED SOMEONE
- ___ MADE A SNACK TO SHARE
- ___ WELCOMED A NEW PERSON
- ___ CONGRATULATED SOMEONE
- ___ MADE JOYFUL SIDEWALK ART
- ___ PRAYED FOR SOMEONE

MY KINDNESS PROJECT

WHO I WILL SHOW KINDNESS TO THIS WEEK

MY ACTION PLAN

WHAT HAPPENED

Never let loyalty and kindness leave you! Tie them around your neck as a reminder. Write them deep within your heart.

PROVERBS 3:3

Address Book

Age Level: ☆★

"I am the vine; you are the branches. Those who remain in me, and I in them, will produce much fruit. For apart from me you can do nothing." JOHN 15:5

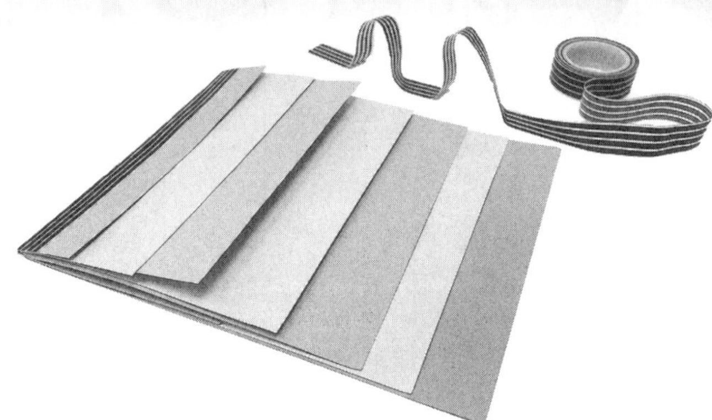

What It's All About

Jesus said that we are the branches and he is the vine. That means we need to stay connected to Jesus to produce spiritual fruit. In the same way, Jesus wants us to stay close to other people. This means keeping track of where they go if they move or if you move. Staying connected to others makes us happier.

What You Need

- Scoring materials (see p. 9)
- Paper Cutting Tools (see p. 8)
- Coloring & Writing Instruments (see p. 8)
- Washi or other decorative tape
- Letter-sized paper, white or colored
- Stapler

Preparation

Cut the following, making one set for each child, or children choose their paper and use scissors and rulers to cut for themselves:

- Cut paper in half to create 5½x8½-inch pieces, five for each child

What Children Do

1. Score and fold a prepared piece of paper 1¼ inch from the top.
2. Score and fold a second prepared piece of paper 2¼ inches from the top. Place the page inside of the first folded paper so that it looks like there are two tabs at the top (image a).
3. Score and fold a third prepared piece of paper 3¼ inches from the top. Place paper inside other folded pages.
4. Score and fold a fourth prepared piece of paper 4¼ inches from the top. Place paper inside other folded pages.
5. Score and fold a fifth prepared piece of paper 5¼ inches from the top. Place paper inside other folded pages.
6. Staple the pages together at the top. Have children put their names on the 1-inch tab at the top.
7. Place a strip Washi or other decorative tape across the top, covering the staples.

a.

Using the Book

8. Children can use each page to write down information about a friend and how to keep in touch with them.

Variations

- Children write their name on the top, and then pass the books around. Other children write or draw something kind and special about that child in their books.
- To make an address book, each child writes their name on the top page and two or three of the letters of the alphabet (in order), on each of the following pages. Children pass the books around. Each child then writes his name and address on the page that has the first letter of their first name.

Hugging Puppet

Age Level: ★★

Please take this gift I have brought you, for God has been very gracious to me. I have more than enough. GENESIS 33:11

What It's All About

Our verse is from a Bible story about two brothers Jacob and Esau who had a big argument and had been separated for a long time. Jacob didn't know what Esau would do when they saw each other again. What Esau did was hug him! (Read the whole story in Genesis 33:1–11.)

Hugs are a way to show someone you care about them. Let's make a puppet gift that can give a hug, when you can't give a hug in person. Have fun mailing hugging puppets to friends and loved ones.

What You Need

- Hugging Puppet Patterns (p. 60)
- Paper Cutting Tools (see p. 8)
- Colored cardstock
- Transparent tape or glue

Optional

- Small photo of your face
- Adhesive-backed Velcro dots

Preparation

Photocopy Hugging Puppet Patterns, making one for each child.

What Children Do

1. Fold a piece of cardstock in half. Place Body Pattern on the folded cardstock, lining up the pattern's dashed line on the edge of the fold.
2. Trace pattern, cut out, and unfold.
3. Draw a face. **Optional:** Cut face out of photo and glue to the head of the puppet.
4. To make clothing, choose additional pieces of cardstock: one for the shirt and another for the pants. Fold cardstock pieces in half, lining up the patterns' dashed lines on the edge of the folds. Cut out.
5. Color and decorate clothing. **Optional:** Make additional shirts and pants.
6. Fold tabs down around puppet body to keep in place. **Optional:** Instead of folding tabs, cut off tabs and attach clothing using adhesive-backed Velcro dots.
7. Take the long tab on each arm and roll to the back of the arm. Tape or glue in place to form a tube (image a).
8. Slip thumb and middle finger into arm tubes. Open and close to make puppet give a hug.

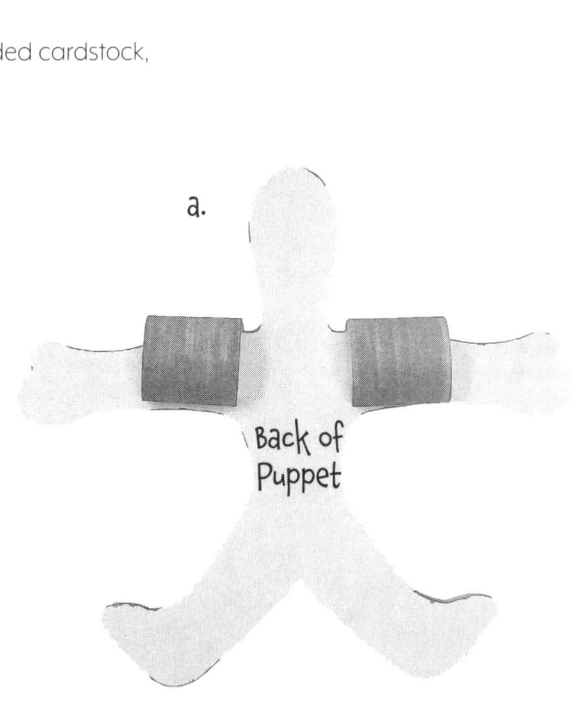

Hugging Puppet Patterns

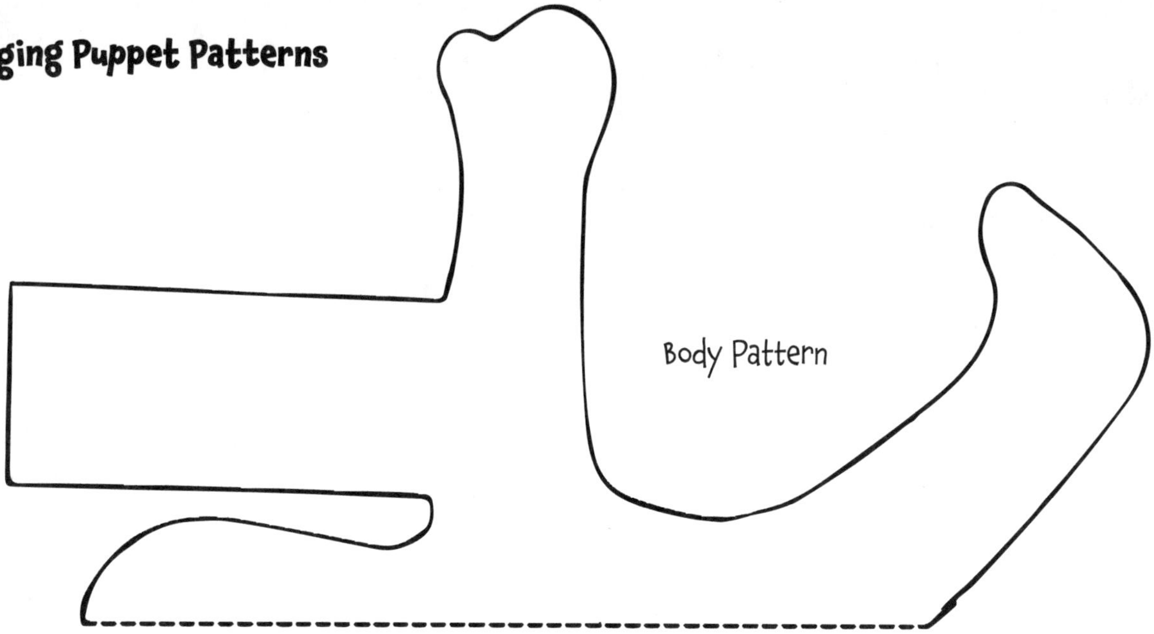

Body Pattern

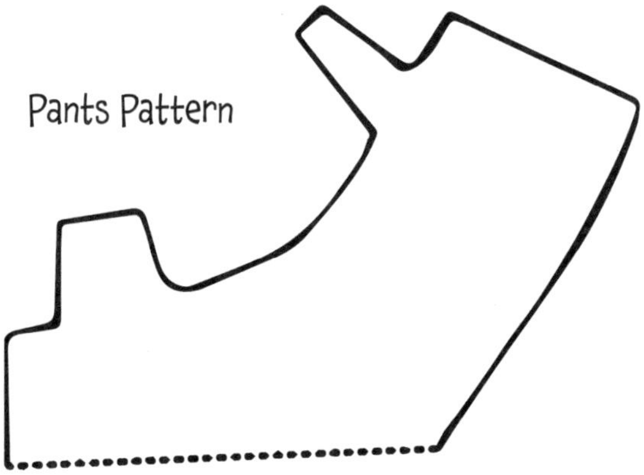

Pants Pattern

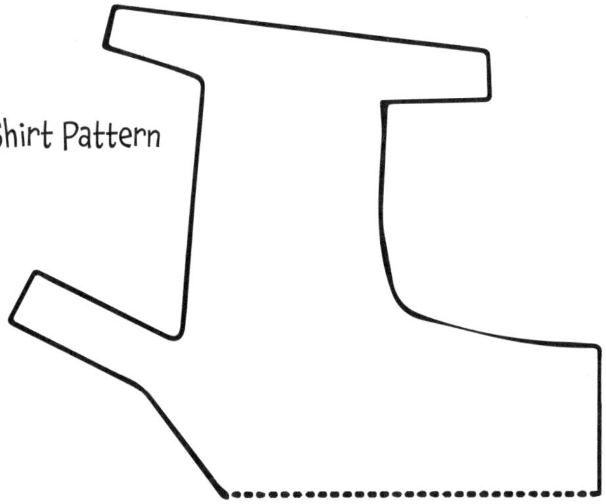

Shirt Pattern

Double Heart Pencil Holder Pattern

Large Double Heart Pattern

Double Heart Pencil Holder

Age Level: ★★

Let us think of ways to motivate one another to acts of love and good works. HEBREWS 10:24

What It's All About

***To encourage* someone is to motivate them. Encourage a friend or study buddy with the gift of a pencil or marker in a little heart holder. It's a simple act of kindness.**

What You Need

- Double Heart Pencil Holder Patterns, below and page 60
- Paper Cutting Tools (see p. 8)
- Patterned paper
- Colored paper
- Pencils
- Hole punch
- Glue

Optional

- Decorating materials (beads, wiggle eyes, glitter, adhesive-backed jewels, craft-foam shapes, paper flowers, stickers, etc.)

Preparation

Photocopy Double Heart Pencil Holder Patterns, making one set for each child.

What Children Do

1. Cut out pattern pieces.
2. Trace the Large Double Heart Pattern onto patterned paper and cut out.
3. Trace the Small Double Heart Patterns onto colored paper and cut out.
4. Punch a hole through all the hearts as shown in the pattern.
5. Lining up the holes you punched, glue the smaller hearts onto the larger hearts.
6. Cut plain paper into strips or a V shape, write a message and glue on hearts without covering holes.
7. Slide pencil through holes

Optional

8. Use decorating materials or markers to add additional decorations to your pencil holder.

Variation

Cut your own shapes and write your own messages. You can cut paper in any shape you want, just remember that there will need to be two holes punched into the shape to hold the pencil.

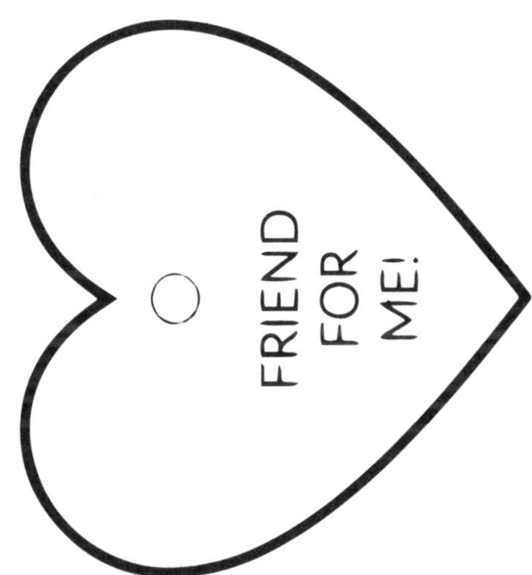

Small Double Heart Patterns

A+ Friendship Banner

Age Level: ★

There are "friends" who destroy each other, but a real friend sticks closer than a brother. PROVERBS 18:24

What It's All About

Before he was king, David became friends with Jonathan, who was the son of King Saul. (***Read about their friendship in 1 Samuel 18:1–4.***) **Throughout their lives and even after Jonathan died, David remained an A+ friend, always loyal, and helpful to each other. Let this banner remind you of qualities that make you an A+ friend.**

What You Need

- A+ Friendship Banner Patterns (pp. 63–64)
- Paper Cutting Tools (see p. 8)
- Cardstock, assorted colors and patterns
- Black cardstock
- Transparent tape
- Glue
- Hole punch
- Thin ribbon in a variety of colors and designs

Optional

- Decorating materials (beads, wiggle eyes, glitter or glitter glue, adhesive-backed jewels, craft-foam shapes, paper flowers, stickers, etc.)

Preparation

Photocopy A+ Friendship Banner Patterns, making one for each child.

Cut the following, making one set for each child, or children choose their cardstock and use scissors and rulers to cut for themselves:

- Black cardstock: two 4x12-inch strips
- Colored or patterned cardstock: two 3x11-inch strips

What Children Do

Make the Banner Base

1. Slightly overlap the prepared black cardstock pieces and tape together to make one long strip 4 inches wide and approximately 24 inches long.
2. Repeat overlapping and taping the prepared colored or patterned cardstock to make a long strip 3 inches wide and approximately 22 inches long. **Note:** In the example image, the cardstock is light gray, not patterned.
3. With taped edges to the back, glue the smaller rectangle on top of the larger one, starting approximately 2 inches from the top of the larger strip (see image).

Make the Shapes

4. Choose either the heart or the hexagon patterns and cut out.
5. On patterned paper, trace and cut seven larger shapes.
6. On coordinating paper, trace and cut seven smaller shapes.
7. Glue the smaller shapes on top of larger ones.

Add the Words

8. Cut out the word strips and the A+ Friend Ideas box on page 64.
9. Glue one word strip to the center of each shape. Glue A+ Friend Ideas box to the back of the banner.
10. Glue shapes onto the front of the banner, spacing them evenly down the length of the banner.
11. Punch two small holes at the top of banner.
12. Cut a 12-inch length of ribbon. Thread each end of the ribbon through a hole from the back to the front. Tie a knot so that the knots are on the front of the banner (see image on p. 62).

Add the Final Touches

13. Use decorating materials to decorate your banner.

A+ Friendship Banner Patterns

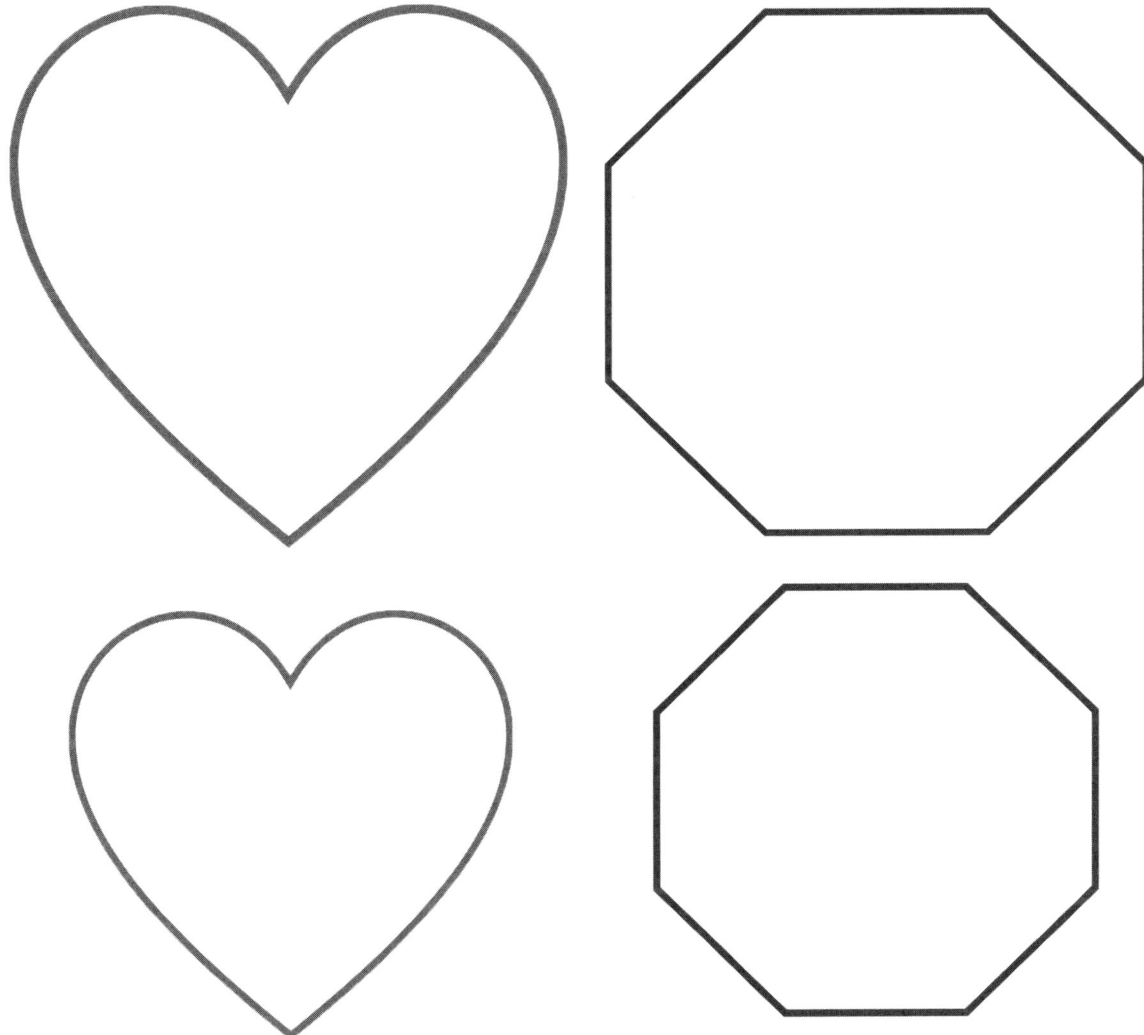

Affirmation

Appreciation

Acceptance

Attention

Adventure

Adaptability

Assurance

A+ Friend Ideas

- Affirmation means showing that you value the person. You congratulate your friend's success and encourage them as they work to learn or master a new skill.
- Appreciation means saying thanks and doing acts of kindness and friendship. Thanking someone shows respect and caring.
- Acceptance means to welcome or receive someone and show they belong in your life. You realize they are unique and wonderfully created by God. You don't try to change the person's personality or basic uniqueness. That is different from letting someone make bad or sinful choices or hurt people.
- Attention means to listen, really listen, and notice your friend. You spend time together. You look the friend in the eye to listen and respond to what he or she says.
- Adventure is to engage in fun together. You try new things including foods, games, and activities. Make sure you stay safe.
- Adaptability means being able to change as circumstances change. As you grow, find new interests, and make more friends, you need to be flexible and make changes as needed.
- Assurance means to let the other person feel safe. You are loyal and trustworthy. You don't share information that would embarrass your friend. You show care about your friend through your words and actions. The best assurance is to share your faith so your friend will also have eternal assurance of Heaven.

Friendship Treat Holder

Age Level: ✩★

If your gift is to encourage others, be encouraging. If it is giving, give generously. If God has given you leadership ability, take the responsibility seriously. And if you have a gift for showing kindness to others, do it gladly. ROMANS 12:8

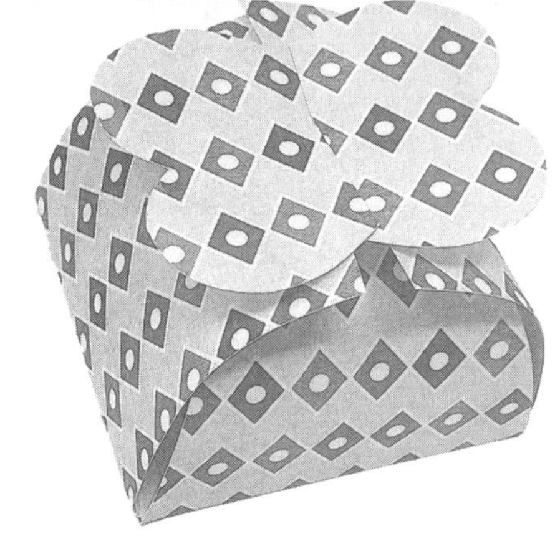

What It's All About

We should give generously to others and show kindness. Giving a friend a little treat makes them feel special and loved. Make it pretty by creating this simple treat holder.

What You Need

- Friendship Treat Holder Pattern (p. 66)
- Paper Cutting Tools (see p. 8)
- Scoring materials (see p. 9)
- Coloring & Writing Instruments (see p. 8)
- Colored or patterned cardstock or paper
- Treats, one for each child (individually wrapped candy, stickers, notes of encouragement, etc.)

Optional

- Decorating materials (beads, wiggle eyes, glitter or glitter glue, adhesive-backed jewels, craft-foam shapes, paper flowers, stickers, etc.)

Preparation

On cardstock or paper, photocopy Friendship Treat Holder Pattern, making one for each child. If the paper is patterned or colored on one side, copy on the non-printed side.

What Children Do

1. Cut out the treat holder. Cut on all the solid lines. To cut the slit, carefully insert one tip of the scissors into the center of the slit and cut to each end.
2. Score and fold on the dotted lines, you will see a square in the middle of the folds (image a).
3. Place one or two treats in the center of the holder.
4. Gently bend in the shorter sides putting the tab into the slit (image b).
5. Gently bend in the longer sides and slide the slits together to form the butterfly on the top of the box.

Optional

6. Use coloring and writing instruments and decorating materials to decorate your box.

Be Creative: Modify the treat holder pattern. Instead of a butterfly shape, trace another shape, cut it in half and replace the butterfly halves. Some shapes to consider:

- Tree
- Apple or pear
- Flower
- Heart
- Bug
- Pumpkin

Friendship Treat Holder Pattern

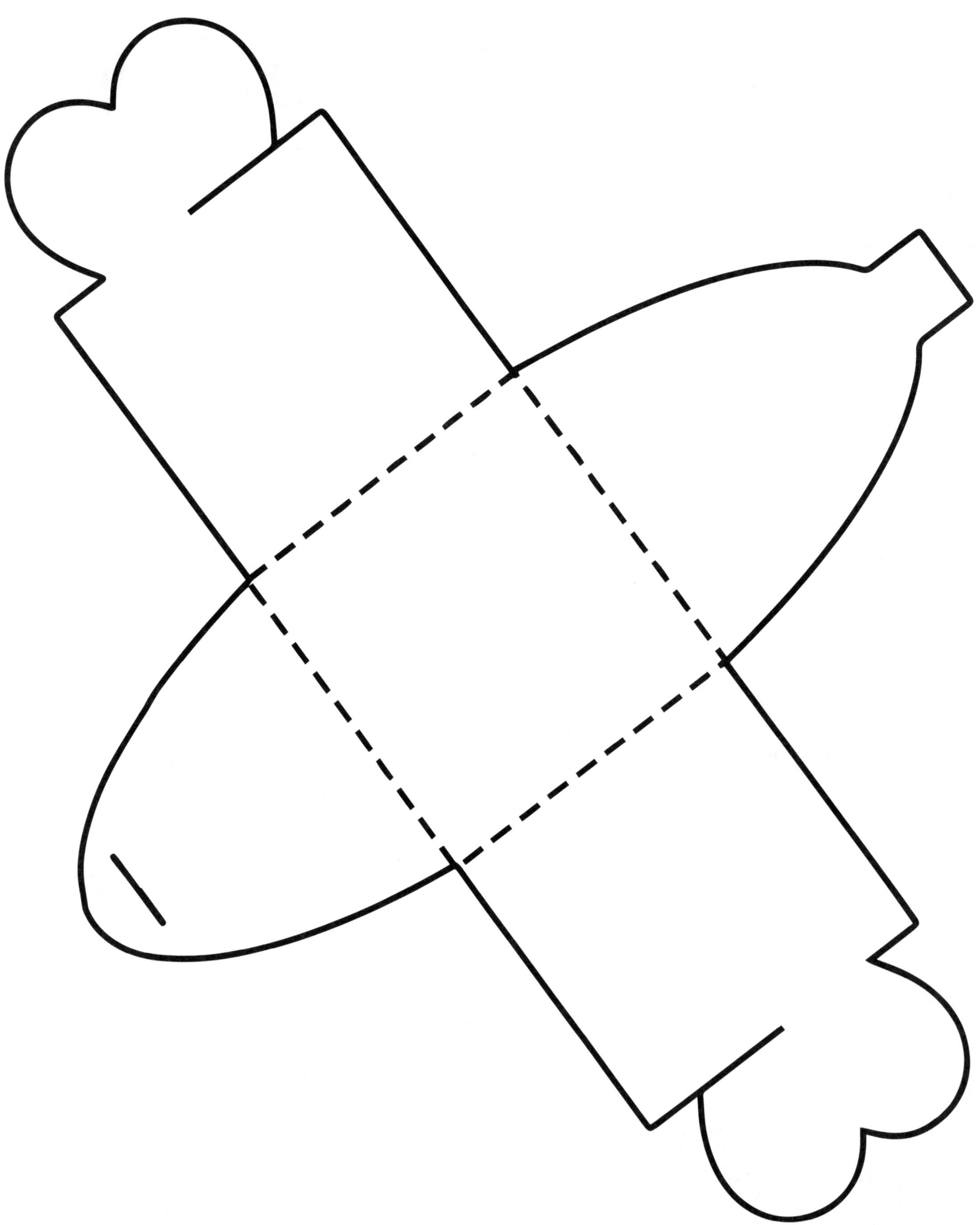

Kindness Vision Board

Age Level: ☆★

"For I know the plans I have for you," says the Lord. "They are plans for good and not for disaster, to give you a future and a hope." JEREMIAH 29:11

What It's All About

God has good plans for us. Let's make a Vision Board and plan ways to be kind to others. A vision board is a place where you can post pictures or ideas for things you'd like to do in the future.

What You Need

- Coloring & Writing Instruments (see p. 8)
- Paper Cutting Tools (see p. 8)
- Variety of colored poster board, one sheet for each child
- Magazines, catalogs, or printed advertisements
- Glue

Optional

- Decorating materials (beads, wiggle eyes, glitter or glitter glue, adhesive-backed jewels, craft-foam shapes, paper flowers, stickers, etc.)

Preparation

Photocopy this page, making one for each child.

What Children Do

1. Write or cut out letters for the top of the board to spell *kindness*.
2. Find pictures in magazines, catalogs, or printed advertisements of people being kind to others. Cut them out and glue them to your board.
3. Ask for ideas of other ways to be kind to others and write words or draw pictures on the poster board.
4. Talk about ways to show kindness and write them down in a list. Post the list on your board (image a).

a.

Optional

5. Use decorating materials to decorate your vision board.

Home Décor

Hospitality means to treat a guest well and make them feel comfortable and happy in your home. Your home and your bedroom are great places to entertain company. That means you want those spaces to look beautiful and be welcoming.

Add decorations that welcome people. This includes centerpieces that fill the middle of a table with beauty and kindness. It can also be signs and artwork you put up to welcome people. Adding a place card with the person's name beside their plate also shows you care.

Greeting people and using words to make them feel special lets people know you are happy to have them visit.

Ways to Be Hospitable

- Smile and greet each guest with kind words and say, "Welcome to my home."
- Ask each guest how they are doing, listen, and respond.
- Compliment the person, perhaps on what they are wearing or for their beautiful smile.
- Let guests go first in games.
- Share your toys.
- Speak words of encouragement.
- Serve your guests if there are refreshments.
- Thank the person for coming.

Snowflake Centerpiece

Age Level: ✩★

Thank you for making me so wonderfully complex! Your workmanship is marvelous—how well I know it. PSALM 139:14

What It's All About

The verse tells us that God made each of us wonderfully complex. We're all unique like snowflakes! Every snowflake is a unique crystal with six points or stems. Let's make a snowflake centerpiece. Put it on your dinner table to remind your family that God made them unique and special.

What You Need

- Paper Cutting Tools (see p. 8)
- Scoring materials (see p. 9)
- Coloring & Writing Instruments (see p. 8)
- White paper
- White, silver, or green pipe cleaners
- Vase or similar container
- Construction paper

What Children Do

Make Paper Snowflakes

1. Fold a top corner of the sheet of paper in half diagonally. You will have a folded triangle with an extra rectangle. Cut off the extra rectangle (image a—dashed line added for clarity).
2. Fold in half again to form a smaller triangle (image b).
3. Fold smaller triangle into thirds (image c).
4. Cut off bottom of folded triangles with a diagonal cut above where the straight line has formed on one side (image d).
5. Cut shapes in the folds of the paper and cut the tip off. See some suggested cuts in image e.
6. Open and see your snowflake. Or cut a little number one shape.
7. Make two or three more snowflakes.

Make the Centerpiece

8. Put pipe cleaner in the center hole of each snowflake and coil the end around a finger (image f). This will help keep the pipe cleaner in place.
9. Press snowflake edges up to form flowers (image g).
10. Arrange several snowflake flowers in vase to make a bouquet.
11. Cut a rectangle from construction paper and write a message such as "You are all special," "God made you unique!" or a message of your choice. Place message card and centerpiece on your dinner table.

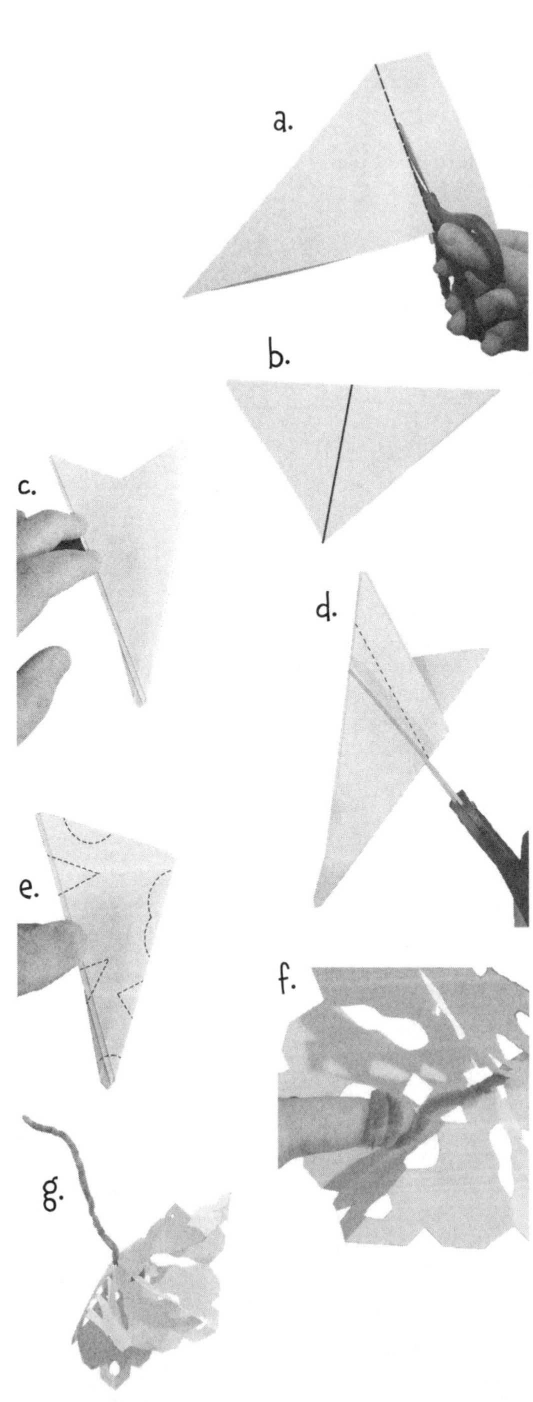

Heart Centerpiece

Age Level: ☆★

We should help others do what is right and build them up in the Lord. ROMANS 15:2

What It's All About

Our verse tells us to build people up. Another way to say that would be to *encourage* others. God told Moses to encourage Joshua who would take over for him as leader of God's people (Deuteronomy 3:28)**. Even leaders need encouragement! Let's make a Heart Centerpiece. Giving it to a leader you know (even your parents) can encourage and cheer them.**

What You Need

- Heart Centerpiece Patterns (p. 72)
- Paper Cutting Tools (see p. 8)
- Coloring & Writing Instruments (see p. 8)
- Styrofoam
- Hot knife, cookie cutter, or dental floss
- Cups, jars, or vases; one for each child
- Patterned paper
- Transparent tape
- Green plant sticks, six for each child
- Glue
- Filler material (tissue paper, nylon netting, or other lightweight and colorful paper or fabric)

Preparation

Photocopy Heart Centerpiece Patterns, making one for each child.

Use hot knife, cookie cutter, or dental floss to cut Styrofoam into pieces to fit snugly in bottom of the cups, jars, or vases. Prepare one container for each child.

Note: To cut with dental floss, cut off a length of dental floss, hold an end in each hand and pull taut. Pull dental floss down through a Styrofoam brick to slice.

What Children Do

1. Cut out the heart pattern. Trace pattern on patterned paper and cut out. Repeat to make twelve paper hearts.
2. On the front of six of the hearts, add notes or references for verses of encouragement. Refer to Encouragement Verses (p. 72), choose your own verses, or write your own words.
3. Tape one end of a plant stick to the back of the hearts with notes.
4. Glue the second six hearts to the back of the first six, sandwiching the plant stick in the middle.
5. Cut out word boxes and glue to blank side of each heart.
6. Place the finished heart into a cup, jar, or vase, making sure the end of the plant stick is securely in the Styrofoam shape at the bottom.
7. Cut and place pieces of filler inside cup to add color and sparkle.

Alternate Ideas

- Instead of using patterned paper, use white paper. Children draw their own designs.
- Instead of plant sticks, you can use food coloring to dye wood skewers green, or use green pipe cleaners.

Heart Centerpiece Patterns

LOVE	HOPE	GLADNESS
CHEER	JOY	DELIGHT

Encouragement Verses

- Psalm 31:24
- Psalm 121:1–2
- Isaiah 40:31
- John 16:33
- Romans 8:31
- Romans 15:5
- 1 Corinthians 16:13
- 1 Thessalonians 5:11
- Hebrews 10:24–25

Sports Centerpiece

Age Level: ★

Therefore, since we are surrounded by such a huge crowd of witnesses to the life of faith, let us strip off every weight that slows us down, especially the sin that so easily trips us up. And let us run with endurance the race God has set before us. HEBREWS 12:1

What It's All About

Celebrate sports and sportsmanship. A centerpiece with various sport symbols and words remind people to be a team player, respect others, lose graciously, and more. Generate conversation about healthy attitudes and actions for playing on a team.

What You Need

- ✯ Sports Centerpiece Patterns (p. 74)
- ✯ Paper Cutting Tools (see p. 8)
- ✯ Scoring materials (see p. 9)
- ✯ Coloring & Writing Instruments (p. 8)
- ✯ Paper Basket Instructions (p. 75); or purchased container, one for each child
- ✯ Tissue paper in local school or professional sports team colors
- ✯ White cardstock
- ✯ 12x12-inch sports-printed cardstock, one sheet for each child
- ✯ 4-inch square of Styrofoam, one for each child
- ✯ Transparent tape
- ✯ Glue
- ✯ 12-inch wooden skewers, six for each child
- ✯ Yarn

Preparation

On white cardstock, photocopy and enlarge to 200 percent the Sports Centerpiece Patterns, making two for each child. On regular copy paper, photocopy Paper Basket Instructions, making one for each child. Cut tissue paper into 4x8-inch rectangles. Cut yarn into 12-inch lengths, one for each child.

What Children Do

Make the Base Container

1. Use a 12x12-inch sheet of sports-printed cardstock to make a basket by following the Paper Basket Instructions.
2. Glue the Styrofoam into the bottom of the basket.

Make the Sports Equipment

a.

3. Cut out equipment shapes. There should be two of each item: baseball bat, baseball, basketball, and football. Color them.
4. Tape the end of a skewer to the back of one of each type of equipment. For the balls, tape the skewer a few inches from the edge of the ball. For the baseball bat, tape the skewer about halfway up the bat (image a).
5. Glue matching shapes on top, sandwiching skewer between the two cardstock pieces.
6. Dip the end of each skewer into glue, and then stick skewer into the Styrofoam at the bottom of your paper basket.

Make Pennants

7. Cut out pennant shapes and color them.
8. On one pennant, print words about good sportsmanship (Team Player, Respectful, Good Sport, Gracious Loser, etc.). On the other pennant, print the verse reference, "1 Corinthians 9:25–26."
9. Tape the end of a skewer to the back of one the pennant shapes. Glue matching shapes on top, sandwiching skewer between the two cardstock pieces.
10. Dip the ends of each skewer into glue, and then stick skewer into the Styrofoam at the bottom of your paper basket.

b.

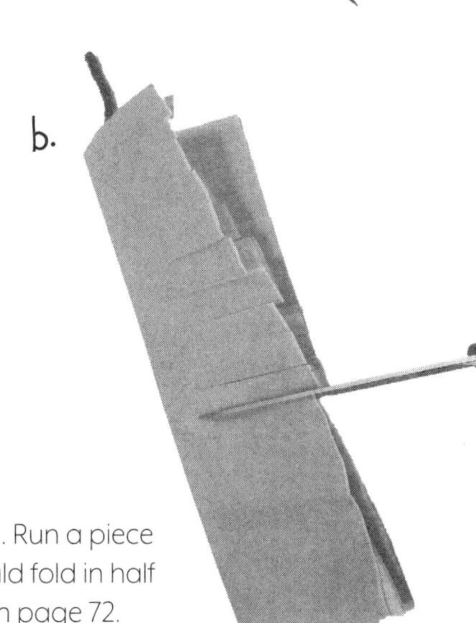

Make Pom-Poms

11. Layer four prepared pieces of tissue. Carefully fold the four layers in half lengthwise. Run a piece of yarn down the center of the folded layers (image b). **Note:** Alternatively, you could fold in half to create longer pom-pom streamers as shown in the photo of the finished craft on page 72.
12. Cut layers into a narrow fringe, from the open edge toward the fold. Stop cutting about an inch from the fold (image b).

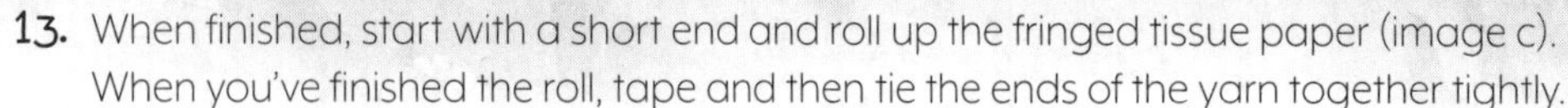

13. When finished, start with a short end and roll up the fringed tissue paper (image c). When you've finished the roll, tape and then tie the ends of the yarn together tightly.
14. Separate the fringes and fluff the pom-pom.
15. Cut your last skewer in half. Tape the center of the pom-pom to the end of the skewer (image d).
16. Dip the end of the pom-pom skewer in glue and stick in Styrofoam.
17. Repeat Steps 11–16 to make a second pom-pom.

d.

c.
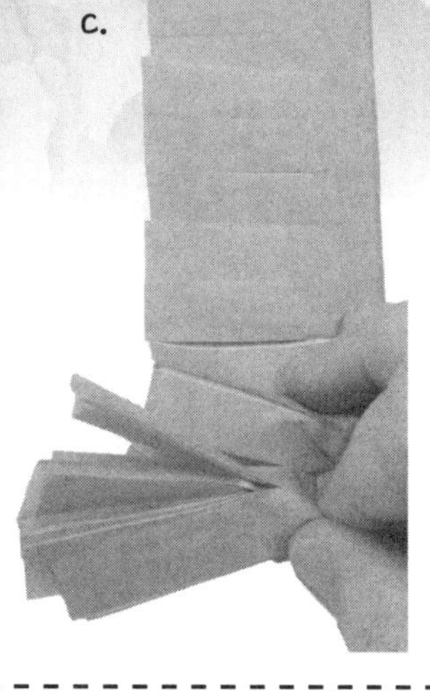

Sports Centerpiece Patterns

Baseball Bat Pattern

Football Pattern

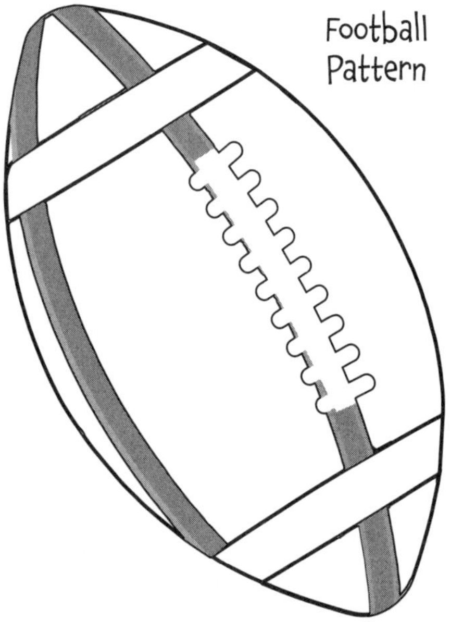

Enlarge these patterns 200%.

Baseball Pattern

Pennant Pattern

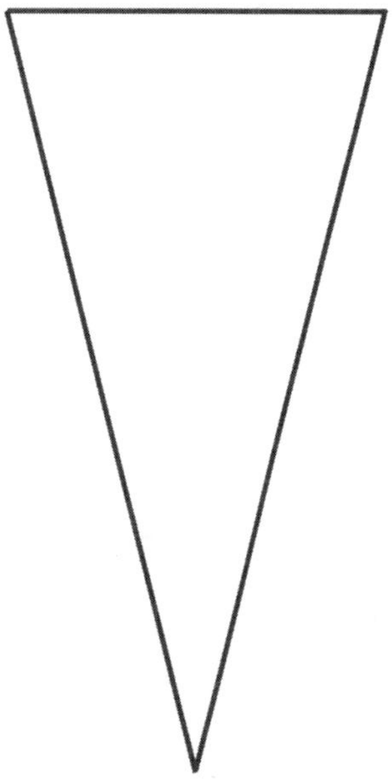

Basketball Pattern

Paper Basket Instructions

What You Need

- Coloring & Writing Instruments (see p. 8)
- 12x12-inch sheet of cardstock, one for each child
- Scoring materials (see p. 9)
- Stapler or glue

What Children Do

1. Before you start, decorate the cardstock with drawings if it is not patterned.
2. Score the cardstock on the inside of the basket (image a):
   - At 4-inch intervals horizontally
   - At 4-inch intervals vertically

   This will divide the paper into 9 sections.
3. Fold along all of the score lines.
4. Open the paper back up and score each of the corner squares diagonally towards the center section. Hint: This is easier if you first put a pencil mark at the corners of the center square (image c).

Assemble the Box

5. Open paper flat.
6. Fold up two sides of the box towards the center.
7. Now fold the diagonal corners in. Place two corners towards each other on the inside of the basket. Staple or glue to secure (image d). If you staple, make sure the smooth side of the staples are on the outside of the basket. **Optional:** You can later decorate with ribbon, washi tape, or other trim to cover the staples.
8. Place the other corners together on the opposite side. Staple or glue to secure.

a.

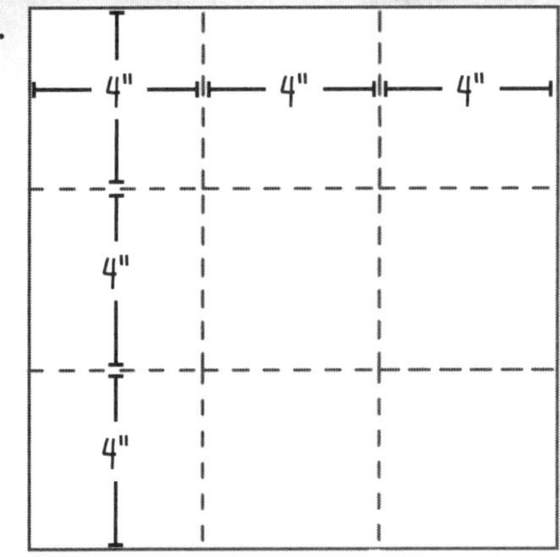

b.

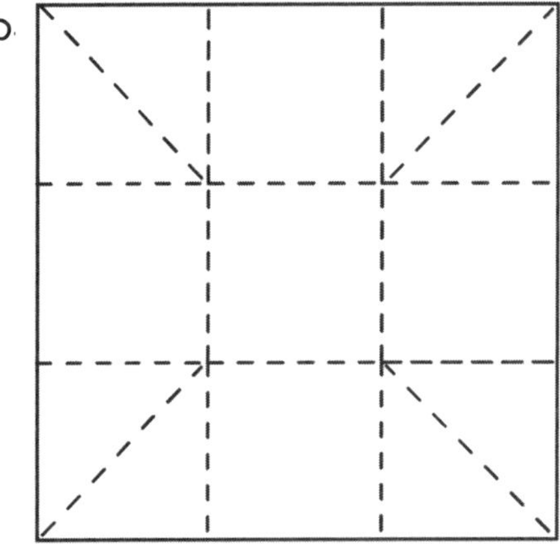

c.

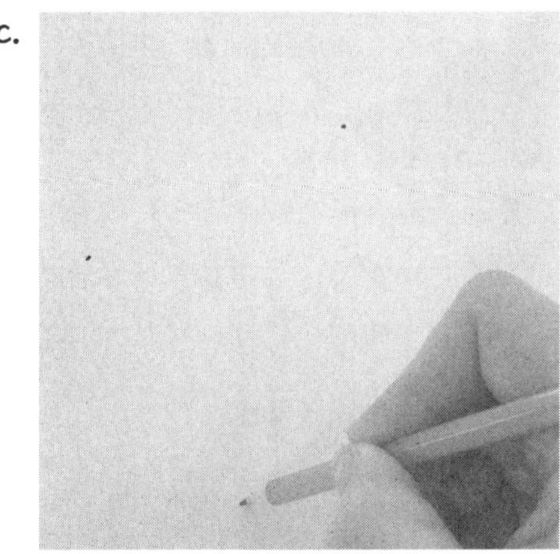

d.

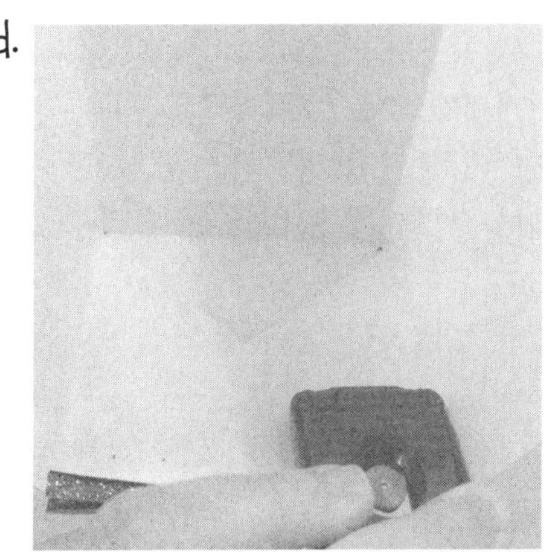

Garden Centerpiece

Age Level: ☆★

Fix your thoughts on what is true, and honorable, and right, and pure, and lovely, and admirable. Think about things that are excellent and worthy of praise. PHILIPPIANS 4:8

What It's All About

Lovely things help us remember to have thoughts that are excellent and worthy of praise. Let's create a fun centerpiece and talk about flowers and other lovely things that God has given us. Let's praise him for all the beautiful things he's given us!

What You Need

- Garden Centerpiece Patterns (pp. 77–78)
- Paper Cutting Tools (see p. 8)
- Coloring & Writing Instruments (see p. 8)
- White cardstock or paper
- Cardstock in three different shades of green
- Green plant sticks
- Clear packing tape
- Glue

Optional

- Decorating materials (beads, wiggle eyes, glitter or glitter glue, adhesive-backed jewels, craft-foam shapes, paper flowers, stickers, etc.)

Alternate Idea

- Instead of plant sticks, you can use food coloring to dye wood skewers green, or use green pipe cleaners.

Preparation

On white cardstock or paper, photocopy Garden Centerpiece Patterns, making one set for each child. Be sure to enlarge patterns 200 percent.

Cut the following, making one set for each child, or children choose their cardstock and use scissors and rulers to cut for themselves:

- Darkest green cardstock: 4½x9-inch strips, one for each child
- Medium green cardstock: 4½x7-inch strips, one for each child
- Lightest green cardstock: 4½x5-inch strips, one for each child

a.

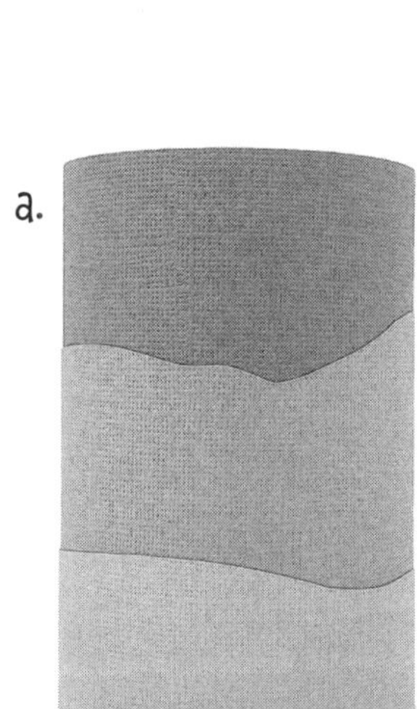

What Children Do

Make the Garden Base

1. For the medium green and light green cardstock pieces, recut the top edge to be wavy (see image a). This will suggest rolling hills.
2. Attach the larger two pieces of cardstock together. Glue or tape it only along the bottom edge. This forms a pocket to put the flowers in.
3. Attach the shortest piece the same way.
4. Curl the sheets together so that they form a cylinder. Glue or tape the seam where the two edges meet up. **Optional:** If using glue, clip on clothespins to hold the top and bottom of the cylinder in place while the seam dries.

Make and Add Flowers

5. Use the patterns or design your own flowers. Cut and color both sides of each flower. **Hint:** If you're going to play the Colorful Meanings Game on page 77, use these colors when you color the flowers.
6. Attach each flower to a plant stick. You can use longer or shorter plant sticks to vary the height of the flowers.
7. Stick the flowers into the pockets, placing them as desired. Set on table or even around a tall vase of real flowers.

Garden Centerpiece Patterns

Enlarge flower patterns 200%.

Family Fun

Make the Garden Centerpiece part of a meal or ceremony and say something as each person adds a flower to the centerpiece. Scriptures in parenthesis can be marked in a Bible and read aloud after reading about the flower's color.

Colorful Meanings Game

Use the information and verses below to talk about virtues:

- White is for purity. Be true to yourself and speak truth (Revelation 3:5).
- Blue of the sky and water reminds us we all share the same earth and should work toward peace (Psalm 65:9).
- Green is the color of plants and grass, a symbol of growth. We should all grow in body and soul (2 Peter 3:18).
- Pink, made from red and white, represents joy (John 15:11).
- Red represents life and love. Let us rejoice in our lives and love one another (Ephesians 1:7).

- Yellow, the color of the sunshine, reminds us to be rays of sunshine spreading hope and a positive attitude. Also, yellow is like gold, reminding us we are all valuable (Matthew 2:11).
- Purple, the color of royalty, reminds us that we are all special and should treat one another as royalty (John 19:2).
- Orange is the color of fire and we should have fired up spirit to encourage and cheer on one another (Acts 2:3–4).

Testimony Time

- Let each person add a flower and mention how has grown and what virtue they want to continue to grow.

Garden Centerpiece Patterns, continued

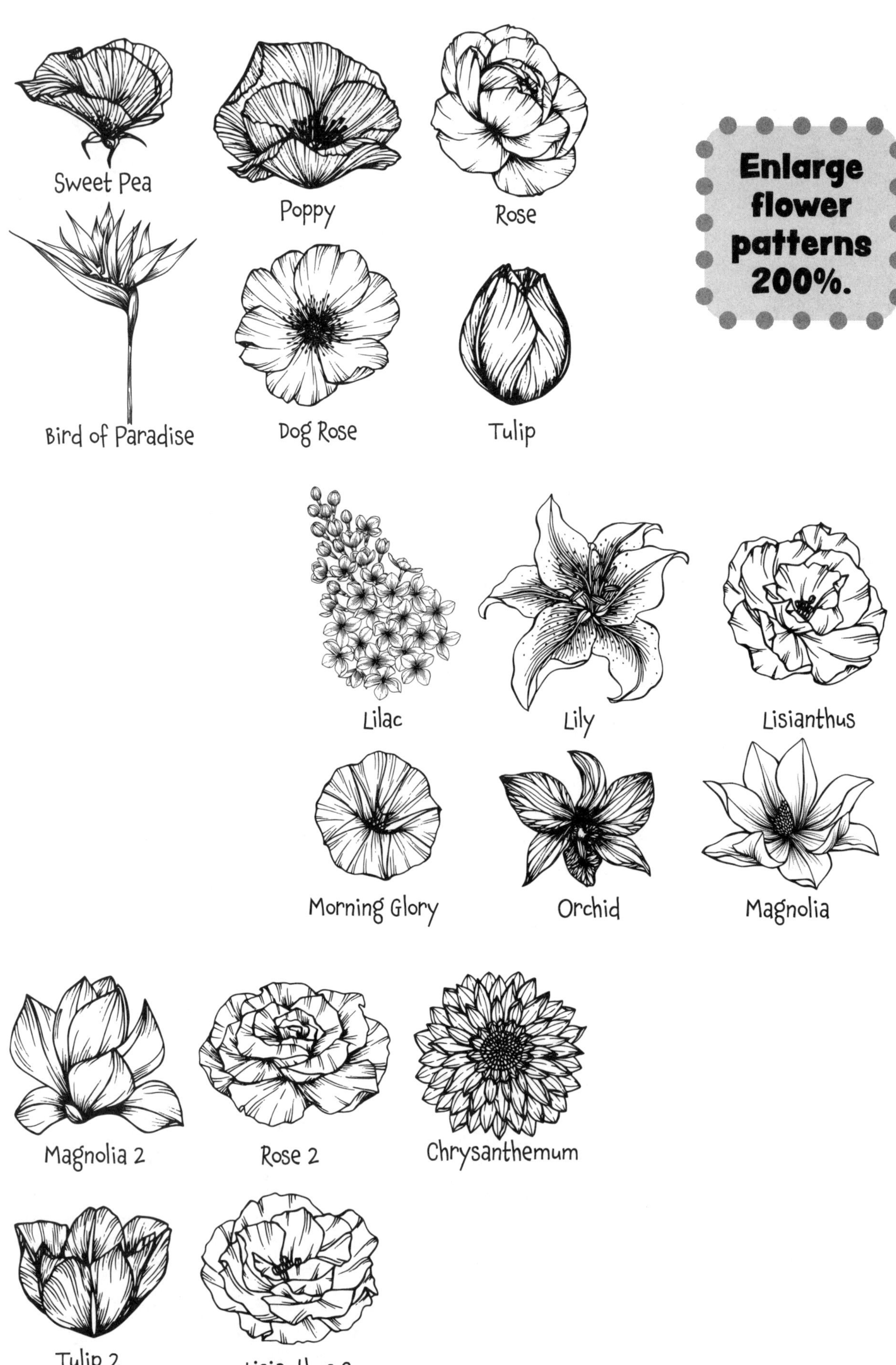

Twirling Centerpiece

Age Level: ★

May God give you more and more mercy, peace, and love. JUDE 1:2

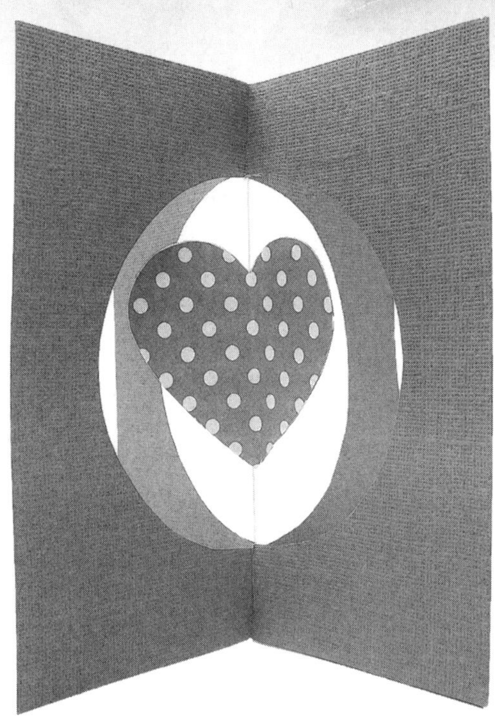

What It's All About

There are two options for this centerpiece. You can either make a heart or a dove. Hearts are symbols of love. A dove is a sign of peace. Decide whether you want to send a message of love or of peace, and choose the appropriate symbol.

What You Need

- Twirling Centerpiece Patterns (p. 81)
- Paper Cutting Tools (see p. 8)
- White or patterned paper
- Colored cardstock
- 8-inch bowls, lids, or other circular objects
- Pencils
- Thread or monofilament fiber (fishing line)
- Transparent tape
- Glue

Optional

- Decorating materials (beads, wiggle eyes, glitter or glitter glue, adhesive-backed jewels, craft-foam shapes, paper flowers, stickers, etc.)

Preparation

For Dove: On white paper, photocopy Dove Body and Dove Wing Patterns, enlarging patterns to 200 percent. Make one set of dove patterns for each child.

For Heart: On the plain, white side of patterned paper, photocopy Heart Patterns, enlarging patterns to 200 percent. Make one set of heart patterns for each child.

Cut the following, making one set for each child, or children choose their cardstock and use scissors and rulers to cut for themselves:

- Four 10-inch squares of cardstock in the same color, one set for each child

What Children Do

Prepare the Base

1. Place an 8-inch bowl, lid, or other circular object in the center back of the cardstock square. Trace the circle onto the cardstock, and then cut out.
2. Use the first sheet of cardstock to trace and cut similar circles from the other three sheets of cardstock. This will ensure the circles are in the same place for all four sheets of cardstock. Remember to trace on the back side of the cardstock.
3. Set two sheets of cardstock aside. On the two remaining sheets, cut slits from the outside of the circle halfway to the circle, as shown in image a. *Do not cut all the way to the circle.*

a.

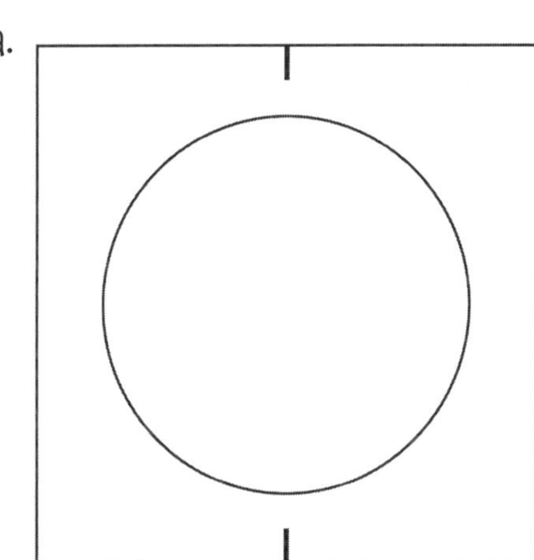

Make the Twirling Object

For the Heart

4. Cut out the hearts from prepared patterned paper. Fold each heart in half lengthwise.
5. Cut a length of thread or monofilament fiber longer than the circle opening. Place the thread over one heart, from top to bottom of the center of the heart. Tape thread in place.
6. Fold each heart in half lengthwise. Glue or tape all three hearts together, gluing one half of each heart to a different heart, forming a three-sided heart with the thread in the middle. Make sure the ends of thread hang out (image b).
7. Pull gently but tightly on thread and center heart in the open window. Tape the thread above and below the window so that the heart will be free to twirl.
8. Glue or tape the second piece of cardstock in which you cut slits to cover the one with the heart, wrong sides together.

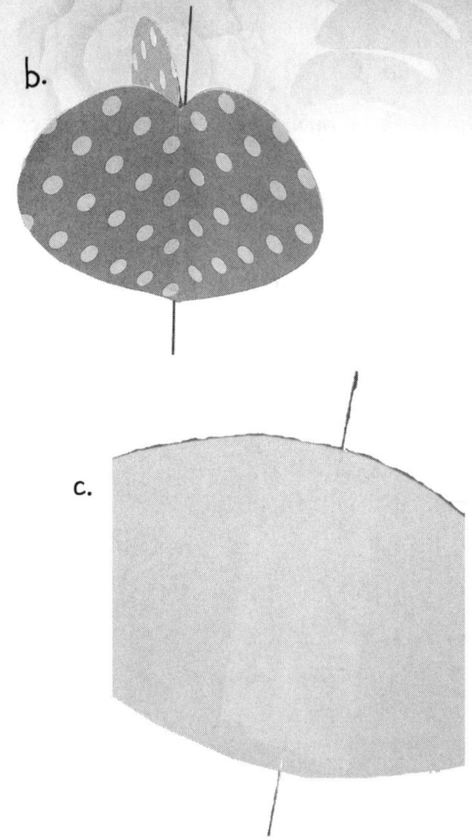

For the Dove

9. Cut out the dove bodies.
10. Cut a length of thread or monofilament fiber longer than the circle opening. Place the thread over one dove, from top to bottom over the center of the dove. Tape thread in place (image c).
11. Glue or tape second dove body over thread and first dove, matching edges, making sure ends of thread hang out.
12. Pull gently, but tightly on thread and center dove in the open window. Tape the thread to above and below the window so the dove will be free to twirl (wings will be added later).
13. Glue or tape the second piece of cardstock in which you cut slits to cover the one with the dove, wrong sides together.

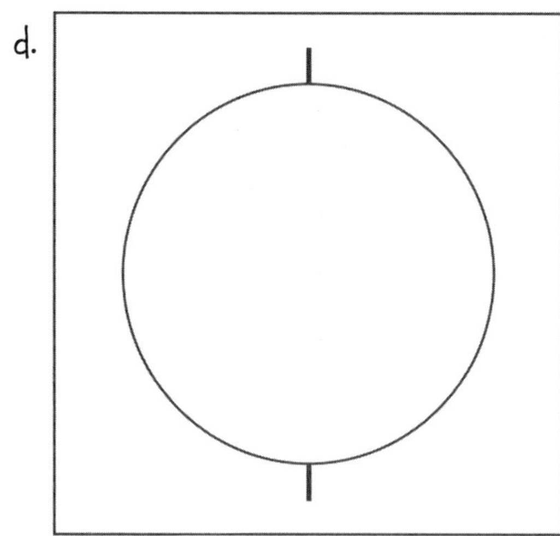

Assemble the Centerpiece

14. Glue other two squares together, wrong sides facing. Cut slits on both the top and bottom of the circle halfway to the edge (image d).
15. Gently bend and slide the square with the twirling object into the opening of the other square. Then slide the top and bottom slits together.
16. If using the dove, cut out the wings and bend at dotted line. Put glue or double-sided tape on the tab and glue on either side of dove's body with the longer section at the top (image e).

Optional

17. Use decorating materials to add your own touch to your centerpiece.

Twirling Centerpiece Patterns

Dove Body Patterns

Dove Wing Patterns

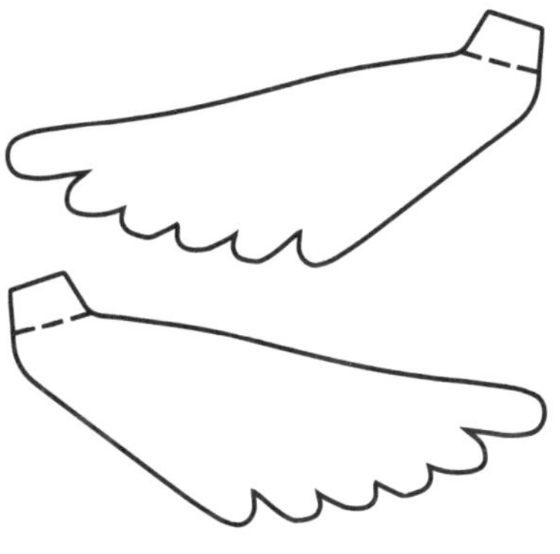

Enlarge all patterns 200%.

Heart Patterns

Changeable Door Sign

Age Level: ☆★

Keep on loving each other as brothers and sisters. Don't forget to show hospitality to strangers, for some who have done this have entertained angels without realizing it! HEBREWS 13:1–2

What It's All About

Our verse talks about hospitality, making people feel welcome in your home. Let's make a sign you can change to welcome friends to your home or to put up as a holiday greeting. Our sign will have an opening to slide in different greetings.

This sign also makes a wonderful welcome gift to a new neighbor.

What You Need

- Message Card Pattern (p. 83)
- Paper Cutting Tools (see p. 8)
- Coloring & Writing Instruments (see p. 8)
- White cardstock
- Cardboard or foam core
- Patterned paper (because of the dimensions needed, wrapping paper is a good option)
- Transparent tape
- Glue

Optional

- Decorating materials (beads, wiggle eyes, glitter or glitter glue, adhesive-backed jewels, craft-foam shapes, paper flowers, stickers, etc.)

Preparation

On white cardstock, photocopy Message Card Pattern, making one for each child. Be sure to enlarge patterns by 200 percent.

- One 1x12-inch strip of cardboard or foam core
- Two 1x8-inch strips of cardboard or foam core

From the scrap cardboard, cut 5x8-inch rectangles to be used as patterns for cutting windows in Step 1 below.

What Children Do

Make the Frame

1. In the center of one of the large (9x12-inch) rectangles, use a 5x8-inch pattern to trace a rectangle (image a). This will make the window of the frame.
2. Cut out the window. **Hint:** Rotate one end of a pair of scissors back and forth to create a hole in the center of the window (image b). Then, cut from the center to the traced rectangle and cut the window from the inside.
3. Cut a piece of patterned paper a couple inches larger than the frame.
4. On the back of the patterned paper use your frame to trace a smaller rectangle inside the window. Then draw diagonal lines to the corners. See dashed lines in image c.
5. Cut inside the smaller rectangle you traced. Cut on the diagonal lines to each corner (image d).

a.

b.

c.

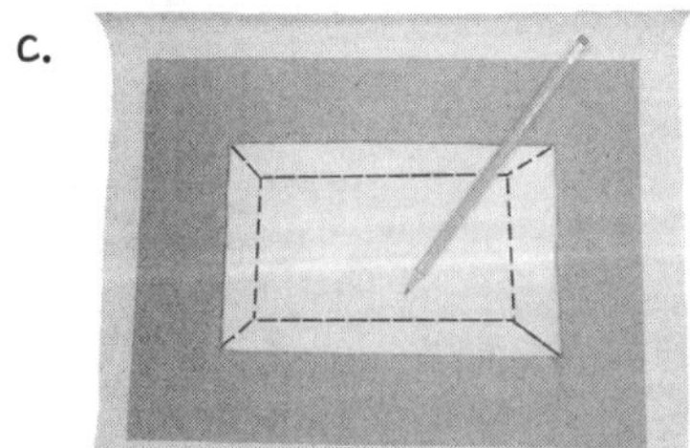

d.

6. Wrap and tape paper in place along the outside edges and inside the window (image e).

e.

Build the Sign

7. Glue the 1x12-inch strip to the-bottom edge of the back of the sign. Glue the 8-inch strips to the-side edges (image f).
8. Apply glue to the bottom and side strips on back of the frame (image f).
9. Carefully place the paper-covered frame on top. Set aside to dry (image g). The top edge of the frame will remain open to insert and remove message cards.

f.

Make the Message Card to Insert

10. Cut out Message Card Pattern.
11. Write a message and color the card. You can make more message papers by cutting out additional pieces of cardstock or colored paper. Each card should be 7x9-inches in size.
12. Place your message in the sign. If you make multiple message cards, you can store them in the frame, behind the message you want to display.
13. Place your sign on a wall at your house or prop it on a table or counter.

g.

Optional

14. Use decorating materials to decorate your Changeable Door Sign and messages.

Younger Elementary Adaptation

To make this craft appropriate for younger elementary children, precut the frame's window. Instead of covering frame with paper, children decorate frame with crayons, paint, or other decorations.

Message Card Pattern

Great Messages for Your Signs

- Welcome to the neighborhood!
- Have a great day!
- You are awesome!
- I love my one-of-a-kind friend!
- We love visitors!

Wall Photo Collage Board

Age Level: ☆★

You were cleansed from your sins when you obeyed the truth, so now you must show sincere love to each other as brothers and sisters. Love each other deeply with all your heart. 1 PETER 1:22

What It's All About

Let's make a collage board. You can fill it with photos of fun times together with family or a friend. Give it to someone in the photos to share happy memories and rejoice with them.

What You Need

- Paper Cutting Tools (see p. 8)
- Fabric or paper (See paper Alternate Idea below.)
- Ribbon in a variety of colors and patterns
- Stapler
- 11x14-inch foam board (or any size you choose)
- Quilt batting
- White glue

Optional

- Pins or thumbtacks

What Children Do

Cover the Board

1. Glue the batting to the foam board.
2. Cut fabric about 3 inches larger than the board on all sides.
3. Lay fabric wrong side up on a table. Place foam board batting side down in the middle of fabric.
4. Wrap edges of fabric over the top of the foam board and staple. Continue around the board folding it in tight at corners. You can either fold in the corners and staple them or fold them in just a little way and cut off the excess fabric.

Add Ribbons

5. Cut ribbon to run diagonally in rows across the front of the board making a crisscross pattern.
6. Staple each ribbon onto the back of the board to hold it down securely. Depending on the fabric and ribbon choices you may need to use staples on the front in a couple of places to secure the ribbons.
7. Add a length of ribbon to the back toward the top to hang the board on a wall.

Decorate Board

8. You can tuck photographs in behind the ribbons. **Optional:** If you are having trouble with the photographs staying you can always use the pins or thumbtacks to hold them down more securely.
9. Give the board to a friend with photos of you rejoicing together or fill it with photos of a special event you shared to remember that event (like a graduation or trip) and words about good memories. Add words about memories around the photos.

Alternate Idea

Cover board as above with batting and then use wrapping paper to cover it and add ribbon or strips of paper and then slide in photos. Be very gentle to not rip the paper.

Nature Wall Art

Age Level: ✮★

Everything on earth will worship you; they will sing your praises, shouting your name in glorious songs. PSALM 66:4

What It's All About

We praise God with all of nature. Let's make artwork we can give someone as a reminder that God is found all around us in nature.

What You Need

- Thin cardboard sheets, one for each child
- Low-temperature glue gun (with adult supervision)
- 4 straight sticks per child
- Nature objects, real or artificial (pebbles, pinecones, flowers, acorns, leaves, sticks, etc.)

For Painted Nature Art

- Paint in a variety of colors
- Paper plates

Optional

- Coloring & Writing Instruments (see p. 8)

Painted Nature Art

Preparation

Pour paint onto the paper plates. Place plates on covered table where children will be working. (See Newspapers and Plastic Tablecloths on p. 8.)

What Children Do

1. Glue the sticks around the edge of the cardboard to make a frame.
2. Dip a nature object into the paint.
3. Press the object onto the cardboard creating a stamp or print of the object. Lift object off.
4. Repeat, using different nature objects and colors. Set aside to dry.

Optional: Use coloring and writing instruments to create a scene with the stamped images as the background.

Glued Nature Art

What Children Do

Arrange the nature objects on cardboard to make a scene or design and glue. Set aside to dry.

Optional: Print words on the cardboard about caring for God's creation or the verse reference, Psalm 66:4.

Place Card Holders

Age Level: ☆★

When Jesus noticed that all who had come to the dinner were trying to sit in the seats of honor near the head of the table, he gave them this advice: "When you are invited to a wedding feast, don't sit in the seat of honor. . . . For those who exalt themselves will be humbled, and those who humble themselves will be exalted." LUKE 14:7–8,11

What It's All About

Today's verse is from a story in the New Testament. Jesus told this story to help his friends know what it means to be humble. Being humble means not thinking of yourself as better than others.

Welcome friends and family to dinner with their names in place card holders. Encourage your guests to enjoy the people seated around them.

What You Need

- Paper Cutting Tools (see p. 8)
- Coloring & Writing Instruments (see p. 8)
- 2-inch binder clips, one or more for each child
- Lightweight cardstock in a variety of colors and patterns
- Tacky glue
- Decorating materials (beads, wiggle eyes, glitter or glitter glue, adhesive-backed jewels, craft-foam shapes, paper flowers, stickers, etc.)

Preparation

Photocopy this page, making one for each child.

Cut cardstock into a 2x3¼-inch strip, making one for each child, or children choose their patterned paper and use scissors and rulers to cut for themselves.

What Children Do

1. Keeping the clip closed, glue a prepared strip of patterned paper around the bottom of the binder clip.
2. Decorate the clip with decorating items. **Optional:** Print words to bless the person, such as "U. R. Special" or "God loves you!"
3. Cut out the pattern of your choice. Trace the shape (or one of your own) onto a piece of cardstock. Print the person's name on the same shape or on another piece of cardstock.
4. Make more place holders as time allows.

Place Card Holder Patterns

Heart Pattern

Star Pattern

Hexagon Pattern

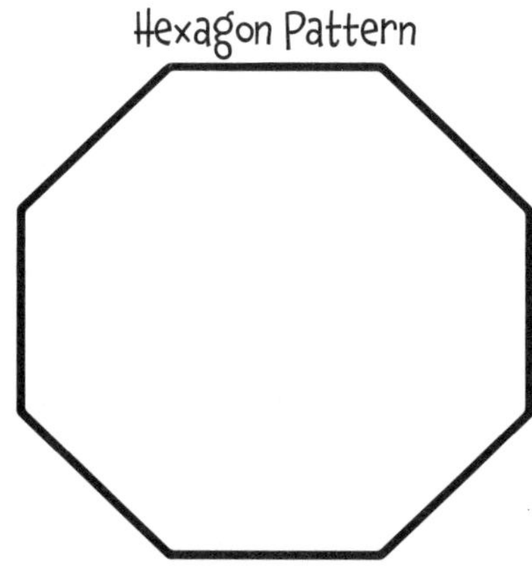

Gifts & Gift Wraps

Gifts are a way to express kindness, love, or friendship. Gifts can be little notes and cards, a treat you cook, or something you make by hand. You can also buy a gift and make it special by adding a card with a note or a pretty bow. The greatest gift any of us can ever receive is salvation through Jesus Christ.

This section includes gifts that can be given to others. There are also ideas for ways to wrap gifts to make them more personal or show someone you care for them. As you make a gift for someone, pray for them. Pray that the gift they are making, or decorating, will bring joy to the recipient and help them feel loved. It takes time to make gifts for others and wrap them up especially for them, the time spent preparing a gift is itself a gift.

Outreach Ideas

Here are a few outreach ideas for the crafts in this section:

- Make Recipe Holders (p. 88) for a church group, especially if they cook for your church. This is a great way to express thanks to them.
- Make the Baby Memory Box (p. 89) for women's shelters or a local crisis pregnancy center. This is one way to share God's love with those who may be struggling.
- Make a Wallet Album (p. 91) for friends and family who have been away.
- Make Bookmarks (p. 95) to give out at a group event or to a group of younger children, especially if you are encouraging them to read.
- Make Gift Coupons (p. 98) for your mom or dad to encourage them. It will show your love and thankfulness for all they do for you.
- Make Gift Bags (p. 100), Gift Boxes (p. 101), and Wrapping Papers (p. 102) to use on upcoming holidays. Sell them to raise money for a cause that your church supports.

Recipe Holder

Age Level: ★★

They worshiped together at the Temple each day, met in homes for the Lord's Supper, and shared their meals with great joy and generosity. ACTS 2:46

What It's All About

Eating together is one way the members of Jesus' new church learned to share life together. This is sometimes called *fellowship*. We're going to make a recipe holder for a favorite cook. It's a gift of kindness, just like their cooking food for others is a gift.

What You Need

- Paper Cutting Tools (see p. 8)
- Scoring materials (see p. 9)
- Heavy cardstock
- Strong craft glue or low-temperature glue gun (with adult supervision)

Optional

- Decorating materials (beads, wiggle eyes, glitter or glitter glue, adhesive-backed jewels, craft-foam shapes, paper flowers, stickers, etc.)

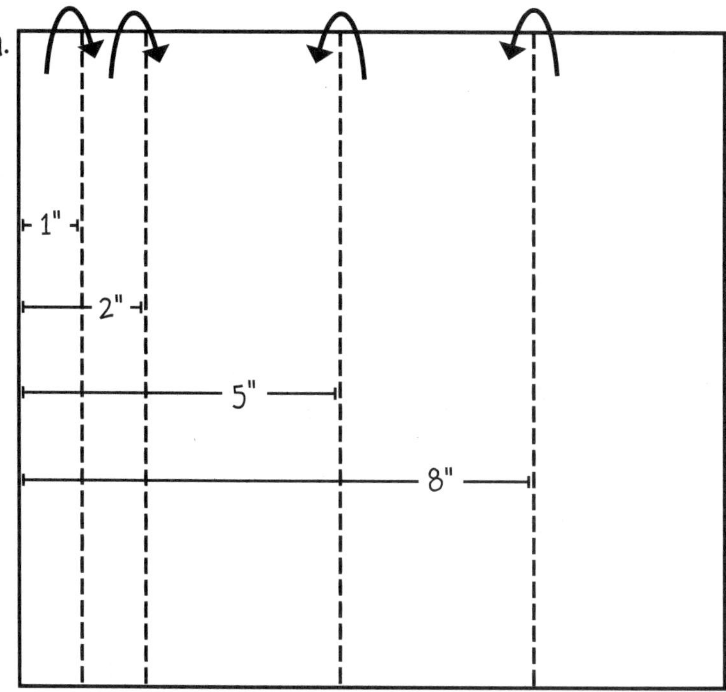

Preparation

Making sure the paper's grain runs along the long edge, cut cardstock into 10x11-inch strips, making one for each child. Or children choose their patterned paper and use scissors and rulers to cut for themselves.

What Children Do

1. Score straight lines across the long side of the rectangle at 1 inch, 2 inches, 5 inches, and 8 inches (image a).
2. Fold the 1-inch score towards the 2-inch score.
3. Fold the 2-inch score in the same direction.
4. Fold the 5- and 8-inch score in the opposite direction of the first two folds, forming a triangle (image b).
5. Glue the first two folds together, making a 1-inch lip.
6. Glue the lip to the bottom edge of the triangle (image b).

Optional: Use decorating materials to decorate holder.

Note: You can use this as a stand for any paper, such as sheet music, craft instructions, etc.

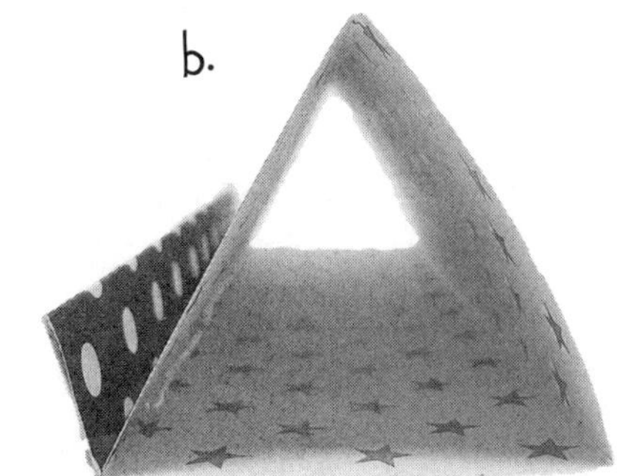

Baby Memory Box

Age Level: ★

After seeing him, the shepherds told everyone what had happened and what the angel had said to them about this child. All who heard the shepherds' story were astonished, but Mary kept all these things in her heart and thought about them often. LUKE 2:17–19

What It's All About

Mary, the mother of Jesus, thought about and remembered all the amazing things that happened when Jesus was born. All mothers love to think about and remember things about the birth of their babies. We're going to make a memory box to give a new mom (or your mom) to store treasured memories to look at and remember in the years to come.

What You Need

- Baby Memory Box Pattern (p. 90)
- Paper Cutting Tools (see p. 8)
- Coloring & Writing Instruments (see p. 8)
- Scoring materials (see p. 9)
- Transparent tape
- 12x12-inch patterned or colored cardstock sheets, one for each child
- Strong craft glue or low-temperature glue gun (with adult supervision)
- Double-sided foam mounting tape (or glue on foam dots)
- Twine or string
- Index cards, several for each child

Optional

- Decorating materials (beads, wiggle eyes, glitter or glitter glue, adhesive-backed jewels, craft-foam shapes, paper flowers, stickers, etc.)

Preparation

Photocopy Baby Memory Box Pattern, making two for each child, and enlarging to 200 percent. Cut twine or string into approximately 12-inch lengths, making one for each child.

What Children Do

Cut and Score the Box

1. Cut out both Box Pattern pieces along the outside lines. Flip one of the pattern pieces face-down and tape to the other one along the hollow dotted line. Your final pattern should look like image a.
2. On the back of a 12x12-inch sheet of cardstock, trace the pattern. Cut on all solid lines. Do not cut the dashed lines.
3. Score the cardstock along the dashed lines.
4. Fold all the score lines in the same direction, toward what will be the inside of the box.

a.

The gray lines indicate the printed side of the paper is facedown.

Glue the Bottom of the Box

5. Place glue on the smaller portion of Flaps B and C (image b).
6. Fold up Flap D and glue it to the glued portions of Flaps B and D.

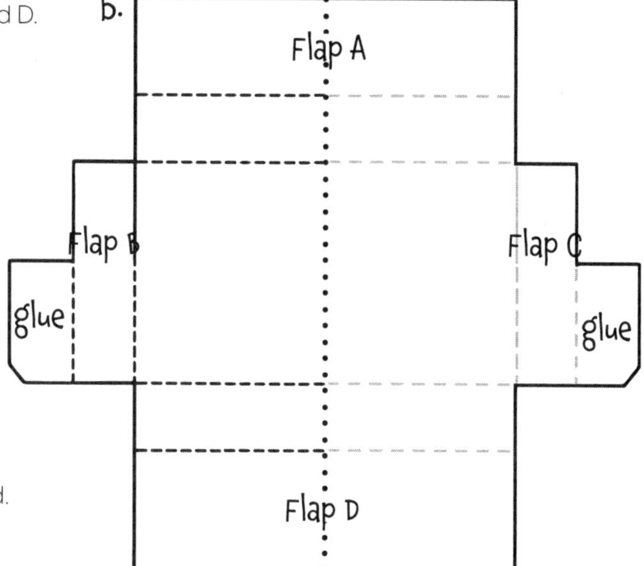

Make Closure

7. Trace the Circle Pattern twice on a contrasting color of cardstock. Cut out.
8. Put a piece of foam tape on the back of one of the circles.
9. Place one end of a length of twine or string on the foam tape. Put a second piece of foam tape on the string.
10. Tape the circle with a string on it in the middle of the outside of Flap A, the top of the box.
11. Take the other circle and put two layers of foam tape on it.
12. Place second circle in the middle of the bottom of the box.
13. Wrap the string around the two circles to keep the box closed.

Make It a Gift

14. Place several index cards in the box.
15. Give this memory box to a new mom. Include a card suggesting she use the cards to quickly write down special moments and memories of her child so she will have them to treasure in her heart. Be sure to include today's verses, Luke 2:17–19.

Optional: Use decorating materials to decorate box.

Baby Memory Box Patterns

It Takes Two

You'll need two enlarged Box Patterns to make a full-sized pattern.

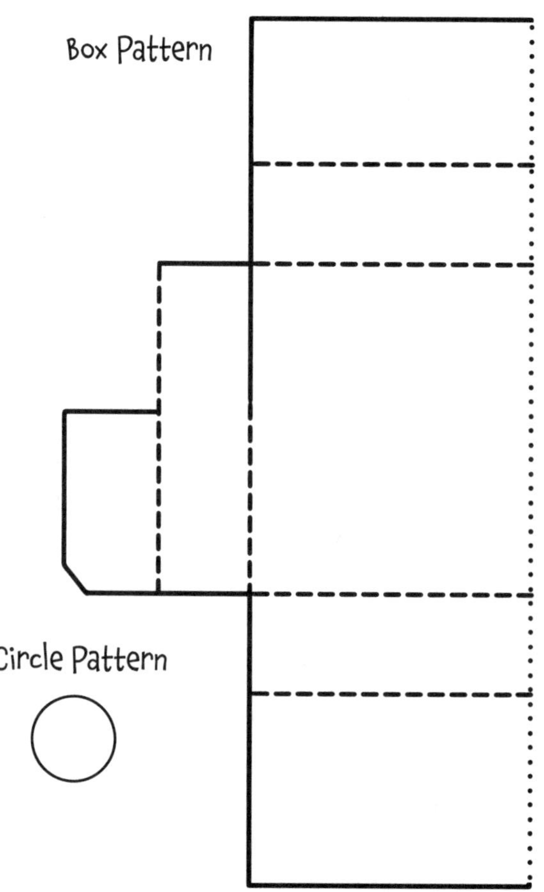

Wallet Album

Age Level: ☆★

After you have read this letter, pass it on to the church at Laodicea so they can read it, too. And you should read the letter I wrote to them. COLOSSIANS 4:16

What It's All About

Paul told the Colossian people to pass on his letters to one another and the people of another church (Colossians 4:16). **We can pass on cheerful notes with Scripture that will encourage others, too. This wallet album can store and protect notes and photos that you might want to pass on to others.**

What You Need

- Paper Cutting Tools (see p. 8)
- Scoring materials (see p. 9)
- Colored or patterned cardstock
- Strong craft glue or low-temperature glue gun (with adult supervision)

Optional

- Decorating materials (beads, wiggle eyes, glitter or glitter glue, adhesive-backed jewels, craft-foam shapes, paper flowers, stickers, etc.)

Preparation

Cut the following for each child; or children choose their cardstock and use scissors and rulers to cut for themselves:

- 4x8-inch rectangle
- 3.5x7.5-inch rectangle
- Two 3-inch squares
- ½x5-inch strip

What Children Do

Score the Cardstock Pieces

1. Score the 4x8-inch piece at 4 inches so it will easily fold in half.
2. Score the 3.5x7.5-inch piece at 3.75 inches to fold it in half.

Make the Inside Pockets

3. On the wrong side of the smaller (3.5x7.5-inch) rectangle, place a thin line of glue on the short sides. Also add a line of glue along one long side, and on either side of the score line (image a).
4. Glue it onto the wrong side of the large (4x8-inch) rectangle, lining up the bottom edges and the score lines (image b). This makes two pockets inside the card to store pictures or notes.
5. Fold the card in half with the pockets on the inside so that you can finish the card.

a.

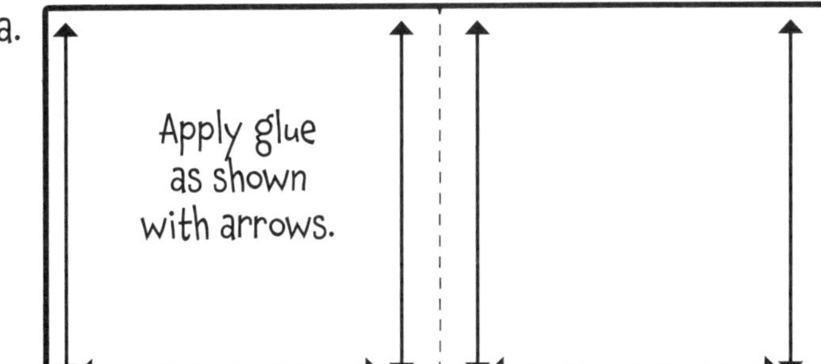

b.

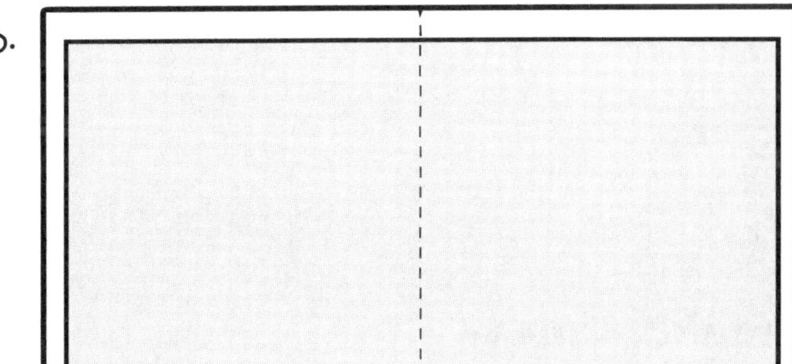

Make Tab Closure

6. Put about 1-inch of glue on end of the ½x5-inch strip of cardstock. Glue it to the middle back edge of the wallet to form the tab closure (image c).
7. Glue one of the 3-inch squares to the middle back of the wallet. Cover the glued end of the tab closure (image c).
8. Place glue on three edges of the other 3-inch square. Place square in the center front of the wallet with the unglued edge facing where the wallet opens.
9. Gently bend the strip of cardstock around the wallet and slip it into the pocket on the front of the card to secure. If strip leaves a gap when bending around the card, cut it shorter.

Optional:
Use decorating materials to decorate wallet.

Paper Flowers

Age Level: ★★

And why worry about your clothing? Look at the lilies of the field and how they grow. They don't work or make their clothing, yet Solomon in all his glory was not dressed as beautifully as they are. MATTHEW 6:28–29

What It's All About

Let's make some beautiful flowers. While it is kind to share things of beauty like these flowers, it is even more important to shine with inner beauty by being caring, loving, and serving others.

Optional: Make these flowers as a way to decorate Gift Bags (p. 100) and Gift Boxes (p. 101).

Accordion-Fold Tissue-Paper Flower

What You Need

- Paper Cutting Tools (see p. 8)
- Tissue paper
- Stapler
- Pipe cleaners

What Children Do

1. Take a large sheet if tissue paper and fold it in half.

2. Cut along the folded edge to make two layers.
3. Starting on the shorter side of the tissue paper, make accordion-folds about ½-inch wide. Fold the length of the tissue paper.
4. In the center, staple through all layers of the tissue paper.
5. Shape both ends of the tissue paper into petal shapes. Depending on how you cut the ends (curved, slanted, fringed, etc.), the flower will look different.
6. Wrap one end of a pipe cleaner around the staple in the center to form a stem.
7. Fluff up the layers of paper to make a flower.

a.
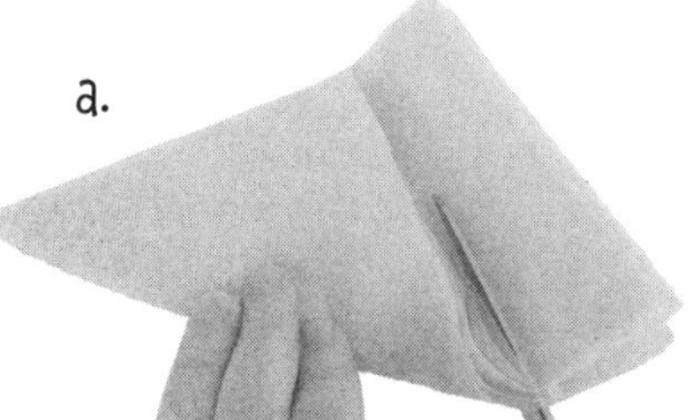

Tissue-Paper Circles Flower

What You Need

- Paper Cutting Tools (see p. 8)
- Tissue paper
- Pipe cleaners

b.
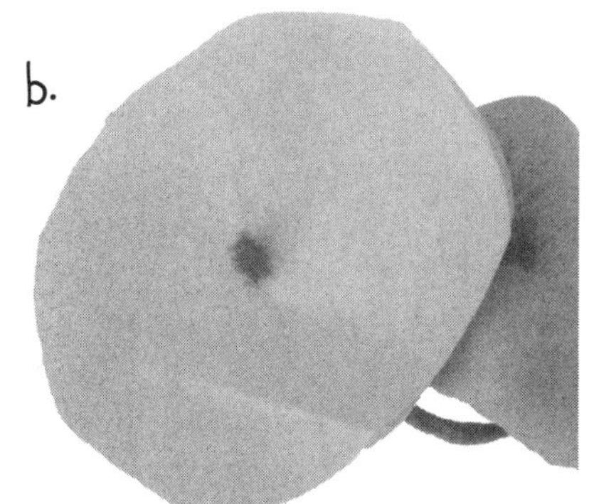

What Children Do

1. Fold a sheet of tissue three times to make eight layers.
2. Diagonally fold layers of tissue by bringing one corner up to the opposite side. Cut off the extra tissue (image a).
3. Unfold to have layers of squares. Cut through all layers at once to round off the corners to make circles (image b).
4. Layer the circles on top of each other.
5. Use the point of the scissors to carefully poke a tiny hole in the middle of the circles.
6. Poke one pipe cleaner up through the hole, pulling about 1 inch through the tissue-paper circles. Twist pipe cleaner to form the center of the flower (image b).
7. On the other side, pinch tissue paper together and wrap pipe cleaner around the pinched end two or three times (image c).
8. Pull up circles one at a time towards the center to create the flower. (image d).

c.
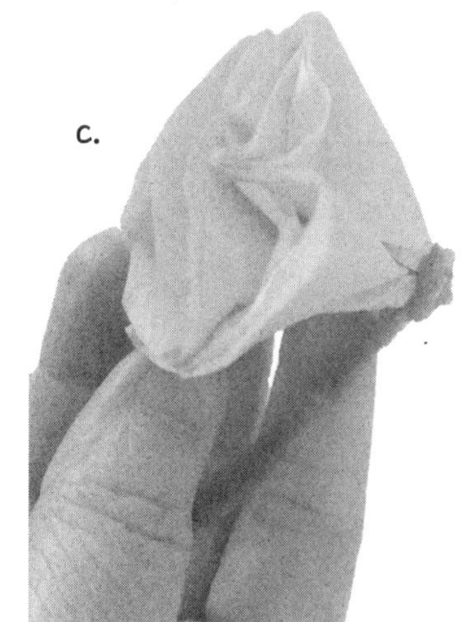

Layered Paper Flower (image on p. 94)

What You Need

- Layered Paper Flower Patterns (p. 94)
- Paper Cutting Tools (see p. 8)
- Variety of colored and patterned paper (construction paper, colored paper, cardstock, etc.)
- Glue or glue dots

Optional

- Foam mounting tape
- Decorating materials (buttons, glitter, beads, glitter glue, adhesive gems, etc.)

d.

Preparation

Photocopy Layered Paper Flower Patterns, making one set of three flowers for each child.

What Children Do

1. Cut out patterns.
2. Trace each pattern piece on a different colored or patterned paper. Cut out flowers.
3. Layer the flowers on top of each other from large to small, alternate the direction of the petals. Glue layers together.

Optional

- To make Layered Paper Flowers more dimensional, use foam mounting tape instead of glue.
- Use decorating materials to decorate Layered Paper Flowers. For example, glue a button or bead to the center of the flower.
- Before layering the Layered Paper Flowers, pinch the end of each petal to form a small crease in it to add more dimension to the flower.

Layered Paper Flower Patterns

Enlarge or shrink flower patterns as desired to have an even larger variety of flower sizes.

Bookmarks

Age Level: ✫★

When [Jesus] came to the village of Nazareth, his boyhood home, he went as usual to the synagogue on the Sabbath and stood up to read the Scriptures. The scroll of Isaiah the prophet was handed to him. He unrolled the scroll and found the place where this was written: "The Spirit of the Lord is upon me, for he has anointed me to bring Good News to the poor. He has sent me to proclaim that captives will be released, that the blind will see, that the oppressed will be set free, and that the time of the Lord's favor has come." He rolled up the scroll, handed it back to the attendant, and sat down. All eyes in the synagogue looked at him intently. Then he began to speak to them. "The Scripture you've just heard has been fulfilled this very day!". LUKE 4:16–21

What It's All About

Jesus knew exactly where to find the words he wanted to read. Bookmarks help us find a place in a book. Bookmarks made from envelopes are easy to use and slip over the corner of a page. Let's make bookmarks you can give as a gift to someone you care for.

What You Need

- ✫ Bookmark Patterns (p. 96)
- ✫ Paper Cutting Tools (see p. 8)
- ✫ Coloring & Writing Instruments (see p. 8)
- ✫ Letter-sized envelopes, one for each child
- ✫ Glue

Optional

- ✫ Small adhesive-backed wiggle eyes

a.

Preparation

Photocopy Bookmark Patterns, making one for each child.

b.

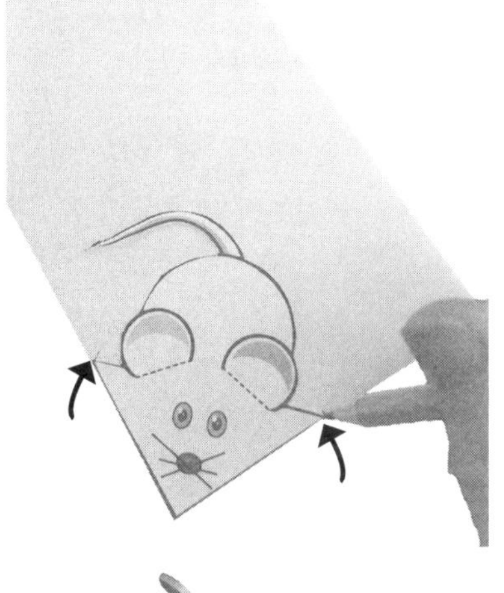

What Children Do

1. Cut out each pattern on all the solid lines. Fold on the dashed lines (image a).
2. Place each pattern on a bottom corner of the envelope. Use pencil to mark the corners of the bookmark triangle on the envelope (image b).
3. Cut off the corners of the envelope (image c). Recycle the rest of the envelope.
4. Glue each bookmark to one of the envelope corners.
5. Color the bookmarks. **Optional:** Stick on adhesive-backed wiggle eyes over the mouse's eyes.

How to Use

6. Slide bookmark onto the corner of a book page. (See image at top right.)

c.

Bookmark Patterns

Fun Tip

You could also use the mouse bookmark as a finger puppet. Just slide it on your finger instead of in a book.

Paper Bead Jewelry

Age Level: ☆★

For wisdom is far more valuable than rubies. Nothing you desire can compare with it. PROVERBS 8:11

What It's All About

While wisdom is better than jewels, we can enjoy creating simple jewels to give to others. Making these beads and stringing the necklaces can remind us of the importance of growing in Godly wisdom.

What You Need

- Paper Bead Patterns (p. 97)
- Coloring & Writing Instruments (see p. 8)
- Paper Cutting Tools (see p. 8)
- White cardstock
- Stringing material (cotton string, leather cording, elastic cording, etc.)
- Yard stick
- Colored or patterned lightweight paper
- Toothpicks or wooden skewers
- Glue

Optional

- Additional beads with wide holes (wooden beads, pony beads, etc.)

Preparation

On card stock, photocopy Paper Bead Patterns, making one set for two or three children. Cut out pattern pieces.

Optional: To improve durability of the patterns, laminate or cover patterns with clear Con-Tact paper or clear packing tape before cutting them out.

Cut stringing material into 36-inch lengths, one for each child.

What Children Do

Make the Beads

1. Choose a bead pattern and a piece of patterned paper. Trace the pattern onto the patterned paper and cut out.
2. Place a toothpick or skewer along the wide end of the bead and roll the paper around it (image a).
3. When you get to the end point of the bead add a drop of glue to seal the end of the bead (image b).
4. Gently remove the toothpick (image c). Set bead aside to dry as you make more beads. Vary the colors and patterns of the beads.

a.

b.

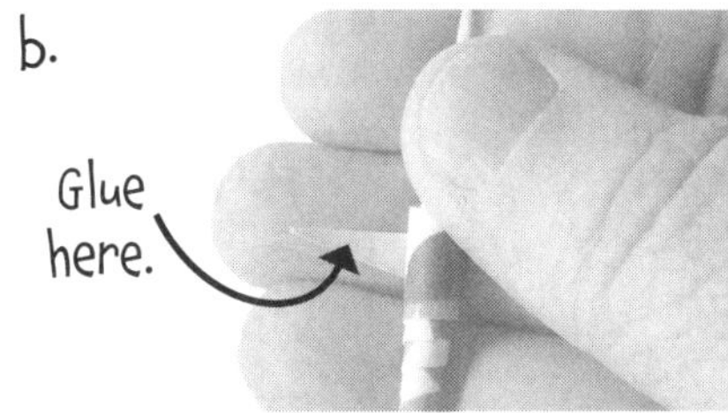

Make a Necklace

5. Tie a knot in one end of a piece of string.
6. Push the beads onto the string. **Optional:** Add additional beads.
7. Tie both ends of the string together. Slip the necklace over your head to wear it or make it as a gift.

Alternate Ideas

- Make a bracelet. Use elastic cording so it will stretch over your hand.
- Make a much longer string and loop it twice around your neck.
- Before cutting out paper, decorate it. Add little spots of glitter glue or metallic markers, paint, markers, etc. Be sure added decorations are dry before cutting and rolling beads.
- Use decorative-edged scissors to cut papers.
- Cut your own triangles. Also experiment with rectangles and other shapes of paper.

c.

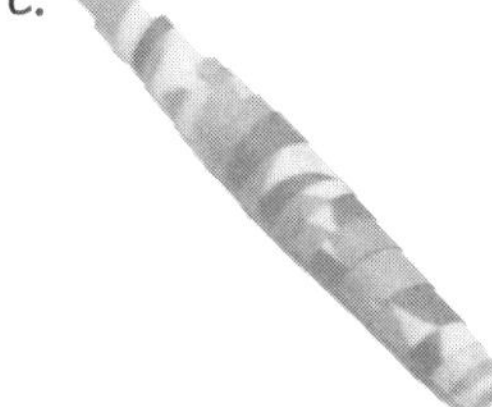

Paper Bead Patterns

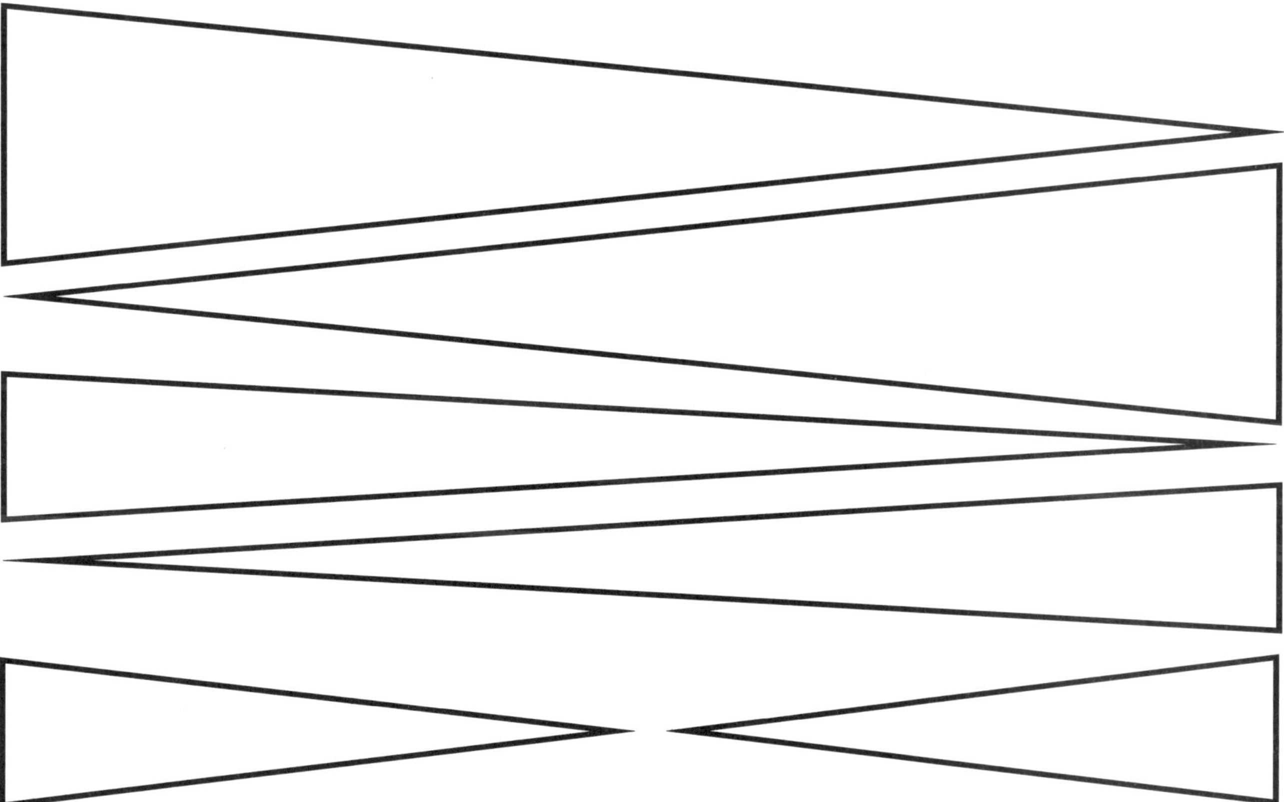

Gift Coupons

Age Level: ☆★

You must each decide in your heart how much to give. And don't give reluctantly or in response to pressure. "For God loves a person who gives cheerfully." And God will generously provide all you need. Then you will always have everything you need and plenty left over to share with others. 2 CORINTHIANS 9:7–8

What It's All About

It pleases God and blesses others when we give of our time and our talents. These coupons are ways you can do that for someone's birthday or other special days.

What You Need

- Gift Coupon Patterns (p. 99)
- Paper Cutting Tools (see p. 8)
- Coloring & Writing Instruments (see p. 8)
- Decorating materials (buttons, beads, pearls, glitter, stamps and stamp pads, stickers, adhesive gems, etc.)
- Stapler
- Ribbon
- Glue

Preparation

Photocopy Gift Coupon Patterns, making one set of coupons for each child.

What Children Do

1. Blank coupons are filled in with things specific to the person to whom children will be giving the coupon book.
2. Decorate the coupons with drawings and decorating materials.
3. Cut out the coupons. Make sure to leave on the strip on the side of each one.
4. Stack up the coupons and staple them together on the side strip.
5. Cut a length of ribbon, thread ribbon through the holes, and tie it in a bow on the front.
6. Give the coupons to someone special. They can tear out each coupon and give it to you when they want you to do something special for them.
7. Create a list of ideas for coupons. Here are a few:
   - Tell a story or joke
   - Organize my desk
   - Clean the bathroom
   - Help with laundry
   - Do not complain or argue all day
   - Make a snack
   - Wash the floor
   - Do the dishes
   - Get the mail
   - Help cook a meal

DO THE
DISHES
GET THE
MAIL
HELP WITH THE
LAUNDRY
GOOD FOR ONE
FOOT RUB
GOOD FOR ONE
SNACK
GOOD FOR A GIANT
HUG

Gift Bag

Age Level: ☆★

Whatever is good and perfect is a gift coming down to us from God our Father, who created all the lights in the heavens. He never changes or casts a shifting shadow. JAMES 1:17

What It's All About

The giving of gifts is an act of serving God and others. Just like we should be thoughtful when we choose a gift to give someone, we can also be thoughtful in how we package the gift.

What You Need

- Paper Cutting Tools (see p. 8)
- Patterned paper, wrapping paper is recommended
- Yardstick
- 5x9-inch box (such as a long tissue box), one for each child
- Ribbon in a variety of colors, widths, and patterns
- Hole punch
- Transparent tape

Optional

- Glue
- Decorating materials (beads, wiggle eyes, glitter or glitter glue, adhesive-backed jewels, craft-foam shapes, paper flowers, stickers, etc.)

Preparation

Cut the following, making one of each for each child; or children choose their paper and use scissors and rulers to cut for themselves:

- From patterned paper cut 12x29-inch rectangles, one for each child
- From the ribbons, cut 14- to 15-inch lengths of ribbon, two for each child

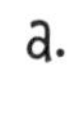

What Children Do

Make the Bottom of the Bag

1. Wrap a piece of prepared paper around the outside of the box leaving about 3 inches of paper below the box.
2. Where the paper overlaps on the box, secure the seam with a piece of tape.
3. Turn the box on its side to prepare the bottom of the bag. Fold in the long sides of the paper and tape them in the middle to each other.
4. Then crease the sides of the paper on the short ends and fold them towards the middle. Add another piece of tape to secure (image a).

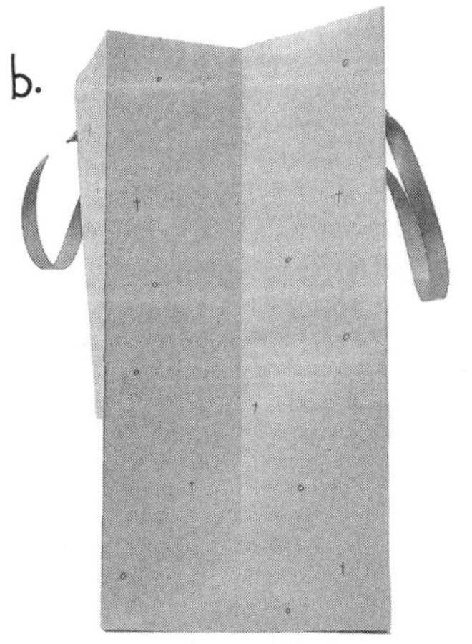

Make the Sides

5. Before taking the box out of the paper, crease the bag at each of the box corners. Crease all the way up to help give the bag shape.
6. Gently slide the box out of the bag and put it aside.
7. Secure the side where the paper meets the length of side with tape or glue to hold bag together.

8. At one top corner of the bag cut a slit about 1 inch long. Starting at the slit you made, fold the top inch of the bag inside itself creasing the top edge all the way around. Tape or glue to secure this neat edge to the top of the bag.

Make the Handle

9. Close top of bag. Use a hole punch to punch two holes through both the front and back of the bag. Make sure the holes are within the 1-inch folded section at the top, and do not punch through the folded sides of the bag.
10. Thread the end of a ribbon through a hole from the inside of the bag to the outside. Leave about an inch of ribbon in the bag. Tie end of ribbon into a knot and tape to the inside of the bag to secure.
11. Thread the other end of the ribbon back into the bag from the other hole on the same side of the bag. Tie end of ribbon into a knot and tape to the inside of the bag to secure.
12. Repeat Steps #10 and 11 on the other side of the bag.

Optional: Use decorating materials to decorate gift bag.

Alternate Ideas

- Make the bag taller. Add a second row of paper that is longer around the outside of the bag and use that to fold down- make sure the papers overlap by at least an inch and secure them together on the inside. The length of the paper should be 1-inch longer than desired new length of bag. To hide the transition on the outside of the bag, glue a ribbon around the bag where the two papers meet.
- If you are putting something very heavy in the bag and want it to be sturdier, cut the bottom out of the box you used to make the bag. Use this piece as a pattern to cut out a piece of cardboard or foamcore to place at the bottom of the gift bag.

Gift Box

Age Level: ☆★

Mordecai recorded these events and sent letters to the Jews near and far, . . . calling on them to celebrate an annual festival on these two days. He told them to celebrate these days with feasting and gladness and by giving gifts of food to each other and presents to the poor. This would commemorate a time when the Jews gained relief from their enemies, when their sorrow was turned into gladness and their mourning into joy. ESTHER 9:20–22

What It's All About

Just as the Israelites celebrated with great joy and gave gifts, we celebrate with gifts, too. What are some days when we give gifts to others? Giving gifts is a way to share God's love and kindness with others.

What You Need

- Paper Cutting Tools (see p. 8)
- Scoring materials (see p. 9)
- 12x12 colored or patterned cardstock, two sheets for each child
- Glue

Optional

- Decorating materials (beads, wiggle eyes, glitter or glitter glue, adhesive-backed jewels, craft-foam shapes, paper flowers, stickers, etc.)

What Children Do

1. Choose a sheet of cardstock to be the box. Score cardstock 2 inches from all the edges (see dashed lines in image a).
2. Fold all of the score lines in the same direction (toward the inside of the box).
3. Reopen the box and cut along both 2-inch score lines on one side of the cardstock until you reach the next score line. This forms slits or tabs 2 inches in from the edge of the paper (see solid lines in image b). These slits form tabs labeled Tab A in image b.
4. Repeat Step 3 on the opposite side (see solid lines in image b).
5. Form the box by folding along the score lines.
6. Put glue on each Tab A.
7. Glue each Tab A under the Tab B (image b) next to them to secure the sides of the box.
8. Repeat Steps 1 through 7 for the second sheet of cardstock to form the box lid, and then place lid on the box.

Optional: Use decorating materials to decorate gift box.

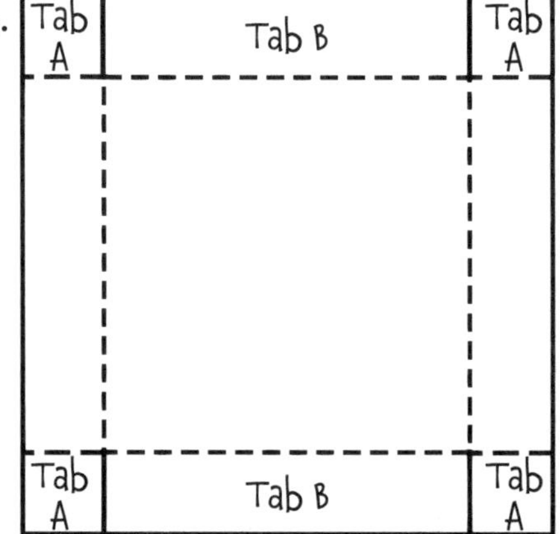

Alternate Idea

Make differently sized boxes using the same steps, but with different widths of score lines for taller boxes.

Wrapping Papers

Age Level: ☆★

The angel reassured them. "Don't be afraid!" he said. "I bring you good news that will bring great joy to all people. The Savior—yes, the Messiah, the Lord—has been born today in Bethlehem, the city of David! And you will recognize him by this sign: You will find a baby wrapped snugly in strips of cloth, lying in a manger. LUKE 2:10–12

What It's All About

Baby Jesus—the greatest gift we ever received—was "wrapped snugly in strips of cloth." When we give a gift, taking time to wrap our gifts in love is like another gift. Let's make some wrapping paper we can use to beautifully wrap gifts.

Marbled Wrapping Paper

What You Need

- Paint, two or more colors
- Disposable cups
- Plastic spoons
- Lightweight paper in white or a light color
- Box large enough to put sheets of paper inside, one for every child
- Marbles

Preparation

Pour each color of paint into disposable cups. Prepare more than one cup of each color, and make at least one cup of paint for each child. Place paint cups and plastic spoons on covered table where children will be working. (See Newspapers and Plastic Tablecloths on p. 8.)

What Children Do

1. Put the paper in the box.
2. Pour a little paint into the bottom of an empty disposable cup.
3. Put a marble into the paint and let it get covered with paint.
4. Lift the marble out with the spoon and drop it in the box with the paper. Move the box around so the marble runs across the paper leaving paint marks across it.
5. Decide whether to wait until the paint is dry or proceed while the paint is wet. If you continue while the paint is wet, the different colors will mix in spots on the paper.
6. Repeat with another color of paint and a differently sized marble. If you want to use the same marble again, rinse it off in a sink before dipping into the new color of paint.
7. You can continue repeating the process until you like the design the paint makes.
8. Set paper aside to dry completely before using it to wrap a gift.

Sponge Paint Wrapping Paper

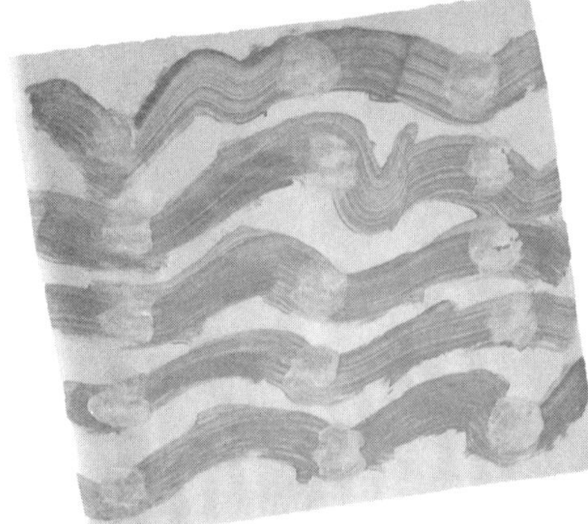

What You Need

- Paper Cutting Tools (see p. 8)
- Lightweight paper
- Liquid paint
- Sponges (such as sea sponges or inexpensive household sponges)
- Paper or plastic plates

Preparation

Pour each color of paint onto a paper or plastic plate.
Prepare at least one plate of each color of paint for every two or three children. Cut sponges into approximately 2-inch shapes (geometric, flowers, letters, etc.) Place one or more sponge in each paint plate and place plates on covered table where children will be working.

What You Say

To use a color of paint, use a sponge that is already on the plate. When you are done using that color of paint, put the sponge back on the plate where it belongs.

What Children Do

1. Lay out the paper and put the paints on disposable plates.
2. Use one sponge for each color of paint.
3. Dip the sponge into the paint and then dab it around on the paper in various areas giving it a lightly painted look. Add more paint to the sponge as needed to get the look you desire.
4. Use another sponge and color of paint and again dab it around the paper you can overlap some of the area from the first paint.
5. Continue using various colors of paint to print on your wrapping paper until you like the design.
6. Set paper aside to dry completely before using it to wrap a gift.

Cookie-Cutter Printed Wrapping Paper

What You Need

- Lightweight paper
- Paint
- Paper or plastic plates and bowls
- Cookie cutters in a variety of shapes

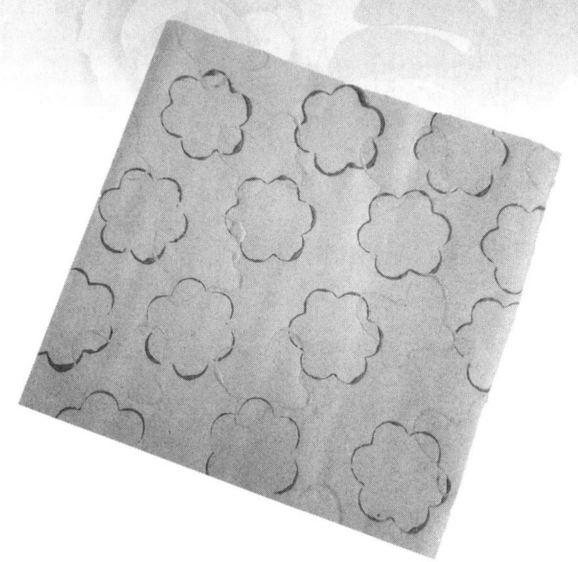

Preparation

Pour each color of paint onto a paper or plastic plate. Prepare at least one plate of each color of paint for every two or three children. Partially fill each bowl with water. Place plates, bowls of water, and cookie cutters on covered table where children will be working.

What Children Do

1. Lay paper out flat on table.
2. Choose a cookie cutter and dip it into a plate of paint. Then, using cookie cutter like a stamp, press it onto the paper.
3. Continue pressing cookie cutter on paper, dipping cookie cutter into paint as needed.
4. When you finish with a color of paint, rinse off the cookie cutter in bowl of water.
5. Dip the same or a different cookie cutter into another color of paint and continue until satisfied with your design.
6. Set paper aside to dry completely before using it to wrap a gift.

Gift Bow

Age Level: ★★

Praise the Lord, the God of Israel, who made the heavens and the earth! He has given King David a wise son, gifted with skill and understanding, who will build a Temple for the Lord and a royal palace for himself. 2 CHRONICLES 2:12

What It's All About

Solomon decorated the temple to honor God. (Read the whole story in 2 Chronicles 3:5–15.) **We show honor to someone when we decorate gift packages that we give them. And even more honor when we make the decorations ourselves.**

This bow looks especially nice made with double-sided patterned paper.

What You Need

- Paper Cutting Tools (see p. 8)
- Colored or patterned paper
- Glue

Optional

- Decorating materials (beads, wiggle eyes, glitter or glitter glue, adhesive-backed jewels, craft-foam shapes, paper flowers, stickers, etc.)

Preparation

Cut colored or patterned paper into 1x8½-inch strips making nine for each child, or children choose their paper and use scissors and rulers to cut for themselves.

What Children Do

1. Place a strip of paper facedown on the table. Place some glue on one end of the strip and then gently bend the paper to glue the ends of the strip together. This will form a teardrop-shaped loop (image a).
2. Continue making the tear drops until you have eight.
3. Place a teardrop-shaped loop on the table. Put some glue on the end opposite the loop. Place the end of another teardrop-shaped loop on top. You should now have double teardrop-shaped loops glued together (image b).
4. Repeat Step 3 until you have four loops.
5. Now take two double teardrop-shaped loops and form a cross. Put a little glue in between to join them together (image c).
6. Repeat Step 5 to make another cross.
7. Put glue in the center of one of the crosses and place the other set at a 45-degree angle to create a bow with eight teardrop-shaped loops on it (image d).
8. Roll the last strip around itself two or three times to form a small circle. Glue the end to the circle, and then glue the circle to the center of the bow (image e).

Optional: Use decorating materials to decorate bow.

Alternate Ideas

- Make smaller or larger bows by changing the length and/or width of the papers.
- Glue a paper flower, bead, or button in the middle of the bow instead of a circle.
- Make similar bows from floral mesh, tissue paper, ribbons, or felt strips.

a.

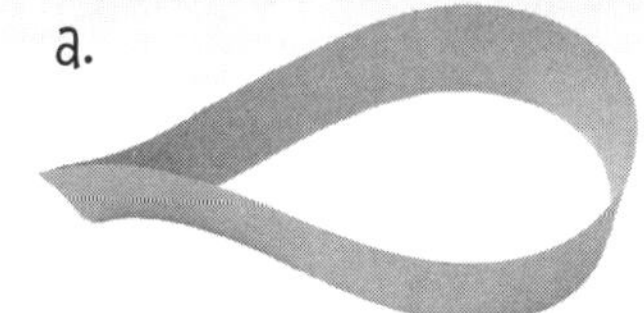

Make 8.

b.

Make 4.

c.

Make 2.

d.

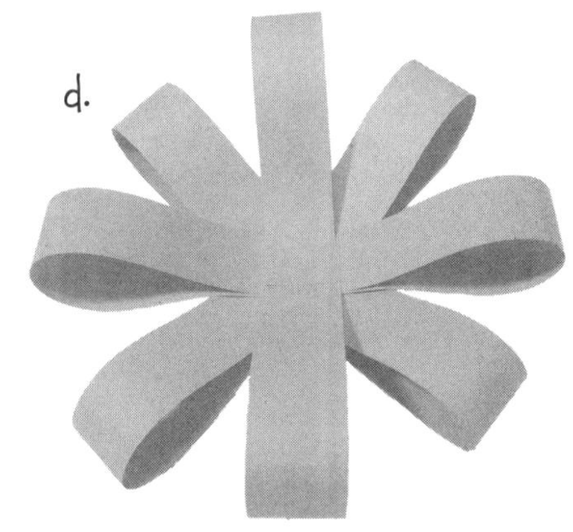

e.

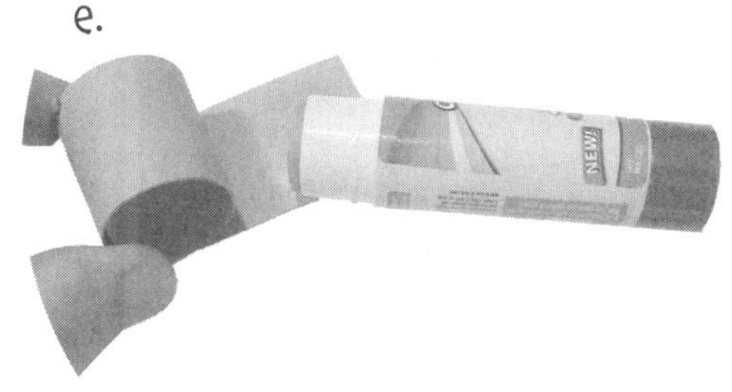

Mobiles & 3-D Art

Mobiles use the power of wind to show movement. They are marvelous designs that employ balance and science to hold the pieces together. Sculptures and other 3-D art made with paper are also three dimensional. God made us to have many dimensions, too.

This introduction into mobiles provides various examples of materials to use.

- **The top hanger** is the holder for the strings or wires that come down from it. These can be anything that could be hung and have strings attached, including hoops, cutout shapes, sticks, paper plates, coat hangers, cylinders made from paper.
- **The strings or wires** hang down to hold the various objects. Multiple items can be added to each string, or each string can hold one object. The strings can be wire, yarn, string, fishing line, pipe cleaners, or even paper clips.
- **The objects** can be natural ones like seashells, or objects made from paper, fabric, or other materials.

Since this book is all about paper art, the mobiles will mainly use paper for the top holder and the objects. Other 3-D objects are made from folding paper or sliding sections of paper together.

Outreach Ideas

Here are a few outreach ideas for the crafts in this section:

- Use art to share Bible stories.
- Use the art as a way to decorate a hospital or nursing home room.
- Make miniatures of mobiles to hang from a stand (form stand with Styrofoam and wire).
- Use the Animal Mobile (p. 113) to celebrate Earth Day.
- Use the Heart Mobile (p. 120) as a gift for parents or a friend.

Other Ways to Learn

- Play with the Heart Mobile (p. 120) to work on balance in art.
- Use a basic mobile structure to design your own mobile.
- Make Calder Sculpture (p. 108) and study Alexander Calder. Learn how he created a new form of art called *mobiles*.
- Create other ways to make the top hangers.
- Think of different ideas to make the basic mobile and work with more balance challenges, such as using sticks and paper clips.

Calder Sculpture

Age Level: ☆★

Get rid of all bitterness, rage, anger, harsh words, and slander, as well as all types of evil behavior. Instead, be kind to each other, tenderhearted, forgiving one another, just as God through Christ has forgiven you. EPHESIANS 4:31–32

What It's All About

We need balance in life and that includes in our speech. We need to balance God's love and forgiveness with wholesome and uplifting words that build people up.

Alexander Calder was an American sculpture famous for his kinetic or movement sculptures and mobiles powered by wind or motors. He pioneered combining art with movement. Enjoy creating a sculpture on a rock or seashell that shows freedom of movement. You will need to balance all the parts.

What You Need

- Paper Cutting Tools (see p. 8)
- Rock or seashell that is flat on one side, and 3 to 5 inches long
- Pipe cleaners
- Pony beads
- Paper
- Hole punch
- Glue

What Children Do

1. Cut small shapes of paper and punch a hole in each one.
2. Wrap a pipe cleaner around the rock and twist it in place.
3. Slide papers or beads onto the ends that stick out. If needed, add a touch of glue to the papers at the end of the pipe cleaners.
4. Add more pipe cleaners and paper cutouts until you feel the sculpture is finished.
5. Blow on your sculpture or sit it in a place where it gets a breeze and watch the parts move.

Optional

6. Use a permanent marker to add words to the base (rock or shell) such as "God is my rock" or "Be kind."

Night Sky Mobile

Age Level: ✩★

He counts the stars and calls them all by name. PSALM 147:4

What It's All About

Stars hanging in the sky amaze us. They also reflect the majesty of God and his presence throughout the universe. Let's make simple mobiles based on the night sky.

What You Need

- Night Sky Mobile Patterns (p. 110)
- Paper Cutting Tools (see p. 8)
- Black cardstock
- Hole punch
- Pictures of constellations (from library or astronomy books, or printed off the Internet)
- Silver or gold markers, gel pens, or crayons
- Paper clips
- Silver or gold pipe cleaners

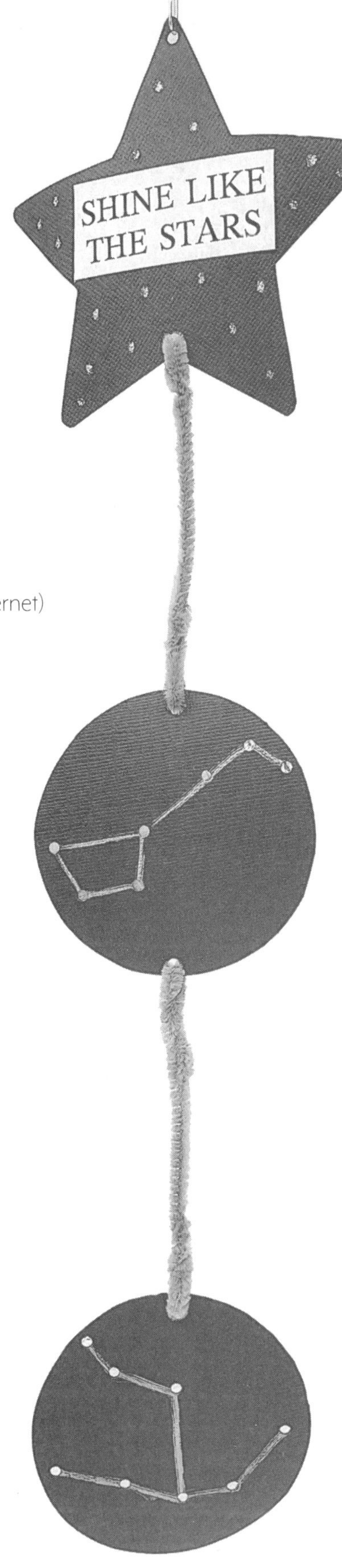

Preparation

Photocopy Night Sky Mobile Patterns, making one for each child.

What Children Do

1. Use Star Pattern to cut a star from black cardstock.
2. Decorate the star with the words from the pattern page, or references for Bible verses about stars such as Genesis 1:16, Psalm 147:4, Daniel 12:3, or Philippians 2:15. Also, draw on it with silver or gold markers, gel pens, or crayons.
3. Punch a hole in the top and bottom.

For Each Constellation

4. Use Circle Pattern to cut two circles from black cardstock.
5. Choose a constellation for your mobile and use silver or gold markers, gel pens, or crayons to draw the constellation.
6. Draw another constellation on the back of the circle.
7. Punch a hole in the top and bottom of the completed constellation circle.
8. Repeat Steps 5–6 to make the second constellation circle. Punch only one hole at the top of this circle.

Optional: Make more than two constellation circles for your mobile.

Assemble the Mobile

9. Mobiles are usually put together from the bottom up. Thread a pipe cleaner through the top hole of the constellation circle with only one hole. Bend pipe cleaner and twist around itself to secure.
10. Thread the other end of the pipe cleaner into the bottom hole of the constellation circle with two holes.
11. Thread a second pipe cleaner through the bottom hole of the star.
12. Thread a paper clip or another pipe cleaner through the top hole of the star to make a hanger.

Night Sky Mobile Patterns

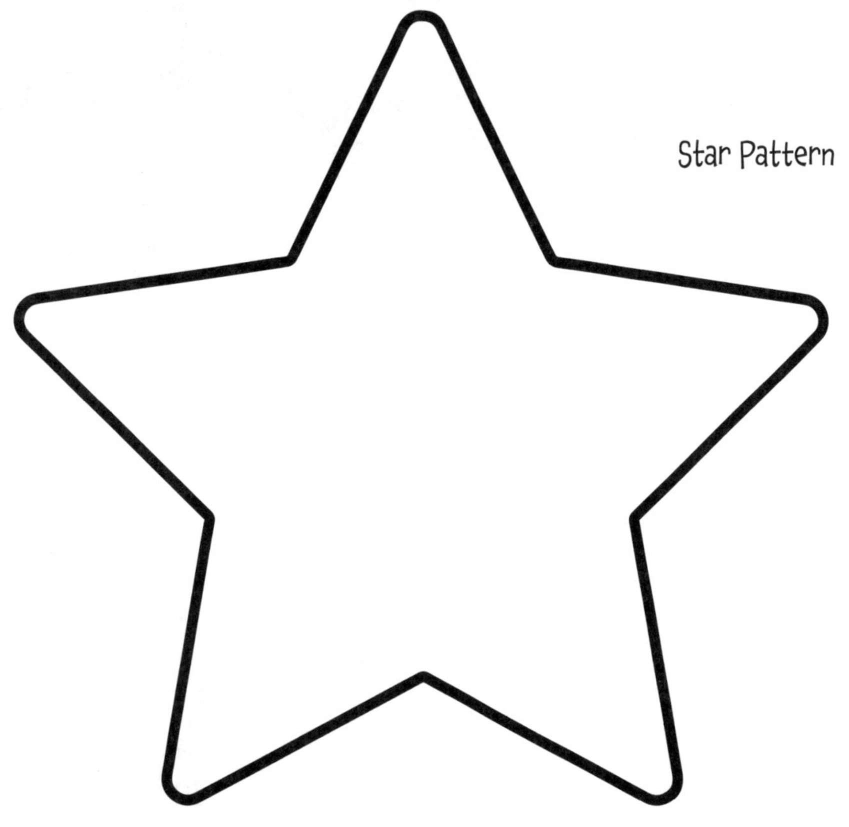

SHINE LIKE THE STARS

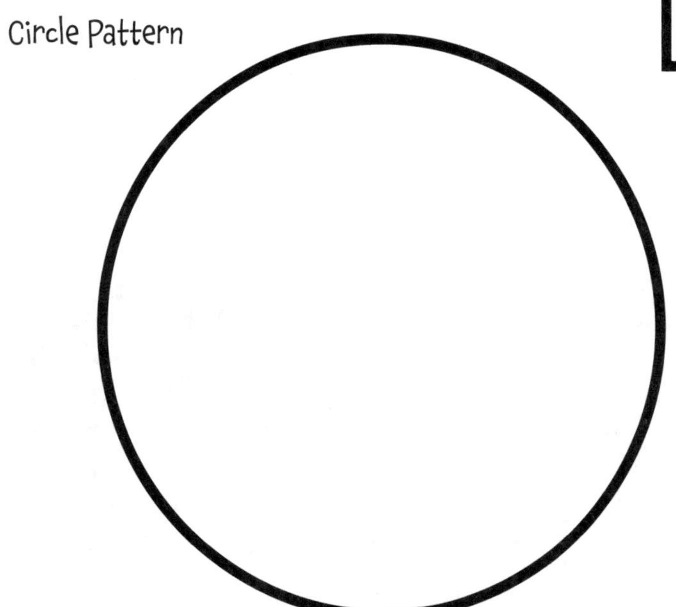

Fruit of the Spirit Mobile

Age Level: ✭★

The Holy Spirit produces this kind of fruit in our lives: love, joy, peace, patience, kindness, goodness, faithfulness, gentleness, and self-control. There is no law against these things! GALATIANS 5:22–23

What It's All About

The Holy Spirit gives us the fruit of the Spirit—fruit that helps us be kind and loving. Let's make a mobile to remember to grow the fruit of the Spirit in our lives.

What You Need

- Fruit of the Spirit Mobile Patterns (p. 112)
- Paper Cutting Tools (see p. 8)
- Coloring & Writing Instruments (see p. 8)
- White cardstock
- Cardstock in a variety of colors
- Glue
- Transparent tape
- Hole punch
- Pipe cleaners

Preparation

On white cardstock, photocopy Fruit of the Spirit Mobile Patterns, making one for each child.

Cut, making one of each for each child; or children choose their cardstock and use scissors and rulers to cut for themselves:

- From cardstock, cut 4x11-inch rectangles, one for each child

What Children Do

Make the Top

1. Cut out and glue the Word Patterns on the cardstock rectangle.
2. Roll into a cylinder and tape in place.
3. Punch three holes evenly spread around the top and thread pipe cleaners through the holes. Twist them together. This forms the hanger.
4. Punch five holes around the bottom of the hanger.

Make the Fruit

5. Color and then cut out each Fruit Patterns, including the slits. Slide matching pieces together.
6. If needed, add a little tape to hold fruits together.

Hang the Fruit

7. Thread a pipe cleaner through each hole at the bottom of the hanger. Twist the end of the pipe cleaner onto itself to secure it.
8. Tape each fruit onto a pipe cleaner. Vary the lengths at which you hang each fruit.

Fruit of the Spirit Mobile Patterns

Word Patterns

THE HOLY SPIRIT GIVES	THE FRUIT OF THE SPIRIT	GALATIANS 5:22–23
LOVE	JOY	PEACE
PATIENCE	KINDNESS	GOODNESS
FAITHFULNESS	GENTLENESS	SELF-CONTROL

Fruit Patterns

Animal Mobile

Age Level: ☆★

God made all sorts of wild animals, livestock, and small animals, each able to produce offspring of the same kind. And God saw that it was good. GENESIS 1:25

What It's All About

Celebrate creatures God made with a mobile. After God created these creatures, he made people and gave us the task of caring for his creation. Be kind to creatures that fly, swim, or move along the ground.

This mobile hangs from a paper bowl with three strands, each holding three creatures.

What You Need

- Animal Mobile Patterns (p. 114)
- Paper Cutting Tools (see p. 8)
- Coloring & Writing Instruments (see p. 8)
- White cardstock
- Paper or plastic bowls, one for each child
- Hole punch
- Pipe cleaners in blue, silver, and green, one of each color for each child plus extras
- Transparent tape

Optional

- Decorating materials (beads, wiggle eyes, glitter or glitter glue, adhesive-backed jewels, craft-foam shapes, paper flowers, stickers, etc.)

Preparation

On white cardstock, photocopy Animal Mobile Patterns, making one for each child.

What Children Do

Make the Holder

1. Punch three equally spaced holes in the rim of the bowl. Use the point of the scissors to poke a hole in the center of the bottom of the bowl.
2. Through center of bowl, thread both ends of a pipe cleaner. Bend and tape the ends to the inside of the bowl. The loop on the outside of the bowl forms the hanger.

Add the Creatures

3. Color and then cut out the animal pattern pieces.
4. Tape the land animals to a green pipe cleaner.
5. Tape the sea creatures to a silver pipe cleaner.
6. Tape the birds to a blue pipe cleaner.
7. Add the three pipe cleaners to the bowl by threading the top end of each pipe cleaner through one of the holes in the rim of the bowl. Bend pipe cleaner and twist it around itself to secure.

Optional

- Use decorating materials to decorate bowl.
- If mobile is not balanced add a little weight to the bowl as needed. Pennies work well.

Animal Mobile Patterns

Land Animal Patterns

Sea Creature Patterns

Bird Patterns

Heavenly Mobile

Age Level: ★

Holy, holy, holy is the Lord God, the Almighty—the one who always was, who is, and who is still to come. REVELATION 4:8

What It's All About

People wonder about Heaven. It's a place God created for us to live happily with him forever. Our verse is from a description of God's throne room, written by John in Revelation 4. Let's make a mobile that shows what is described. Use your mobile to tell others what the Bible tells us about Heaven.

What You Need

- Heavenly Mobile Patterns (pp. 116–119)
- Paper Cutting Tools (see p. 8)
- Coloring & Writing Instruments (see p. 8)
- White cardstock
- Metallic gold cardstock
- Paper Cutting Tools (see p. 8)
- Glue
- Monofilament fiber or yarn
- Tapestry needle, one for each child

Preparation

On white cardstock, photocopy Heavenly Mobile Patterns on pages 116–118, making one for each child.

On metallic gold cardstock, photocopy crown patterns on page 119, making one for every two children.

What Children Do

Make the Top Hanger

1. Color and cut out rainbows, including the slits.
2. Slide the two rainbow pieces together at the slits.

Make the Objects

3. Color and cut out the Four Creatures Patterns (man, lion, eagle, ox).
4. Color and cut out the four objects (door to Heaven, trumpet, lamp with flame, and lightning) that are mentioned in Revelation 4.
5. Color and cut out the throne.
6. Color and cut out the jewels for the ruby, emerald, and jasper described.
7. Cut out the crowns (which stand for the 24 crowned elders) and glue them to the rainbow.

Assemble the Mobile

8. Cut a length of monofilament fiber or yarn and thread it onto the needle.
9. Use the needle to poke a hole near the top of one of the gems. Pull all but the last inch or so of the fiber through the hole. Tape the end of the fiber to the back of the gem.

10. Continue stringing the other gems and the throne on the same piece of fiber. For this object you'll poke a hole from the front bottom to the back, and then poke a hole from the back through a hole near the top to the front. Tape the fiber to the back of the object.
11. Attach fiber with the throne and jewels to the hanger by making a hole near the bottom center of the rainbow. Remove needle and tape the top of the fiber to the rainbow.
12. In the same way, string one object and one of the four creatures on four additional fibers. Attach each strand to one of the four ends of the rainbows.
13. Cut a short length of fiber and knot into a loop. Tape to the center top of the rainbows to make a hanger.

Heavenly Mobile Patterns

Four Creatures Patterns

Throne and Other Objects Patterns

Rainbow Patterns

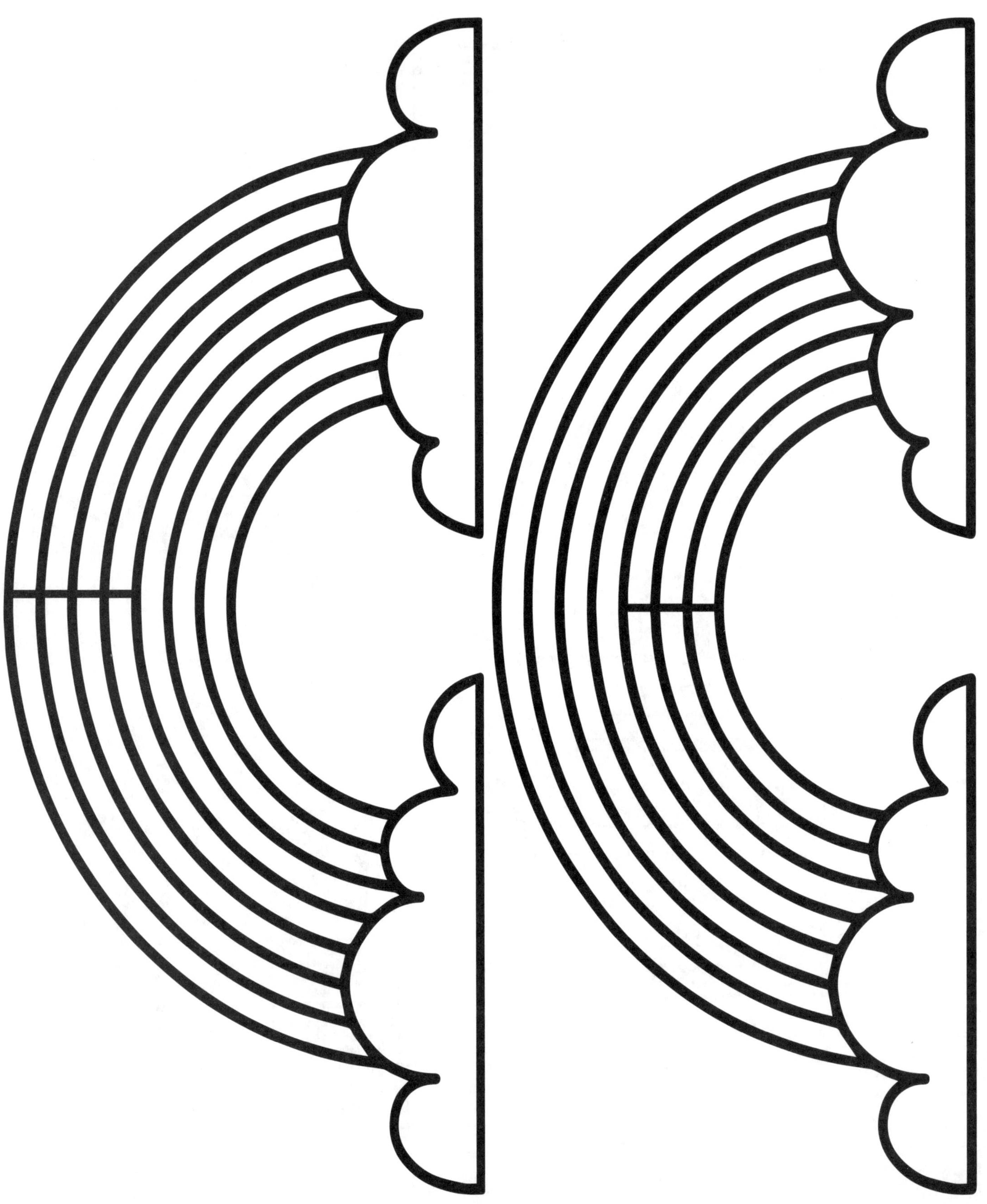

Crown Patterns

Heart Mobile

Age Level: ☆★

If I could speak all the languages of earth and of angels, but didn't love others, I would only be a noisy gong or a clanging cymbal. If I had the gift of prophecy, and if I understood all of God's secret plans and possessed all knowledge, and if I had such faith that I could move mountains, but didn't love others, I would be nothing. If I gave everything I have to the poor and even sacrificed my body, I could boast about it; but if I didn't love others, I would have gained nothing. Love is patient and kind. Love is not jealous or boastful or proud. 1 CORINTHIANS 13:1–4

What It's All About

We can express love in many ways. This mobile lets you hang hearts that share different love messages. Create your own messages, too. The mobile uses skewers to create balance. Play with where to hang each heart.

What You Need

- Heart Mobile Patterns (p. 121)
- Paper Cutting Tools (see p. 8)
- Coloring & Writing Instruments (see p. 8)
- Wooden skewers, two for each child
- 1-inch cube of Styrofoam, one for each child
- Colored or patterned cardstock in a variety of pinks, reds, whites, and purples
- Yarn, monofilament fiber, or string
- Thin ribbon or rickrack trim
- Glue
- Decorating materials (aluminum foil, beads, wiggle eyes, glitter or glitter glue, adhesive-backed jewels, craft-foam shapes, paper flowers, stickers, etc.)

Preparation

Photocopy Heart Mobile Patterns, making one for each child.

What Children Do

Create Mobile Hanger

a.

1. Push one skewer through the center of one side of the Styrofoam cube to the other evenly. Repeat with other skewer through the other two sides of the cube, at a slightly different height.
2. Optional: Cover the cube with cardstock (image a).
3. Cut four 2- or 3-inch lengths of thin ribbon or rickrack trim and wrap around the end of each skewer. Glue to secure.
4. Cut a 10- to 12-inch length of yarn, monofilament fiber, or string. Tie each end around one skewer, on both sides of the cube. This forms a loop to hang the mobile.

Make the Hearts

5. Use Heart Patterns to cut paper hearts of various sizes.
6. Use gel pens, markers, or colored pencils, and the decorating materials to decorate each heart. Create your own designs and messages or use some of the ideas below:
   - Cut out the sayings from the pattern page. Glue each one to a different heart.
   - Cut an open heart inside of a larger heart. Write, "Be open to love."
   - Cut a foil heart smaller than a paper heart, glue it on, and write, "Reflect God's love."
   - Cut two arms and hands and glue ends to the back of the heart. Bend arms around to the front of the heart. Write "hug and kisses" or draw Xs and Os for hugs and kisses.

Assemble the Mobile

7. Attach a length of yarn, monofilament fiber, or string to each heart. You may wish to add more than one heart to each strand of hanging material.
8. Create a loop at the other end of each strand to slide onto skewers. Move strands around to balance the mobile.

Heavenly Mobile Patterns

Egyptian Diorama

Age Level: ☆★

The Lord will deliver me from every evil attack and will bring me safely into his heavenly Kingdom. All glory to God forever and ever! Amen. 2 TIMOTHY 4:18

What It's All About

After Jesus was born, King Herod was jealous that a new king had been born and wanted to have Jesus killed! God led Joseph to take Mary and Jesus and escape to Egypt so they would be safe. (Read the whole story in Matthew 2:1–18.)

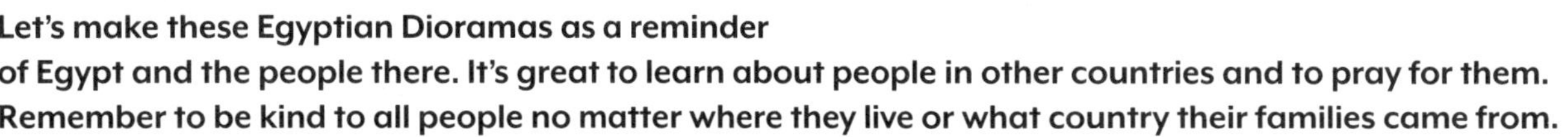

Let's make these Egyptian Dioramas as a reminder of Egypt and the people there. It's great to learn about people in other countries and to pray for them. Remember to be kind to all people no matter where they live or what country their families came from.

What You Need

- Egyptian Diorama Patterns (p. 123)
- Paper Cutting Tools (see p. 8)
- Coloring & Writing Instruments (see p. 8)
- Blue and white cardstock
- Brown or gold pipe cleaners, one for every three children
- Glue
- Sandpaper
- Yarn, string, or monofilament
- Transparent tape

Preparation

On white cardstock, photocopy Egyptian Diorama Patterns, making one for each child.

Cut one 8½-inch square of blue cardstock, making one for each child, or children use scissors to cut for themselves.

Cut pipe cleaners into thirds, making one 4-inch length for each child.

What Children Do

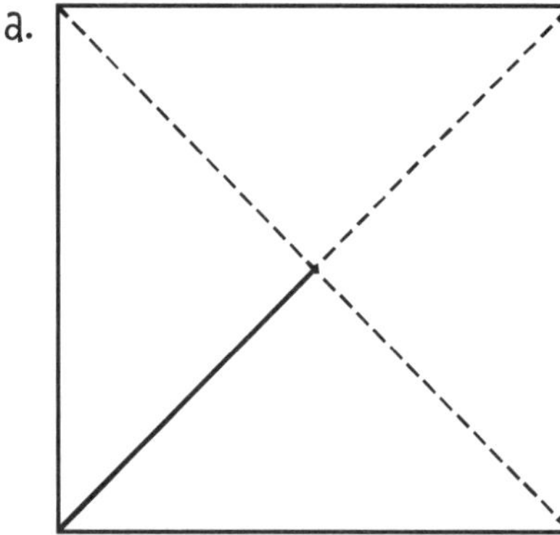

1. Fold a blue cardstock square in half diagonally to form a triangle. Fold in half again, and then open paper flat on the table.
2. The creases in the paper make four triangles. Cut along one creased line to the center of the square (solid line in image a). Slide one of the separated triangles over the other. Glue it in place. This forms a three-sided container for the diorama.
3. Cut a piece of sandpaper to fit the floor of diorama and glue in place.
4. Color and cut out all pattern pieces.
   - **For Pyramid:** Fold along dashed lines and glue tab under opposite edge of the pyramid. Place in diorama.
   - **For Bird:** Bend bird's wings a little to give dimension. Cut a length of yarn, string, or monofilament and tape to back of bird. Tape other end to the roof of the diorama.
   - **For Palm Tree:** Glue to one end of pipe cleaner. Coil the other end of the pipe cleaner and tape inside diorama.
   - **For Camel:** Fold along dashed line and place in diorama.
   - **For Sphinx:** Fold tabs at dashed lines. Glue ends of tabs together at the back. Place in diorama.

Egyptian Diorama Patterns

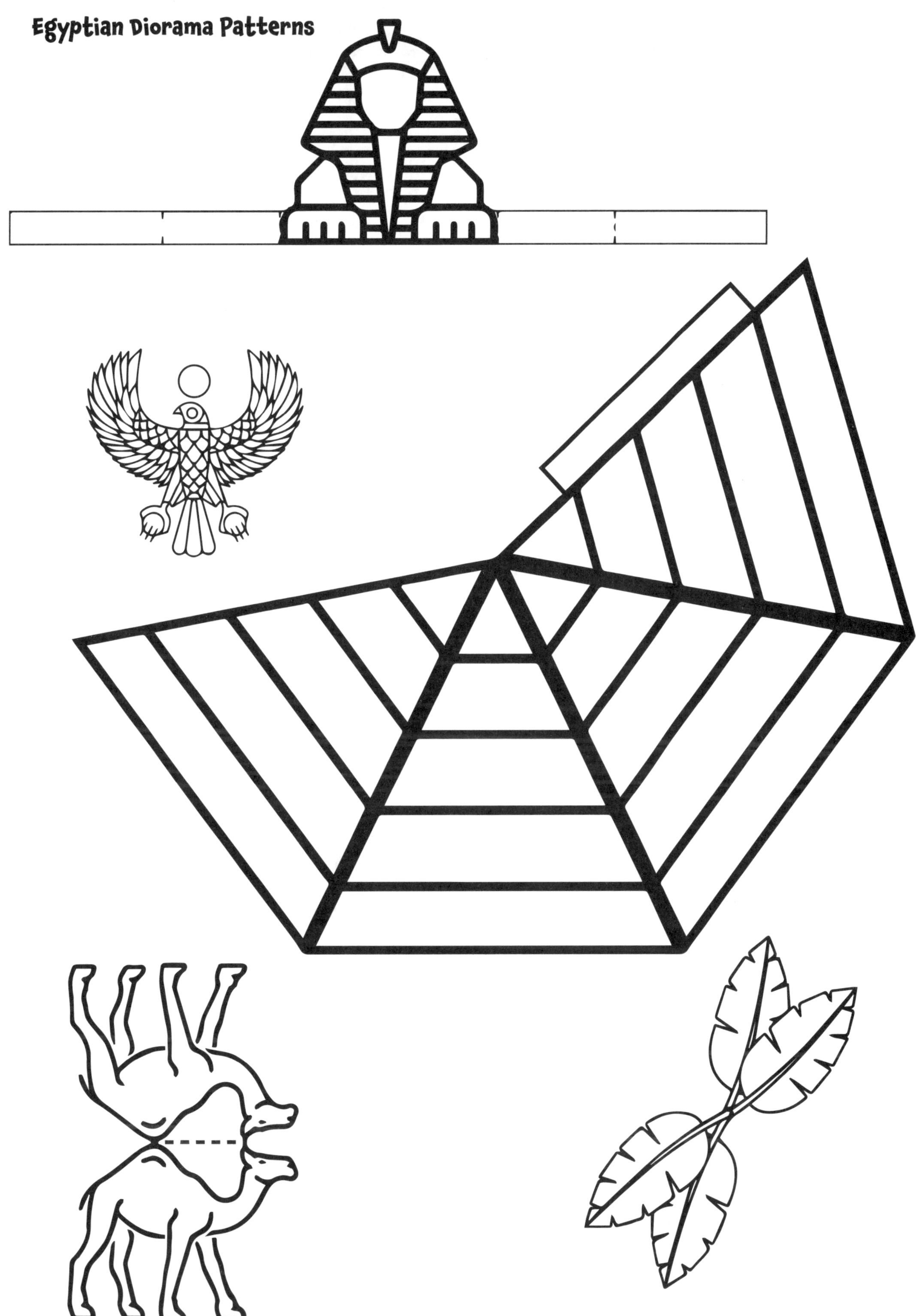

Pop-Up Angels & Owls

Age Level: ✯★

He will order his angels to protect you wherever you go. PSALM 91:11

None of them could stand against the wisdom and the Spirit with which Stephen spoke. ACTS 6:10

What It's All About

Today we'll make cards that open up for three angels or owls to pop up. The angels remind us of Psalm 91:11 which tells us God provides angels to protect us.

The owls remind us of Acts 6:10 and that we can receive the wisdom Stephen had through the Holy Spirit.

You can put three or four cards back to back like a diorama to remember these great blessings from God.

What You Need

- Pop-Up Angels & Owls Patterns (p. 125)
- Paper Cutting Tools (see p. 8)
- Scoring materials (see p. 9)
- Coloring & Writing Instruments (see p. 8)
- Cardstock for card, blue or other desired color
- Glue

Optional

- Decorating materials (glitter, stamps and stamp pads, stickers, adhesive gems, wiggle eyes, etc.)

Preparation

Photocopy Pop-Up Angels & Owls Patterns, making two for each child.

Cut the following or children choose their cardstock and use scissors and rulers to cut for themselves:

- 4x7-inch rectangles, four for each child

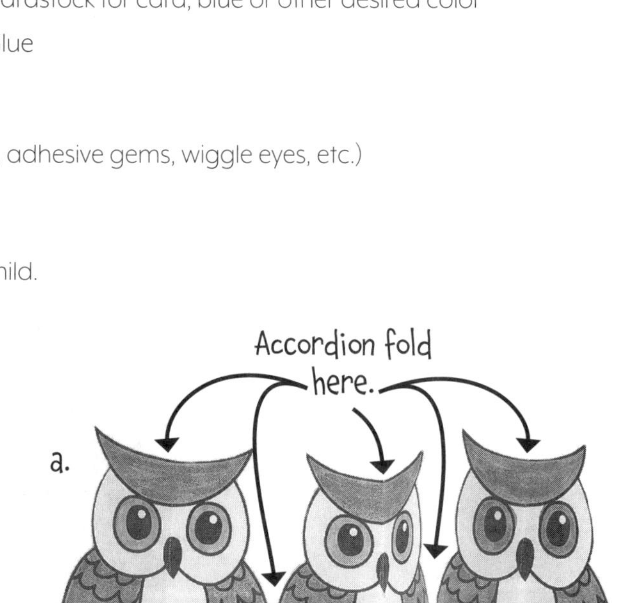

What Children Do

Make the Pop-Ups

1. Fold each 4x7-inch rectangle in half to make 3½x4-inch cards.
2. Cut out patterns. Be sure to keep the angels and owls connected at their wings.
3. Accordion fold each strip of angels or owls, folding at the point where the shapes meet and at the half way point (image a).
4. Color the cutouts as desired, adding features to all, waves for feathers on owls, and hands holding objects on angels (such as cross, heart, star, trumpet, anchor).
5. Center the middle angel or owl in the inside center of card. Glue the left and right sides of the figures to the inside of the card. The angels or owls will pop up when card is opened partway. **Note:** Cards only open partway. They will not extend all the way to lay flat on a table.

Make the Covers

6. Cut out message squares. Glue to the covers of the cards. Be sure to put messages about angels on angel cards and messages about wisdom on owl cards.

b.

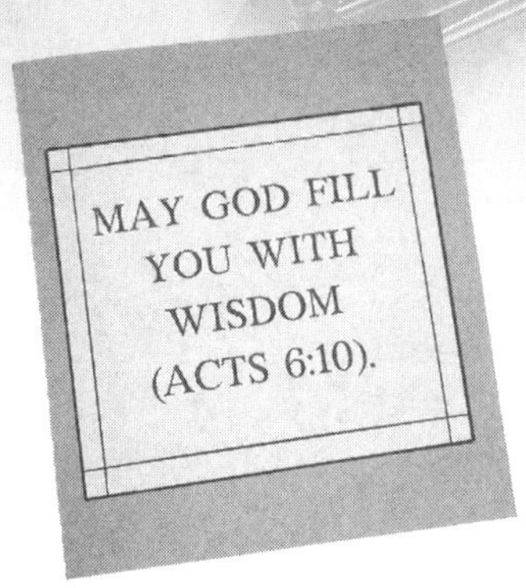

7. Center the middle figure in center of card and glue sides of outer figures to card. The figures will pop up when card is opened part way.
8. Make four cards.
9. Place three or four cards back to back to form a circle.

Optional: Use decorating materials to decorate cards.

Make More!

To make other pop-up cards, accordion fold strips of paper, and then cut out other designs such as hearts, stars, or crosses. First, draw a pattern for your shape, and then fold the pattern in half. Place the folded pattern on your folded strip and cut out.

Pop-Up Angels & Owls Patterns

MAY GOD FILL
YOU WITH
WISDOM
(ACTS 6:10).

MAY GOD
SEND ANGELS
TO PROTECT
YOU
(PSALM 91:11).

Christmas Crafts

Each year we come together to celebrate the birth of Christ—the greatest gift any of us has ever received. As we celebrate Christmas, we think about giving, sharing, and caring for others. It is a time when people come together with families and friends. We reach out and get back in touch with those from whom we have not seen or heard in a while.

These festive activities may include making crafts to decorate our homes as well as gifts to give to others. Christmas is a great time to share with others about Christ's love as the world stops to celebrate his birth. It is a time to tell others about Jesus and his love for every person.

This wonderful time filled with joyous celebrations and music can also be a difficult time for those who have lost loved ones or are dealing with other troubles. If you know someone who is struggling, maybe you can invite them to some of your celebrations. Some families hold an open house party during the Christmas season for friends, relatives, and neighbors to drop by and share the joy together.

Outreach Ideas

Here are a few outreach ideas for the crafts in this section:

- Create an Advent Calendar (p. 128) for a family with young children to help them have something to look forward to each day as they await the celebration.
- Create Christmas Tree Tunnel Cards (p. 145) and Stained Glass Window Art (p. 135) and bring them to area nursing homes to share Christmas joy with the residents.
- Celebrate good deeds in your household by making Paper Chains (p. 138) together.
- Create Gift Tags (p. 147) to put on presents for family and friends.
- Create decorations to give to neighbors. As you deliver them, take time to see how the person is doing. If they don't have a church of their own, invite them to celebrate Christmas with your family at your church.

Advent Calendar

Age Level: ☆★

His government and its peace will never end. He will rule with fairness and justice from the throne of his ancestor David for all eternity. The passionate commitment of the Lord of Heaven's Armies will make this happen! ISAIAH 9:7

He will be very great and will be called the Son of the Most High. The Lord God will give him the throne of his ancestor David. LUKE 1:32

What It's All About

People waited a long time for the birth of Jesus, our Savior. We wait each year for Christmas to come to thank God for sending Jesus. An advent calendar helps us wait. Make your own with little windows to open, and put words or pictures about the Christmas story inside the windows.

What You Need

- Advent Calendar Patterns (pp. 129–130)
- Paper Cutting Tools (see p. 8)
- Coloring & Writing Instruments (see p. 8)
- White cardstock
- Glue

Optional

- Decorating materials (glitter, stamps and stamp pads, stickers, adhesive gems, wiggle eyes, etc.)

Preparation

On white cardstock, photocopy Advent Calendar Patterns, making one set for each child.

What Children Do

1. Color and cut out patterns (image a).
2. For the Calendar Top, cut the numbered squares on the solid lines. Fold on the dashed line to make a hinge. The squares are now little windows.
3. Place a line of glue around the top, bottom, and sides of the back of Calendar Top. Carefully glue over Calendar Bottom.

Optional: Use decorating materials to decorate calendars.

a.

Advent Calendar Patterns

Calendar Top

Calendar Bottom

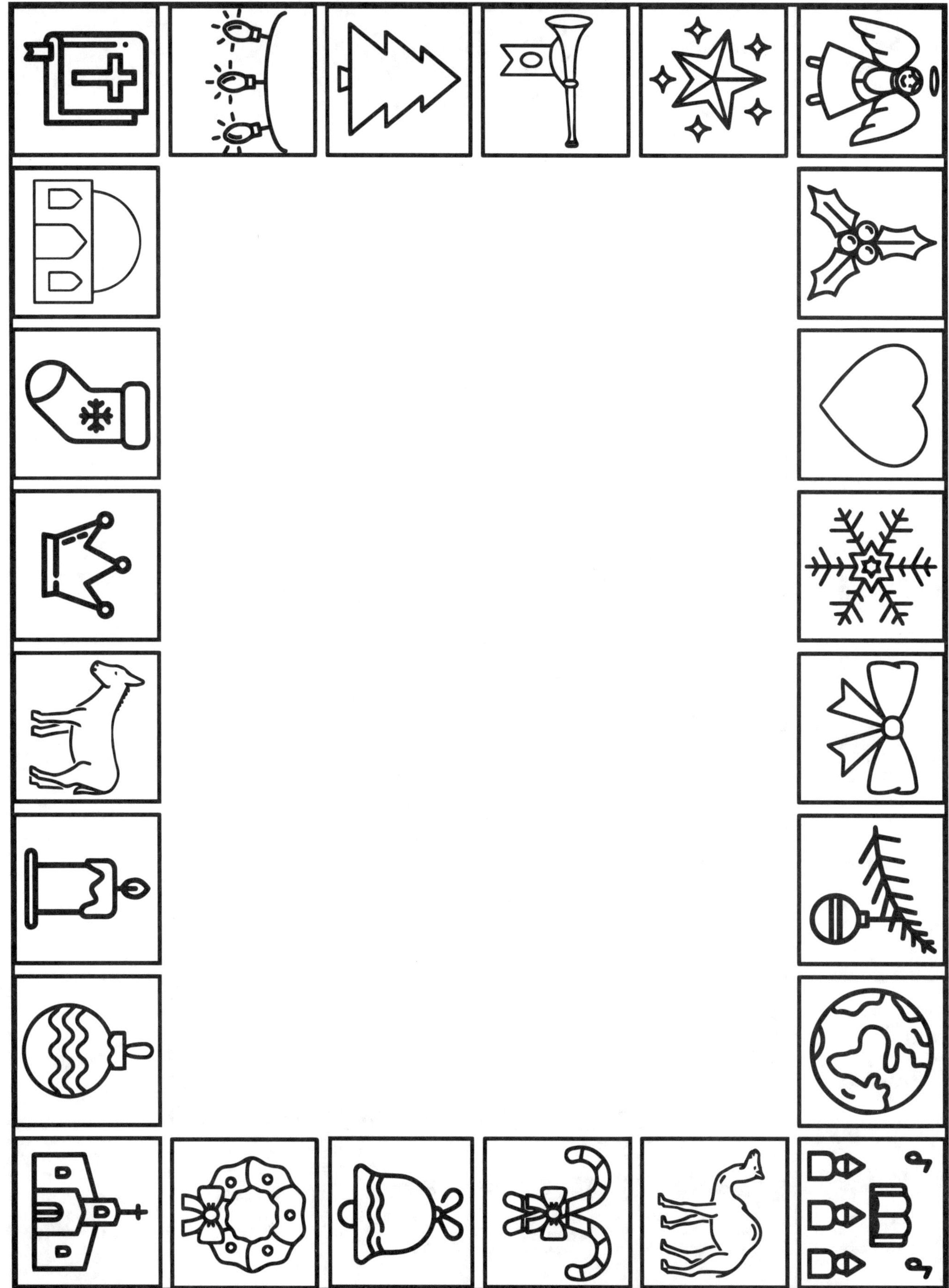

Christmas Wreath

Age Level: ✫★

O Lord, God of Israel, there is no God like you in all of heaven above or on the earth below. You keep your covenant and show unfailing love to all who walk before you in wholehearted devotion. 1 KINGS 8:23

What It's All About

Today's verse is from a prayer King Solomon prayed at the dedication of the Temple he built in God's honor. In 1 Kings 7:27–37 we read how the Israelites decorated God's Temple. One of the things they used as decorations were wreaths. At Christmas, it's traditional to decorate our homes and other buildings with wreaths. We can make this wreath to help our family remember that our house is a place for God to live and dwell with us just like the temple was God's dwelling place in Israel.

What You Need

- Christmas Wreath Patterns (p. 132)
- Paper Cutting Tools (see p. 8)
- Red cardstock
- Green lightweight paper (such as copy paper or construction paper)
- Transparent tape

Optional

- Decorating materials (glitter, stamps and stamp pads, stickers, adhesive gems, etc.)

Preparation

On red cardstock, photocopy Christmas Wreath Patterns, making one set for each child.

What Children Do

Make the Wreath

1. Fold a piece of green paper in half lengthwise.
2. Starting at the folded side cut slits in the paper about every ½ to 1 inch stopping 1 inch from the opposite side (image a).
3. Unfold the paper and curl it around to make the uncut long edges meet. Seal these edges together with tape.
4. Make a second green paper tube with slits by repeating Steps 1–3.
5. Attach tubes together to make one long tube. Make sure slits are on the same side of both tubes and then tape them together with slits.
6. Curve the long tube into a circle forming a wreath a tape to secure.

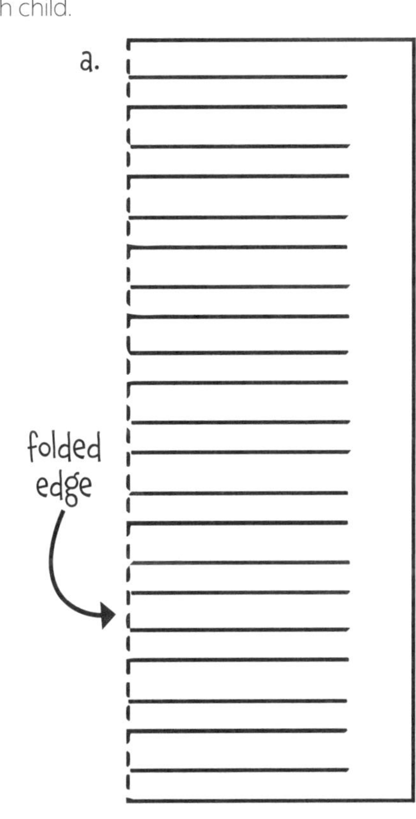

Decorate the wreath

7. Cut out pattern pieces and glue to wreath.

Optional: Use decorating materials to decorate calendars. Consider adding red glitter glue to the bow and berries.

Christmas Wreath Patterns

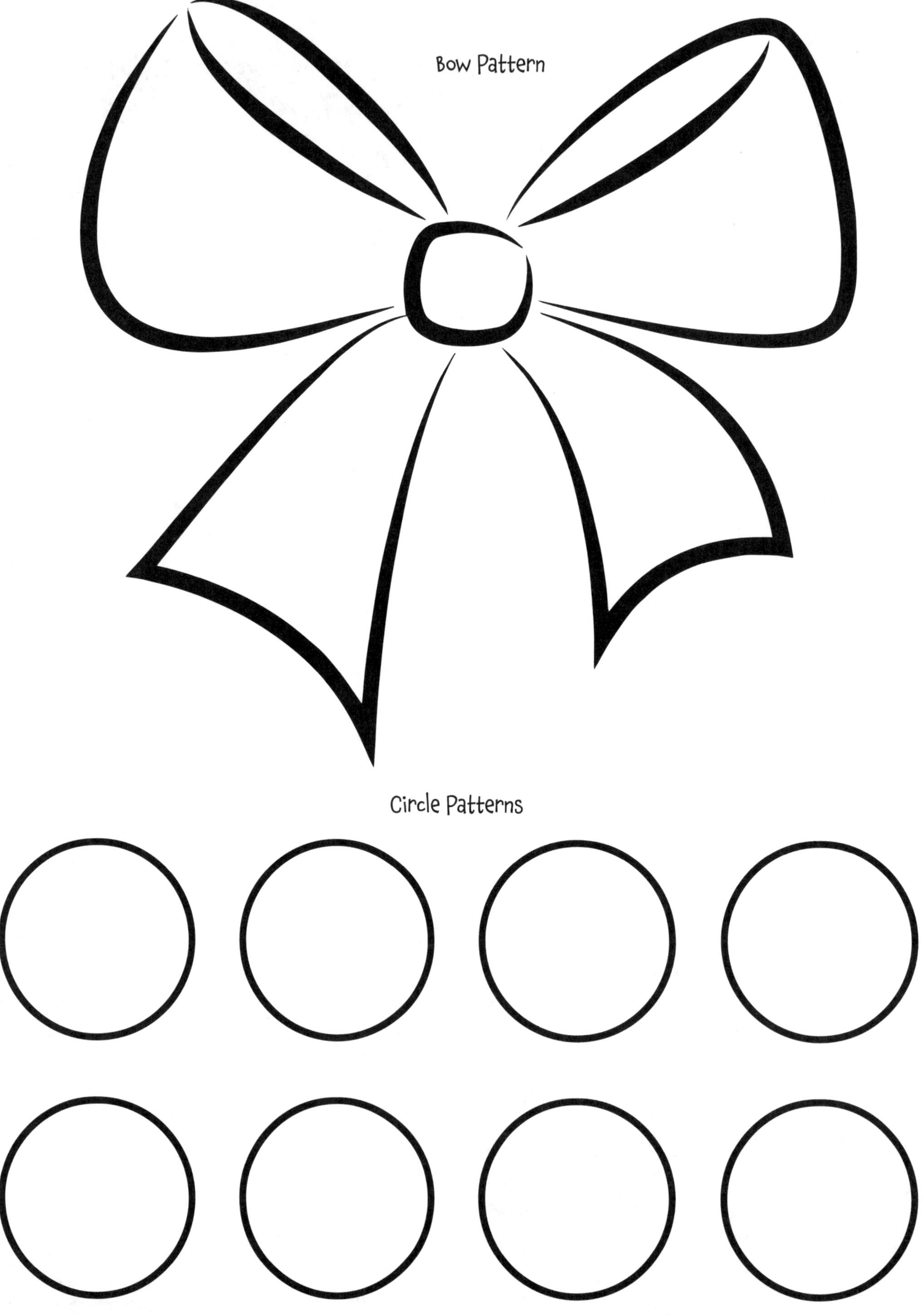

Paper Cone Christmas Tree

Age Level: ★★

"O Israel, stay away from idols! I am the one who answers your prayers and cares for you. I am like a tree that is always green; all your fruit comes from me." HOSEA 14:8

What It's All About

The Lord is like an evergreen tree and he helps us bear good fruit, like kindness, goodness, gentleness and so on. We can make this tree and tell others how God is like an evergreen tree.

What You Need

- Paper Cone Christmas Tree Patterns (p. 134)
- Paper Cutting Tools (see p. 8)
- Coloring and Writing Instruments (p. 8)
- Toilet-paper cardboard tube, one for every two children
- Cardstock in brown and yellow or metallic gold
- Green lightweight paper (such as copy paper or construction paper)
- Glue
- Transparent tape

Optional

- Decorating materials (glitter, stamps and stamp pads, stickers, adhesive gems, etc.)

Preparation

Photocopy Paper Cone Christmas Tree Patterns, making one set for each child.

Cut toilet-paper cardboard tubes in half, making smaller tubes about 2 inches in length.

What Children Do

1. Cut out patterns.

Make the Base of the Tree

2. Trace and cut the cone pattern out of brown cardstock.
3. Glue the tab under the other side of the shape to create a cone.
4. Glue to a 2-inch piece of toilet-paper tube, which forms the tree trunk.

Make the Branches

5. Cut green paper into 4-inch strips.
6. Gently fold the paper in half. Use a very thin line of glue to glue opposite edges together, forming a tube.
7. Starting at the folded side cut into the paper every ⅛ to ¼ of an inch. Stop about ¼ inch from the glued side together (image a).
8. Push the fold towards the glued side to form loops along the length of the tube.
9. Wrap the strip around the bottom of the tree. Tape in place and trim the excess.
10. Continue layering rows of the strips until you reach the top of the tree.

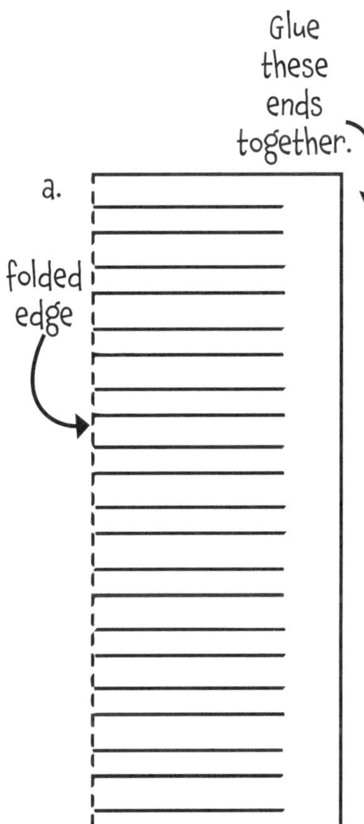

Make the Star Topper

11. Trace and cut star pattern out of yellow cardstock, cutting on all solid lines, including slits.
12. Slide the star shapes together. If needed, use tape to secure and glue star to the top of the tree.

Optional: Use decorating materials to decorate trees.

Paper Cone Christmas Tree Patterns

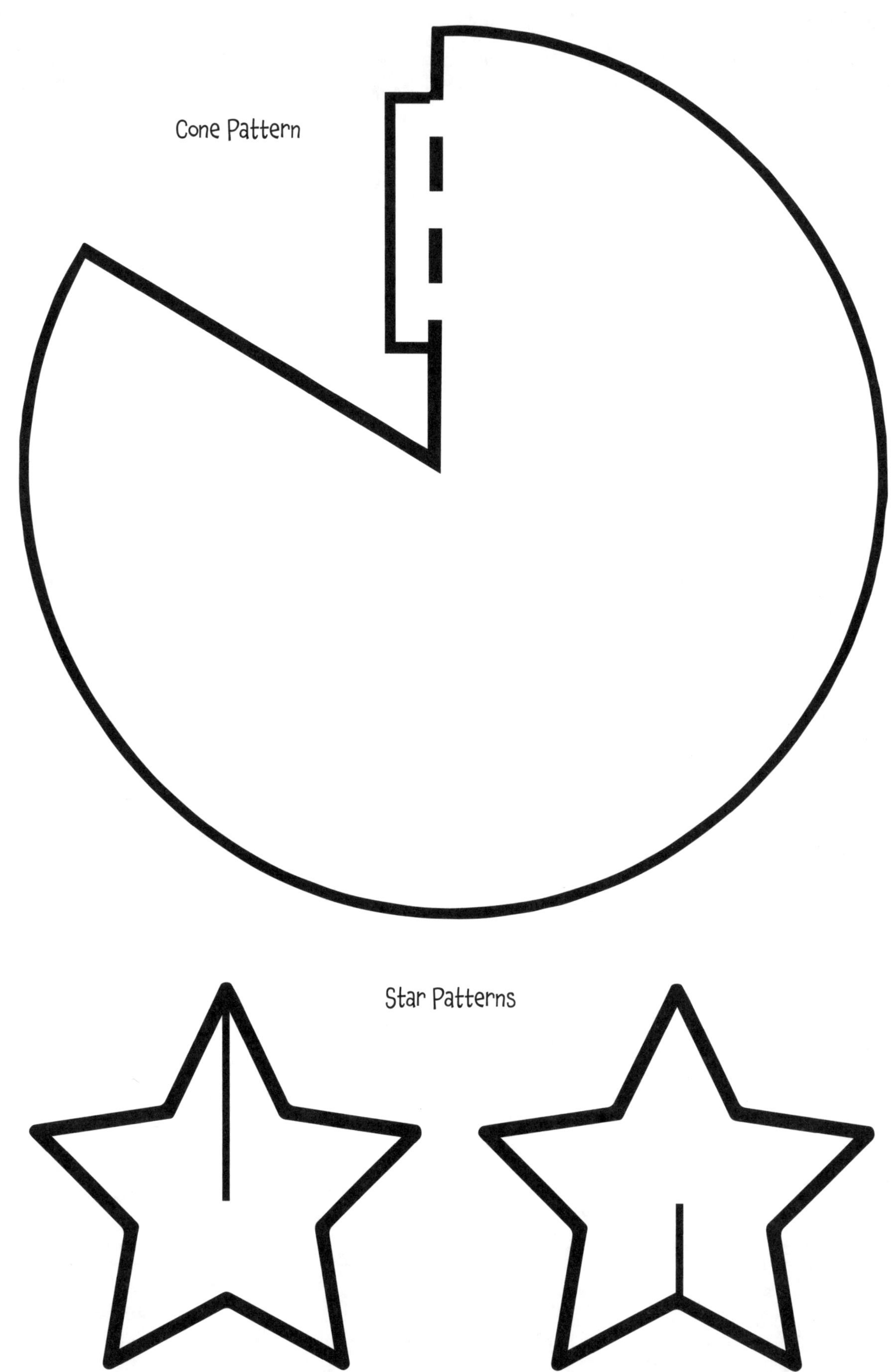

Stained Glass Window Art

Age Level: ✮★

You are the light of the world—like a city on a hilltop that cannot be hidden. No one lights a lamp and then puts it under a basket. Instead, a lamp is placed on a stand, where it gives light to everyone in the house. In the same way, let your good deeds shine out for all to see, so that everyone will praise your heavenly Father. MATTHEW 5:14–16

What It's All About

Putting this stained glass hanging in our windows can remind us to be lights for others, pointing them to Jesus through our attitudes and kindness.

What You Need

- Stained Glass Window Art Patterns (pp. 136–137)
- Acetate sheets, two for each child
- Masking tape
- Colored permanent markers
- Hole punch
- Yarn, string, or monofilament

Preparation

Photocopy Stained Glass Window Art Patterns, making one set for each child.

What Children Do

1. Place a pattern sheet on the table and tape it down.
2. Place a sheet of acetate over the pattern sheet and tape it down.
3. Using permanent markers, trace the design from the paper onto the acetate.
4. Use permanent markers to color the design.
5. Punch a hole in the top of the acetate.
6. Thread the yarn, string, or monofilament through the hole to create a hanger for the stained glass window art.

Alternate Ideas

- Instead of using patterns, children draw their own designs.
- Instead of acetate, use printable transparency sheets. Color on the rough side of the sheet. You can also color with colored pencils.

Stained Glass Window Art Patterns

Paper Chains of Good Deeds

Age Level: ☆★

Be careful how you live. Don't live like fools, but like those who are wise. Make the most of every opportunity in these evil days. Don't act thoughtlessly, but understand what the Lord wants you to do. EPHESIANS 5:15–17

What It's All About

It is wise to walk in kindness and love. As we do good deeds for others, we walk in kindness. Let's make a paper chain that can remind us of good deeds we can do for others.

What You Need

- Coloring & Writing Instruments (see p. 8)
- Paper Cutting Tools (see p. 8)
- Colored and patterned paper in red, green, white, metallics, etc.
- Glue

Optional

- Decorating materials (glitter, stamps and stamp pads, stickers, adhesive gems, etc.)

Preparation

Cut the following, making one of each for each child; or children choose their paper and use scissors and rulers to cut for themselves:

- Rectangles approximately 1 inch wide and at least 8 inches long

What Children Do

Making Links

1. Ask children to share their ideas for good things they have done for others (cleaned up after a meal, set the table, did some of the laundry, shared with a friend, etc.) or that they plan to do. Hand a paper strip to children for each idea.
2. Children write or draw on the paper strip about the good deed.

Making and Using the Chain

3. Glue the short ends of a paper strip together to make a circle.
4. Add another paper strip by threading it through the first loop before gluing the ends together. Continue adding links.
5. Decorate classroom, a church Christmas tree, or give as a gift to another group. Or have children create their own chains to take home with extra papers so that their family can add to their good deeds chain.

Optional: Use decorating materials to decorate chain links.

Alternate Ideas

- You can make the chains with the pictures and words on the inside so people don't know what the good deeds are unless they take the chain apart or you can put them on the outside and celebrate with each other the ways we are helping others.
- You can also add a scripture or kind words on the opposite side of the paper.

Photo Ornaments

Age Level: ✩★

See how very much our Father loves us, for he calls us his children, and that is what we are! But the people who belong to this world don't recognize that we are God's children because they don't know him. Dear friends, we are already God's children, but he has not yet shown us what we will be like when Christ appears. But we do know that we will be like him, for we will see him as he really is. 1 JOHN 3:1–2

What It's All About

We are all God's children and can celebrate that we are a part of God's family tree by putting pictures of ourselves and others on our Christmas trees.

What You Need

- Photo Ornaments Patterns (p. 140)
- Paper Cutting Tools (see p. 8)
- Coloring & Writing Instruments (see p. 8)
- Instant camera or camera and printer
- White cardstock
- Transparent tape
- Glue
- Hole punch
- Yarn, string, or monofilament
- Decorating materials (buttons, glitter, stamps and stamp pads, stickers, adhesive gems, etc.)

Preparation

On white cardstock, photocopy Photo Ornaments Patterns, making one for every two children.

What Children Do

1. Color and cut out patterns.
2. As children color and cut, take a photo of each one or of the child and a friend. If not using an instant camera, print out photos.
3. Trim the photo into a circle and glue in place as indicated on patterns.

Make the Hanger

4. Punch a hole in the top of the ornament.
5. String a length of yarn, string, or monofilament through the hole and tie a knot to make it into an ornament hanger.
6. Use decorating materials to decorate ornaments.

Alternate Idea

In the days before teaching this craft, contact children's parents and ask them to send a wallet-sized photo of their child.

Photo Ornaments Patterns

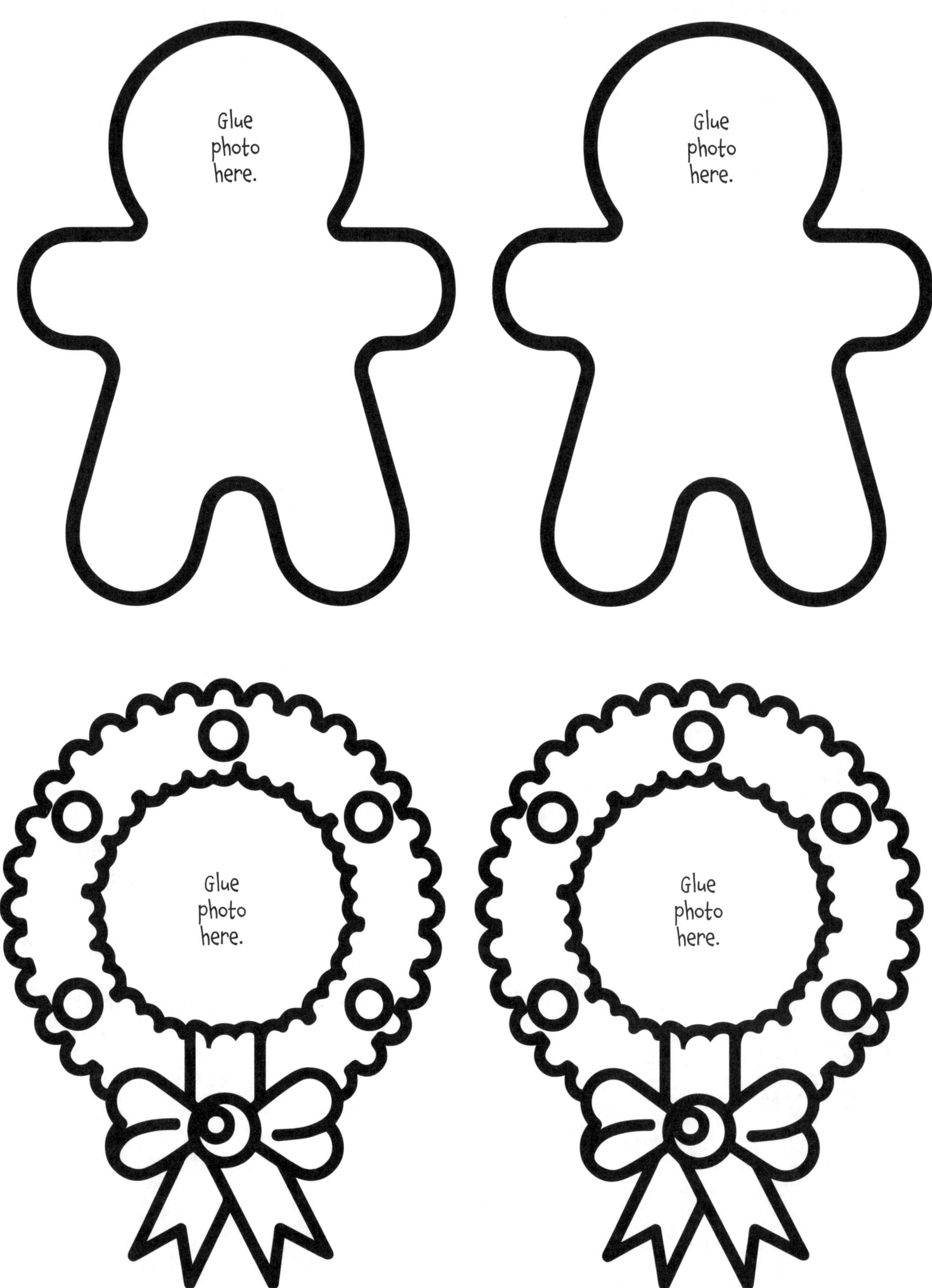

Envelope-Corner Village

Age Level: ☆★

The one who is the true light, who gives light to everyone, was coming into the world. He came into the very world he created, but the world didn't recognize him. He came to his own people, and even they rejected him. But to all who believed him and accepted him, he gave the right to become children of God. JOHN 1:9–12

What It's All About

Jesus came for all people and those who believe become children of God. Use envelopes to make a village as a reminder to pray for people around the world and to celebrate all believers.

What You Need

- Envelope-Corner Village Patterns (pp. 142–143)
- Paper Cutting Tools (see p. 8)
- Coloring & Writing Instruments (see p. 8)
- Envelopes, four for each child
- Glue
- Decorating materials (buttons, glitter, stamps and stamp pads, stickers, adhesive gems, etc.)

Preparation

Photocopy Envelope-Corner Village Patterns, making one set for each child.

What Children Do

1. Color and cut out each pattern on all the solid lines.
2. Seal the envelope closed. Glue a pattern piece to each corner of an envelope.
3. Cut out patterns.
4. Pop each pattern piece open enough to stand upright (see image a). **Note:** If needed, make a small paper cylinder to go under the house to help it stand.
5. Use decorating materials to decorate buildings and trees.

Optional

Use the houses as finger puppets to talk about Christmas around the world.

a.

Alternate Ideas

- Place your village into another uncut envelope to take home.
- Recycle by using used envelopes.

Envelope-Corner Village Patterns

Luminary

Age Level: ✮★

Jesus was born in Bethlehem in Judea, during the reign of King Herod. About that time some wise men from eastern lands arrived in Jerusalem, asking, "Where is the newborn king of the Jews? We saw his star as it rose, and we have come to worship him." MATTHEW 2:1–2

What It's All About

This beautiful light can shine to show the story of Jesus' birth. Jesus brought the light of hope into the world and sharing that story still brings hope.

Luminary, or *luminaria*, are from Mexico. Their name means "festival lights." They were originally used to line paths, the thought being that the lights would lead people to the Christ child.

What You Need

- Luminary Patterns (below right)
- Paper Cutting Tools (see p. 8)
- Black paper
- Pencil
- Glue
- White lunch bag (or brown lunch bags), one for each child
- Battery-operated tea lights, one for each child

Preparation

Photocopy Luminary Patterns, enlarging to 200 percent, making one set for each child.

What Children Do

1. Cut out the patterns and trace onto the black paper with a pencil.
2. Cut out the patterns from the black paper.
3. Glue the black pattern pieces onto the white paper bag near the bottom. On one side put the scene with Mary, Joseph, and Jesus.
4. Put the tea light in the bag and turn it on.

Tips

- For a better effect turn off the lights and look at the light shining through the bag.
- If you are placing the luminary outside (which is traditional), place some sand or a rock in the bottom of the bag so it won't be disturbed by the wind. Also, be sure to bring it inside if it starts to rain or snow.

Luminary Patterns

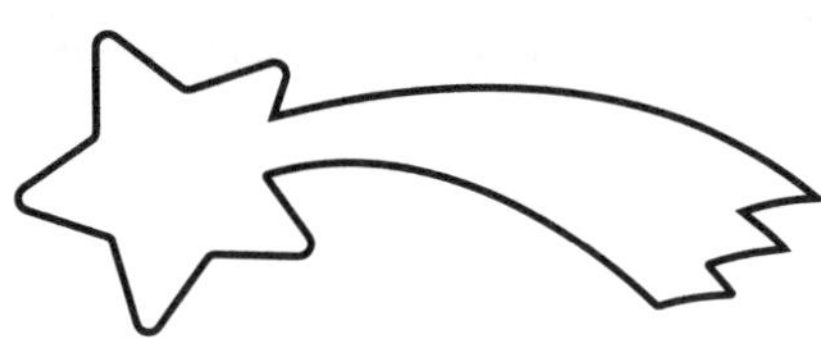

Christmas Tree Tunnel Card

Age Level: ☆★

A good tree can't produce bad fruit, and a bad tree can't produce good fruit. A tree is identified by its fruit. Figs are never gathered from thornbushes, and grapes are not picked from bramble bushes. A good person produces good things from the treasury of a good heart, and an evil person produces evil things from the treasury of an evil heart. What you say flows from what is in your heart. LUKE 6:43–45

What It's All About

Jesus is the reason for the Christmas season. Trees and lights and all the decorations help us celebrate the birth of God's only son. Jesus once said that a good tree bears good fruit. Let the ornaments on trees remind us to speak kind words as encouragement is like good fruit.

What You Need

- Christmas Tree Tunnel Card Patterns (p. 146)
- Paper Cutting Tools (see p. 8)
- Scoring materials (see p. 9)
- Cardstock in red, green, yellow, and black or Christmas patterns
- Double-sided tape or glue

Optional

- Decorating materials (glitter, stamps and stamp pads, stickers, adhesive gems, etc.)
- Decorative-edged scissors

Preparation

Photocopy Christmas Tree Tunnel Card Patterns, making one for each child. Be sure to center the pattern on the page. Trim papers to 5x7¾ inches.

Cut the following for each child; or children choose cardstock and use scissors and rulers to cut for themselves:

- One 5½x8½-inch piece of red cardstock for the outside cover
- One 4½x5-inch piece of green cardstock
- One ¾x2-inch piece of yellow cardstock
- One 3¾x5-inch piece of black or Christmas patterned cardstock
- Two 1x5-inch strips of black or Christmas patterned cardstock
- One 1-inch square of black or Christmas patterned cardstock

What Children Do

Make a Tunnel Card

This card is created in much the same way as described on page 16.

1. Score and fold red cardstock in half to make the front cover.
2. Glue 3¾x5-inch black or Christmas patterned cardstock piece to the center front of card (image a).

3. Score and fold green and yellow cardstock in half. Glue green cardstock to the inside center of the card, and yellow cardstock piece right above it.
4. Score and fold the 1-inch square of black cardstock. Glue below the green paper, centered.

Make the Windows

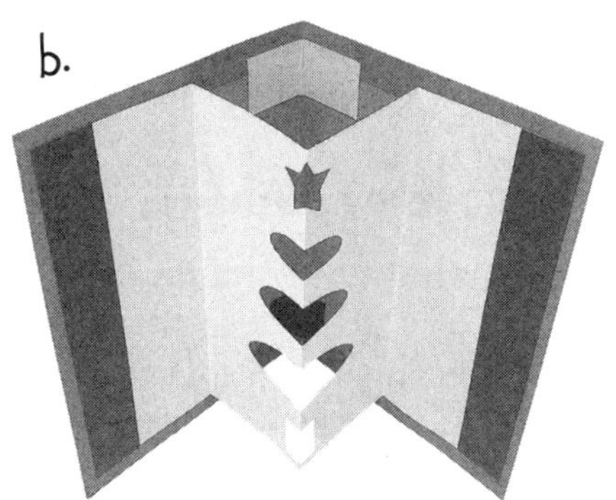

5. Fold white paper in half and then fold each side in the opposite direction to the center of the paper (to the fold already made).
6. Cut out the windows on the white paper.
7. Glue edges of white paper to 1x5-inch black cardstock strips. Glue strips and side edges of white paper ⅜ inch from the inside edges of the card (image b).

Optional

- Use decorating materials to decorate cards.
- Use decorative-edged scissors to trim the sides of the white paper before gluing it to the black strips.

Christmas Tree Tunnel Card Patterns

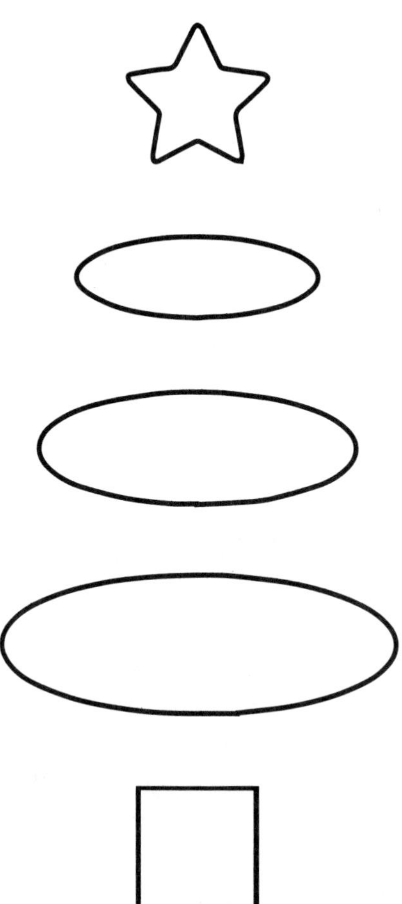

Gift Tags

Age Level: ✯★

Most important of all, continue to show deep love for each other, for love covers a multitude of sins. Cheerfully share your home with those who need a meal or a place to stay. God has given each of you a gift from his great variety of spiritual gifts. Use them well to serve one another. 1 PETER 4:8–10

What It's All About

God has given us many gifts. What are some of the gifts God has given you? Just as God has given us gifts, it makes him happy when we give gifts to others.

It is kind to give gifts to one another. At Christmas we often put tags on gifts to let others know who the gift is for and who it is from. Use these tags to share God's loving kindness with others.

What You Need

- Gift Tag Patterns (p. 148)
- Paper Cutting Tools (see p. 8)
- Coloring & Writing Instruments (see p. 8)
- White cardstock
- Ribbon, yarn, or string
- Hole punch
- Glue
- Decorating materials (buttons, glitter, stamps and stamp pads, stickers, adhesive gems, etc.)

Note: Striped baker's twine, as used in the photos, is a nice seasonal touch.

Preparation

On white cardstock, photocopy Gift Tag Patterns, making one for each child.

What Children Do

1. Cut out tags.
2. Color one side of the tag and write "To" and "From" on it, leaving space to add names later.
3. Decorate other side of cards with drawings and decorating materials.
4. Punch a hole at the top of the tag and thread a length of ribbon, yarn, or string through it.

Variations

- Photocopy patterns on the back (blank) side of Christmas patterned or colored cardstock.
- Cut your own tag shapes like a Christmas tree or heart.
- Children make gift tags using old Christmas card fronts. Or they could cut out images from the card fronts and glue to tags along with layers of patterned paper and designs they draw. Use foam tape to attach some elements to give the tag more dimension.

Gift Tag Patterns

Angel Tree Topper

Age Level: ★★

Suddenly, the angel was joined by a vast host of others—the armies of heaven—praising God and saying, "Glory to God in highest heaven, and peace on earth to those with whom God is pleased." LUKE 2:13–14

What It's All About

The angel Gabriel spoke to Mary about God choosing her to be the mother of Jesus, the Savior (Luke 1:26–38)**. Angels filled the sky the night of the birth of Jesus and spoke to shepherds. Those shepherds saw Jesus and then shared the good news with everyone. Share the news of Christ's birth.**

What You Need

- Angel Tree Topper Pattern (p. 150)
- Paper Cutting Tools (see p. 8)
- Coloring & Writing Instruments (see p. 8)
- Cardstock in white or metallic colors, also patterned white or metallics
- Decorating materials (buttons, beads, pearls, glitter, stamps and stamp pads, stickers, adhesive gems, etc.)

Optional

- Paper doily
- Glue
- Hole punch

Preparation

On white cardstock, photocopy Angel Tree Topper Pattern, making one for each child.

Cut the following for each child; or children choose cardstock and use scissors and rulers to cut for themselves:

- One 12-inch square of white or metallic cardstock

What Children Do

Make the Angel Tree Topper

1. Cut out pattern.
2. Fold the white or metallic cardstock in half. Place long dotted line on the fold. Cut along the solid outside lines. Unfold the cardstock.
3. Cut two slits on opposite sides of the angel, following the lines on the pattern for the left and right-side slits.
4. Slide the slits together to form the angel.

Decorate the Angel Tree Topper

5. Draw a face and arms on the front of the angel. You could also have the angel holding something like a heart or a cross.
6. Draw the halo.
7. Decorate angel with other drawings and decorating materials. **Optional:** Cut out sections from a doily and glue to the angel for a lacy look. Or punch a row of holes on each wing.

Angel Tree Topper Pattern

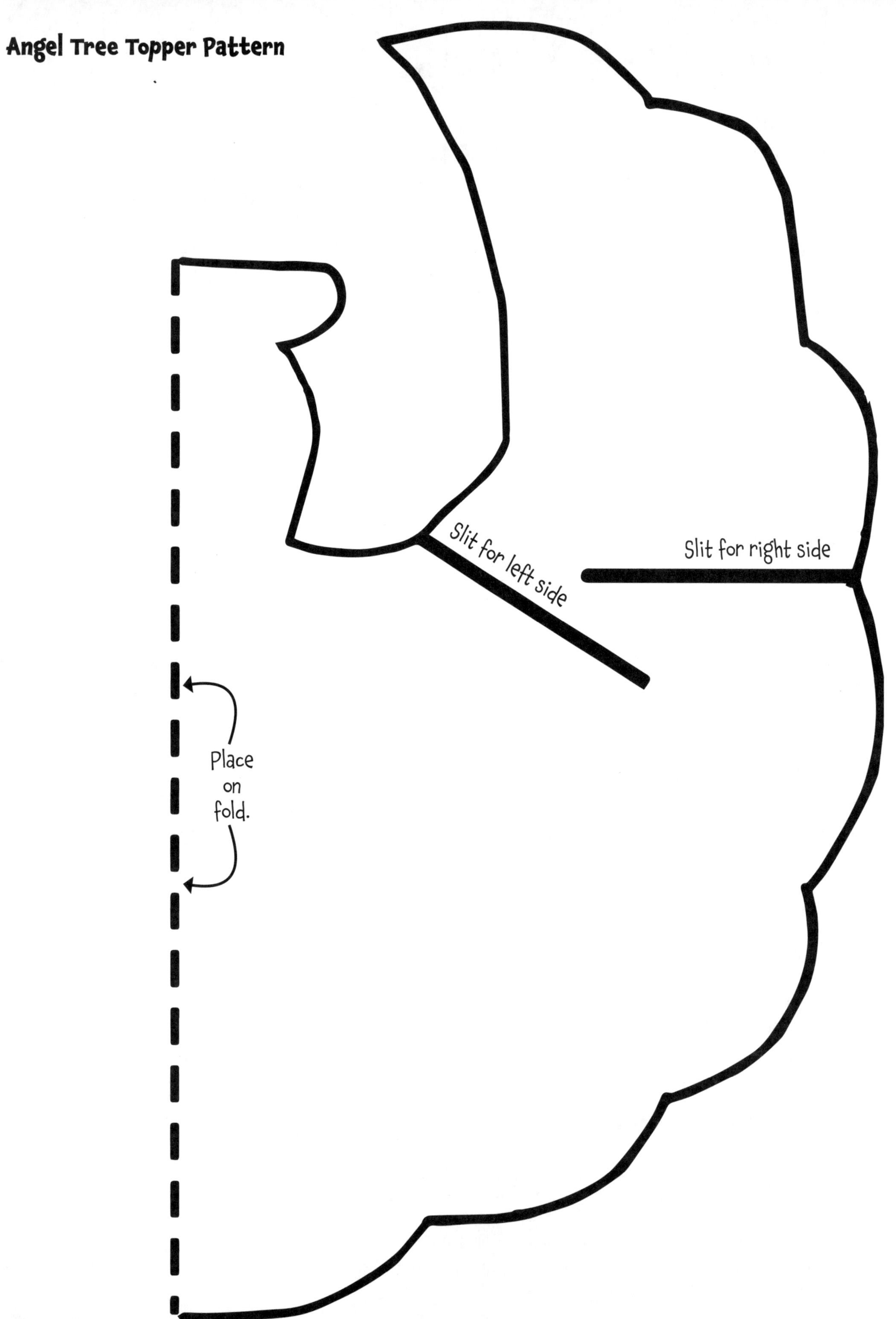

Diversity Crafts

It's good to read Psalm 139 and consider how much care God puts into the start of a person's life. He wants us to live in peace and celebrate the uniqueness of the people we meet and pray for all to come to have faith in him. God looks at the heart and not the outward appearance and we should follow that example.

Celebrate that our hands can hold one another, pray for one another, and help one another. We can go further to understand cultures of people who come from different parts of the world. We can also consider ways to live in peace and rejoice for everyone we meet and each person's talents and beauty.

Discussion Ideas

Here are a few ways to spark discussion about inclusiveness while making the crafts in this section:

- Read about children from around the world and find out where there is religious freedom and where there is religious persecution. Pray for those who are not allowed to practice faith in Jesus.
- Appreciate differences and notice differences in all creation from flowers and dogs to people. God has a great imagination to make us different and unique.
- Share about respect and acceptance of people who are not like you. Talk about how everyone has the desire to be respected and accepted. Everyone is made in the image of God. In accepting and including all the people God made, we are honoring God.
- Life is precious, so use diversity to also share about caring for the lives of all people from those still growing inside the womb to those who are of advanced age.
- Make the Woven Heart Basket (p. 157) using a variety of colors to represent different skin tones. Write notes to fill the heart with encouragement and kind thoughts.
- Discuss ways to have peace and live together in harmony.
- Celebrate differences by using some of the crafts as decorations for a party where you play games from different countries, learn phrases in different languages, and taste foods from around the world.

Diversity Coils

Age Level: ☆

Instead, I want to see a mighty flood of justice, an endless river of righteous living. AMOS 5:24

What It's All About

God wants righteousness and justice to flow from us like a stream. That means that loving others and treating others fairly should be natural and flow from our hearts.

What You Need

- Diversity Coils Patterns (p. 153)
- Paper Cutting Tools (see p. 8)
- Coloring & Writing Instruments, especially in skin tones (see p. 8)
- Paper in white and blue
- Brad
- Yarn, string, monofilament, pipe cleaners or paper clips

Preparation

Enlarge patterns 200 percent as you photocopy Diversity Coils Patterns, making one in each color for each child. Use the Clockwise Coil Pattern for one color, and the Counter-Clockwise Coil Pattern for the other color.

What Children Do

1. Cut out the circle. Do not cut the inside spiral yet.
2. Color lines across the white pattern in all directions, in colors for people's skin (various shades of beige, brown, pink, etc.).
3. Cut along the spiral lines.
4. Cut out the second circle and the spiral.
5. Place the colored coil on top of the blue coil. Grab the center of the two circles and lift it up to let the rest fall down. This forms two spirals that intertwine. Say, **The colored lines on the one coil represents people of all colors. The blue coil represents a flowing river of the Holy Spirit as well as justice flowing from us like a river.**
6. Add a brad through the tops of both coils (image a).
7. Add a length of yarn, string, monofilament, a pipe cleaner or unbend a paper clip to make a hanger.

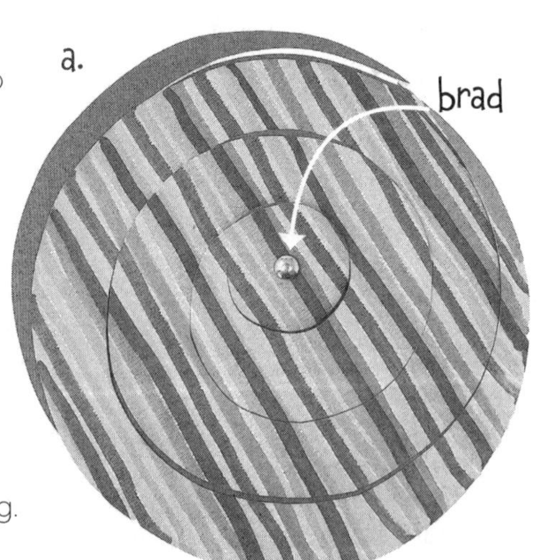

Variations

Use green instead of blue paper to symbolize people on earth getting along.

Diversity Coils Patterns

Enlarge coil patterns 200%.

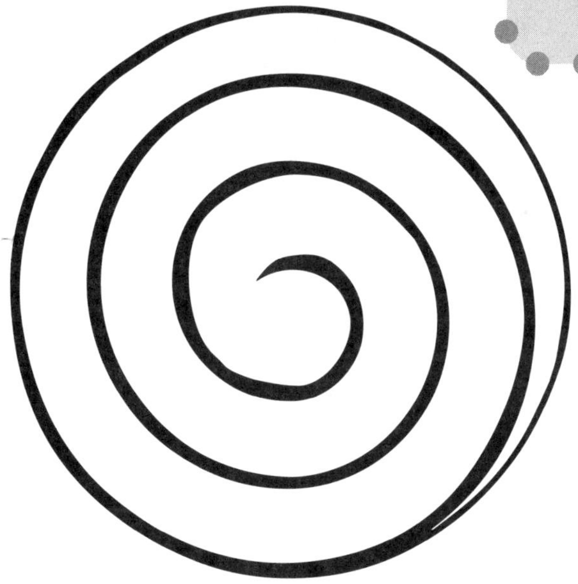

Clockwise Coil Pattern

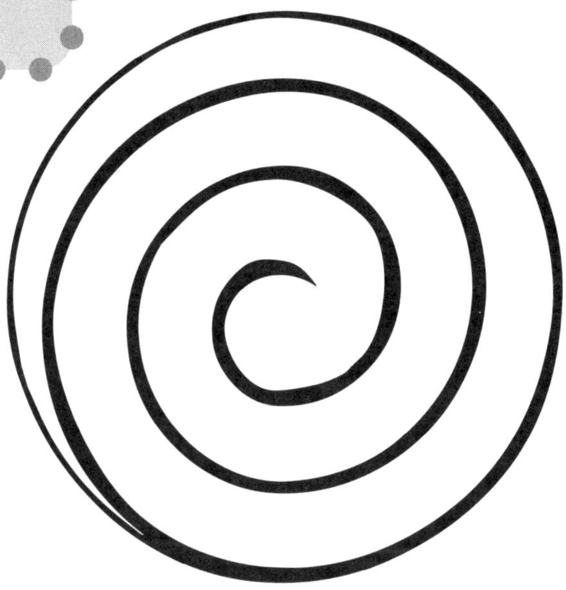

Counter-Clockwise Coil Pattern

Diversity Circle Cutout Patterns (for craft on p. 154)

Diversity Circle Cutout

Age Level: ☆★

For this is how God loved the world: He gave his one and only Son, so that everyone who believes in him will not perish but have eternal life. JOHN 3:16

What It's All About

We're going to make a circle of children. Between each child is a heart to remind us to love one another. In the center of the circle will be a cross to remind us of Jesus' sacrifice on the cross. Our verse tells us that Jesus died so that EVERYONE—no matter how they look or where they live—can become a member of God's family.

What You Need

- Diversity Circle Cutout Pattern (p. 153)
- Paper Cutting Tools (see p. 8)
- Coloring & Writing Instruments (see p. 8)
- White paper

Preparation

Photocopy Diversity Circle Cutout Pattern, making one copy for every three children. (There are three patterns on the page.)

What Children Do

Prepare the Paper

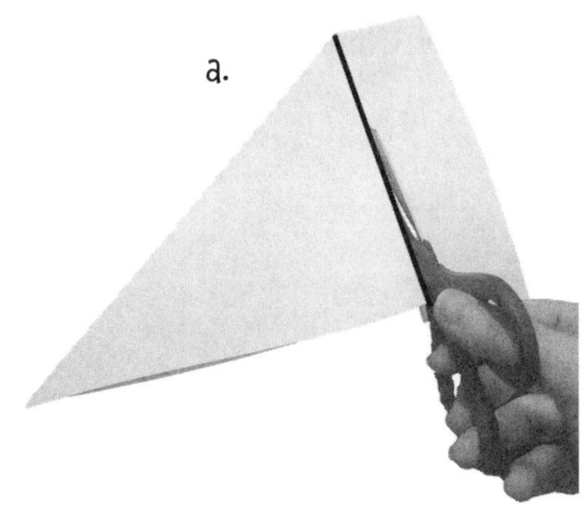

1. Fold a piece of paper in half diagonally. Cut off the excess paper (image a).
2. Fold in half again, and then once more. You will have a triangle shape with one edge rounded.

Prepare the Pattern

3. Cut out the pattern.
4. Place pattern on folded paper so that the sides of the pattern run along the folded sides of the paper. Trace pattern onto folded paper (image b).
5. Cut folded paper on the lines you traced.
6. Open the circle.
7. Color in the children using different skin colors and their clothing.

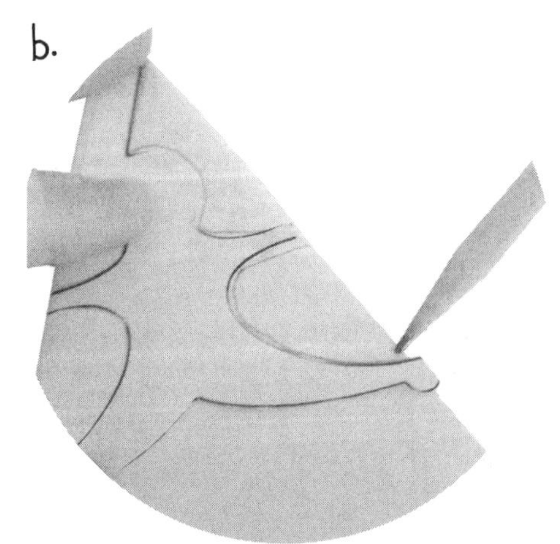

Talk about It

- Talk about ways kids can show love and kindness to everyone.
- Sing songs that celebrate Jesus' love for all the children of the world.

Handy Diversity Booklet

Age Level: ☆★

Do to others whatever you would like them to do to you. This is the essence of all that is taught in the law and the prophets. MATTHEW 7:12

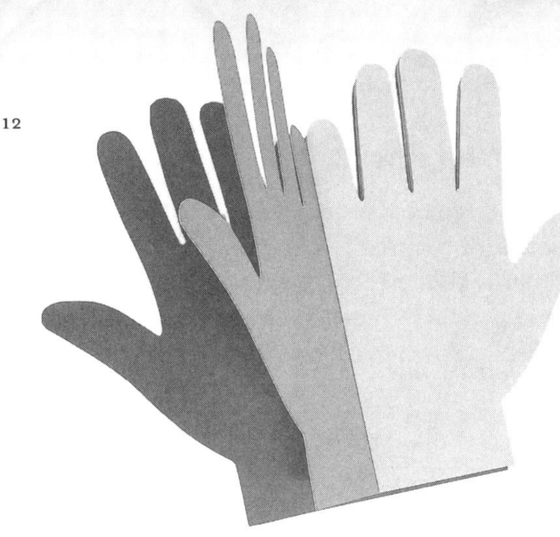

What It's All About

Jesus spoke the words in our verse. Sometimes this is called "The Golden Rule." These wise words remind us to be kind if we want people to be kind to us. We're going to make a booklet you can use to write about how you will treat others.

What You Need

- Paper Cutting Tools (see p. 8)
- Coloring & Writing Instruments (see p. 8)
- Cardstock in a variety of skin colors
- Stapler and staples

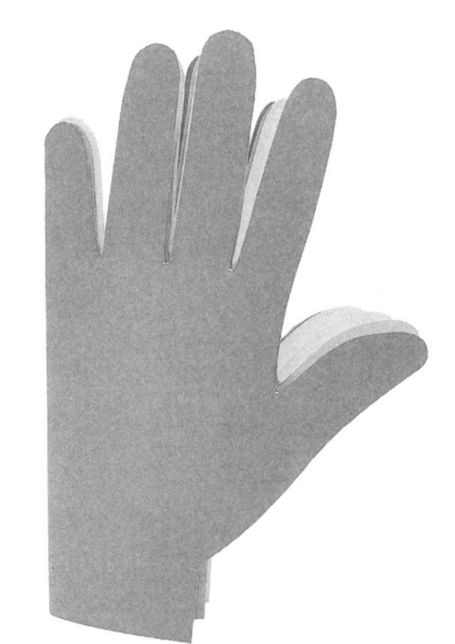

What Children Do

1. Fold a piece of cardstock in half. Trace your hand with the little finger against the fold.
2. Cut out and use as pattern. Be sure to keep it folded!
3. Trace your pattern onto additional sheets of folded cardstock. Be sure to use in different colors.
4. Open all the hands and layer them to make a booklet. Staple them together along the center fold line.
5. Say, **Use the booklet to write notes about how to treat others, prayers for friends, and notes about how you want to be treated. Also write notes about what you learn from friends of different cultures.**

Ideas of What to Write

- How you want to be treated when you play with friends and how you will then treat them.
- Write about different foods and customs of people from other places.
- Prayers for friends who are bullied.
- Write how you will stand up for friends who are bullied.
- Write notes about how we are all different. That includes our ages, looks, and abilities.
- Write about a friend who has a disability or learning disorder and how you will help that person. Write about any help you need because of your own difficulties.
- Write about how Jesus treated and healed people like those who were sick, blind, deaf, or crippled.

Peace Prayer Basket

Age Level: ☆★

God blesses those who work for peace, for they will be called the children of God. MATTHEW 5:9

What It's All About

We are called to be peacemakers. That means to put others first, settle differences, and agree to get along and respect others even when you have different beliefs. We're going to make baskets in which to store verse and prayer requests for peace. The baskets will be colored with different skin tones to celebrate all the colors of the people God made.

What You Need

- Paper Cutting Tools (see p. 8)
- Scoring materials (see p. 9)
- White 12x12-inch cardstock
- Crayons, gel pens, markers or colored pencils in various skin tones
- Transparent tape
- Hole punch
- Brads, two for each child
- Scrap paper

Preparation

Cut cardstock as listed below, making one of each for each child; or children use scissors and cut for themselves:

- 6-inch squares (one 12-inch square sheet yields four 6-inch squares)
- ½x6-inch strips

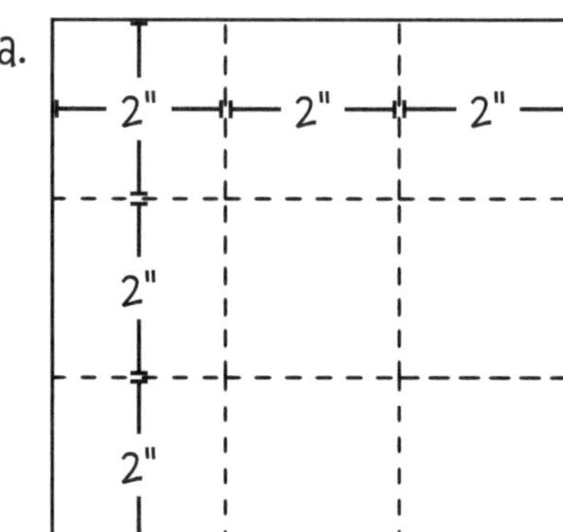

b.

What Children Do

Make the Basket

1. Color both sides of your cardstock square with the different colors. You can make a drawing or just draw patterns: stripes, circles, other shapes, or faces.
2. Score the paper into thirds both vertically and horizontally. The lines will be two inches apart (image a).
3. Cut the top and bottom fold lines to make slits (image b).
4. Fold along all lines to form the basket.
5. On each side that has slits, fold side pieces over the center until they meet. Tape in place.
6. Punch a hole through all layers, near where you taped the sides.

Make the Handle

7. Punch a hole at both ends of a ½x6-inch strip.
8. Thread a brad through one of the basket holes, and then one of the handle holes. Open on the inside of the basket to secure (image c).

How to Use the Basket

9. Write out scriptures and quotes or thoughts about peace. Put them in the basket and use them to pray for peace.

c.

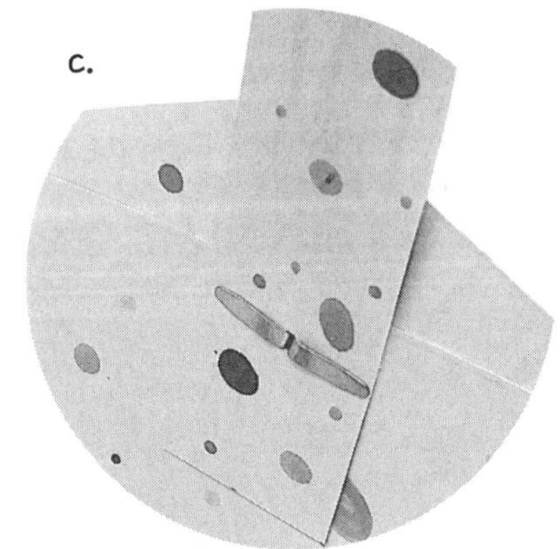

Woven Heart Basket

Age Level: ★

All of you should be of one mind. Sympathize with each other. Love each other as brothers and sisters. Be tenderhearted, and keep a humble attitude. 1 PETER 3:8

What It's All About

Love binds people together with joy and makes it easier to forgive one another and sympathize with one another's troubles. These hearts are woven together with paper and can hold small notes or treats. They originated in Denmark in the 1800s and were used as Christmas decorations.

What You Need

- Paper Cutting Tools (see p. 8)
- Woven Heart Basket Patterns (p. 158)
- Construction paper in two different skin colors, one of each color for each child
- Crayons, gel pens, markers or colored pencils in various skin tones

Optional

- Decorating materials (buttons, beads, pearls, glitter, stamps and stamp pads, stickers, adhesive gems, etc.)

Preparation

a.

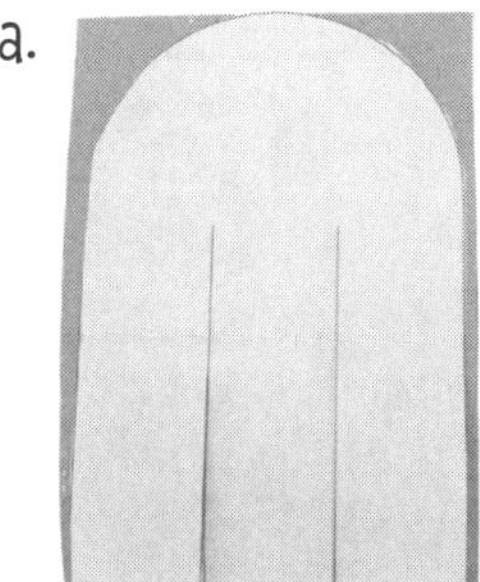

Photocopy Woven Heart Basket Patterns, making one copy for every two children.

Cut construction-paper sheets in half lengthwise, making 4½x9-inch pieces, one of each color for every child.

What Children Do

1. Cut out pattern, including the slits.
2. Fold each sheet of construction paper in half making a 6x9-inch rectangle.
3. Place pattern on one of the sheets of paper, with the dashed line along the fold (image a). Cut out; cut slits. Repeat for second sheet of paper.
4. Start weaving the hearts together. Starting with the first loop of the right-hand heart, thread it through the loop formed by the first strip of the other paper (image b).
5. Next, thread the second sheet's middle strip through the loop of the first sheet (image c).
6. Finally, weave the strip through the loop formed by the third strip of the other paper, like you did in Step 4.
7. Repeat for the next two strips. **Note:** For the second strip you will start with thread the second sheet's strip through the first sheet's, then the first sheet's through the second sheet, and finally the second sheet's strip through the first sheet. The third strip is done the same as the first.

b.

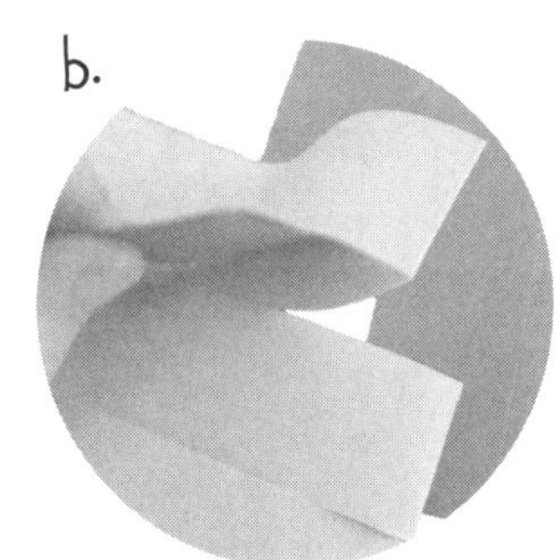

Optional: Decorate Woven Heart Basket with decorating materials.

Variations

c.

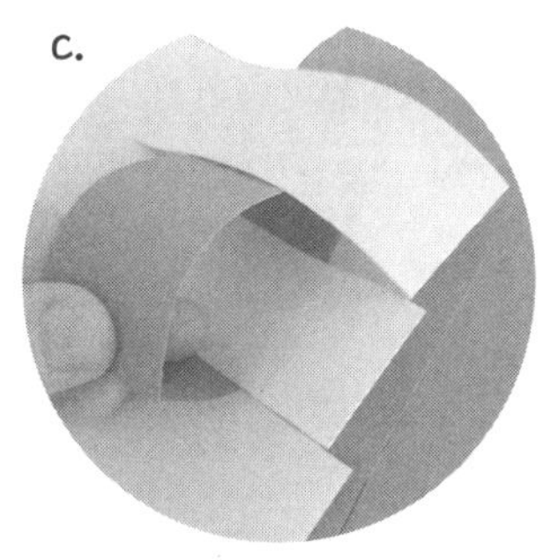

- Make a handle or hanger with a pipe cleaner, strip of paper, or length of yarn.
- Make larger or smaller hearts by enlarging or shrinking the pattern.
- Cut wiggly lines for an interesting woven pattern.
- Cut white paper and color the loops a variety of skin colors before weaving them.

Woven Heart Basket Patterns

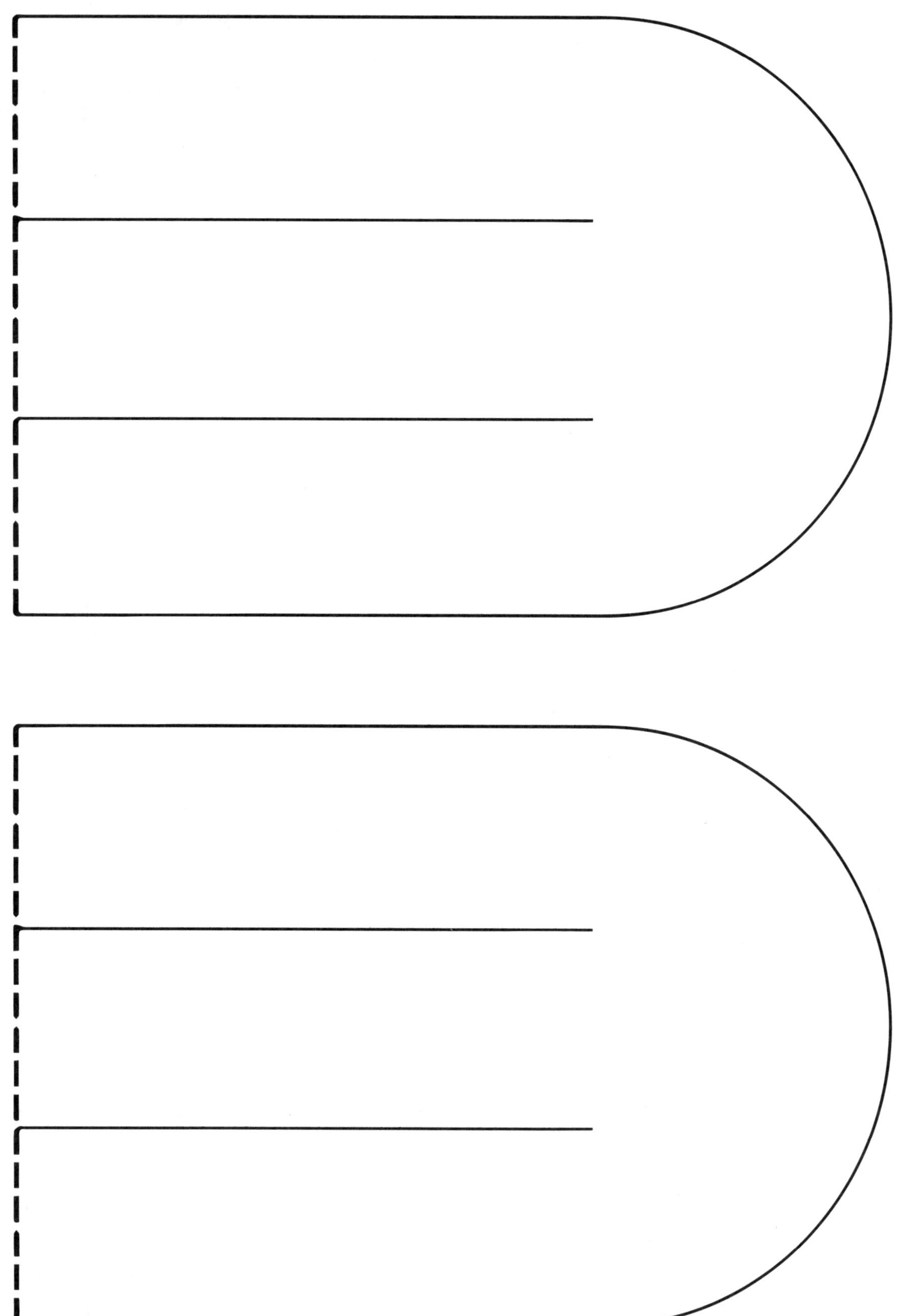

Hand Puzzles

Age Level: ☆★

Is there any encouragement from belonging to Christ? Any comfort from his love? Any fellowship together in the Spirit? Are your hearts tender and compassionate? Then make me truly happy by agreeing wholeheartedly with each other, loving one another, and working together with one mind and purpose. Don't be selfish; don't try to impress others. Be humble, thinking of others as better than yourselves. PHILIPPIANS 2:1–3

What It's All About

Encourage others and learn to cooperate by working together. This develops a sense of unity and team spirit. We're going to make hands in several different skin tones to represent people of all colors. Then, we'll team up to play a game.

What You Need

- Paper Cutting Tools (see p. 8)
- Cardstock in skin tones
- Pencils

What Children Do

1. Trace a hand onto a piece of cardstock.
2. Cut out.
3. Children continue to make two or three hands each as time allows.

How to Play

4. Children form teams of three or four players.
5. Use the hands to make designs, like putting puzzle pieces together. Instruct teams to use the hands to:
   - Form one large heart to represent loving everyone.
   - Make a rainbow with the hands separated into rows by color as a reminder that God's promises are for everyone.
   - Create a circle to represent the world and all the people in it.
   - Make a cross to represent how Jesus died for all people.
   - Pair up hearts and put thumb and pointer fingers together to form hearts.
6. Encourage children to come up with their own ideas and race to complete those as well:
7. For each round, the team that finishes first repeats the verse together.

Rolling with Joy

Age Level: ☆★

Always be full of joy in the Lord. I say it again—rejoice! Let everyone see that you are considerate in all you do. Remember, the Lord is coming soon. Don't worry about anything; instead, pray about everything. Tell God what you need, and thank him for all he has done. Then you will experience God's peace, which exceeds anything we can understand. His peace will guard your hearts and minds as you live in Christ Jesus. PHILIPPIANS 4:4–7

What It's All About

God wants everyone to rejoice and live in peace with one another. Have fun making this a rolling reminder of joy. Make a rolling cylinder and put a child inside that is different in looks and skin color on the other side. These rolling racers can be a reminder to rejoice with others.

What You Need

- Rolling with Joy Pattern (below)
- Paper Cutting Tools (see p. 8)
- Coloring & Writing Instruments (see p. 8)
- White and colored cardstock
- Stapler

Preparation

On white cardstock, photocopy Rolling with Joy Pattern, making one for each child.

Cut colored cardstock into 4½x11-inch strips, making one for each child, or children choose cardstock and use scissors and rulers to cut for themselves.

What Children Do

1. Fold colored cardstock in half lengthwise, making it 2¼-inches wide. Write words on one side like *joy* and *love*.
2. Curve the length of the paper to overlap ends, to form a tube. Overlap the ends so that tube is 3 inches in diameter and staple.
3. Cut out pattern piece.
4. Color each side to show two different children. Color tabs to match the tube.
5. Fold all the tabs on the child in the same direction. Staple tabs inside tube so children are standing up in the tube.

How to Play

6. Use masking tape to make start and finish lines and have races.
7. Use masking tape to make paths for the racers to follow.

Rolling with Joy Pattern

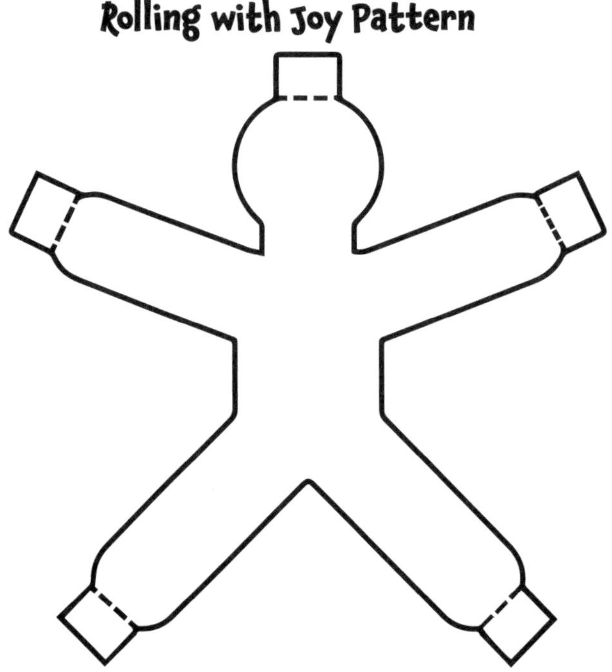

Thumb-Body Special

Age Level: ☆★

You formed me with your hands; you made me, yet now you completely destroy me. Remember that you made me from dust—will you turn me back to dust so soon? You guided my conception and formed me in the womb. You clothed me with skin and flesh, and you knit my bones and sinews together. You gave me life and showed me your unfailing love. My life was preserved by your care. JOB 10:8–12

What It's All About

Each person is special, carefully created by God, lovable, and full of potential. You are special right down to your fingertips—each fingerprint is one of a kind! Celebrate that you and everyone else is unique with fingerprint designs.

What You Need

- Coloring & Writing Instruments (see p. 8)
- Stamp pads of ink in skin tones
- White paper
- Moistened towelettes

What Children Do

1. Press the thumb of your non-dominant hand into an ink pad or a thin layer of paint.
2. Press your thumb on a sheet of white paper. Wipe thumb clean with a moistened towelette.
3. Use pens or colored pencils to draw designs to add arms, legs, faces, hats, and other items that show them doing things: cooking, playing an instrument, running, etc.
4. Repeat with other colors of ink and other fingers. Make one that shows what you like to do.
5. Make additional thumbprint people to represent family and friends.

Diversity Jewelry

Age Level: ★

Jesus said, "Let the children come to me. Don't stop them! For the Kingdom of Heaven belongs to those who are like these children." MATTHEW 19:14

What It's All About

Jesus loved children and told his friends, "Let the children come to me." Make a pendant of various skin tones as a reminder that Jesus wants all the children of the world to become members of God's family.

What You Need

- Paper Cutting Tools (see p. 8)
- Cardstock in a variety of skin tones, at least 5 different colors
- Glue
- Hole punch
- Yarn, string, or baker's twine

Preparation

Cut colored cardstock into 1¾-inch squares, making one for each child, or children choose cardstock and use scissors and rulers to cut for themselves.

What Children Do

1. Starting with a 1¾-inch square, cut a slightly smaller square from a different color of cardstock. The differently colored square should be approximately ⅛ inch smaller than the first.
2. Cut up to eight more slightly smaller squares. Make each smaller square a different color. The smallest square should be approximately ⅜-inch square.
3. Glue the second square cut on top of the first one. Let dry.
4. Repeat with next smaller square until all squares have been glued.
5. When the layers dry, punch a hole in one side for stringing yarn through it. Brush glue over the whole pendant to give it a glossy finish.
6. Attach yarn to make it into a necklace. Tie the ends of the necklace at the length that can slip easily over your head.

Younger Child Adaptation: Younger children use fewer layers or larger pendants with approximately ¼-inch difference between sizes. Precut squares for very young children.

Variations

- If desired, cut a tiny bit off each square's corners to make the points less sharp.
- Cut other shapes like diamonds or circles.
- Make the beads from the Paper Bead Jewelry craft (pp. 96–97) using paper in a variety of skin tones. String the beads into a bracelet.
- Add a heart bead to the necklace as a reminder to people of all colors.

Celebration Crafts

Eat, play games, be merry, CELEBRATE! We love to find joy in things and holidays give us that time. Throw a party to celebrate God's love. Play music and praise him! Make decorations. Invite friends! Plan food and games!

Through the year there are times we celebrate one another and other holidays. The crafts here give us opportunities to spread joy as we celebrate birthdays and babies. They also give us an opportunity to celebrate God's creation with a May Day Basket (p. 172). We can be thankful to God and celebrate our salvation as well with activities. Many of the crafts can be used with different images or words to celebrate other days.

Outreach Ideas

Here are a few outreach ideas for the crafts in this section:

- Make Party Favor Holders (p. 166) to give small gifts to people for any celebration.
- Make Party Banners (p. 168) to celebrate events in your group as well as achievements that individuals or groups make.
- Make Baby Cards (p. 175) and give them to a crisis pregnancy center with gift cards for new moms who are struggling.

Invitations

Age Level: ✩★

He must enjoy having guests in his home, and he must love what is good. He must live wisely and be just. He must live a devout and disciplined life. TITUS 1:8

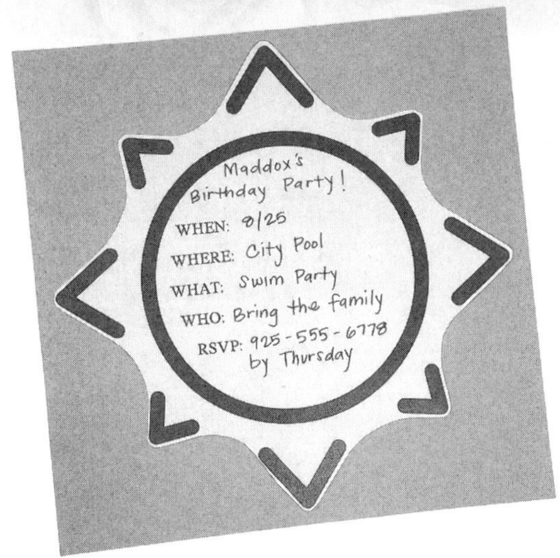

What It's All About

Just as Jesus welcomed the disciples back from a night of fishing (Read the story in John 21:9–13)**, and our verse encourages us to show hospitality to strangers, the invitations we will be making welcome guests to an event. Hospitality starts with a welcoming invite to make guests feel you care about them.**

An invitation is all about what guests need to know in order to enjoy your event. You can use a regular piece of paper and choose either a horizontal or vertical orientation—although most invitations use a vertical one where the card opens from side to side.

What You Need

- Coloring & Writing Instruments (see p. 8)
- Colored cardstock
- Paper

Optional

- Decorating materials (buttons, beads, pearls, glitter, stamps and stamp pads, stickers, adhesive gems, etc.)

What Children Do

1. Put the name of the event in the middle of the top of the paper. Example: Ashley's Birthday Party
2. Then add the important details underneath. Write down each of the following:
   - **When:** What day and time is the event planned to happen?
   - **Where:** Give an address or a known location (if it is at a house it should include an address but could also say the name of the person's home. If it is at a church, you can use the name of the church and don't have to include the address).
   - **What:** Tell a little about what is happening or what people should bring. If it includes a meal, that is nice to tell people so they can plan for it, if they need a swimsuit or other special gear you should tell them this as well.
   - **Who:** Is it only for them or is the family invited to attend?
3. Near the bottom of the card, write R.S.V.P. and give a phone number they can call or text to let you know they are coming.
4. Now that you have given all the important information, draw some pictures in the corners to decorate the invitation.

Optional: Use decorating materials to jazz up your invitation.

More Creative Options

- Cut the invitation in a shape related to the event such as a teacup for a tea party or a football for a sports party.
- Use Invitation Pattern on page 165. Fill in the information, make photocopies (one for each person you wish to invite) . Then cut out the paper and glue it to a piece of cardstock to make a card that looks like the one at the top of this page.

WHEN:
WHERE:
WHAT:
WHO:
RSVP:

Party Favor Holder

Age Level: ★

If your gift is to encourage others, be encouraging. If it is giving, give generously. If God has given you leadership ability, take the responsibility seriously. And if you have a gift for showing kindness to others, do it gladly. Don't just pretend to love others. Really love them. Hate what is wrong. Hold tightly to what is good. Love each other with genuine affection, and take delight in honoring each other. ROMANS 12:8–10

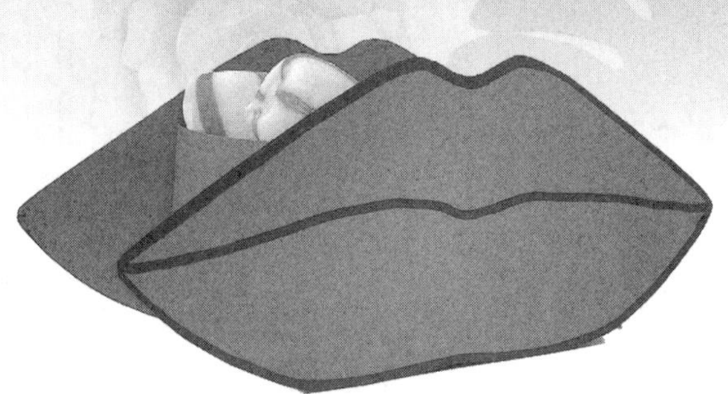

What It's All About

We are to use the gifts God gave us to build up others. He wants us to be kind and loving. Use these boxes to remind you to use kind words and show love towards others.

What You Need

- Party Favor Holder Patterns (p. 167)
- Paper Cutting Tools (see p. 8)
- Scoring materials (see p. 9
- Red cardstock
- Glue or double-sided tape
- Small treats (individually wrapped candies, stickers, erasers, etc.)

Optional

- Decorating materials (buttons, beads, pearls, glitter, stamps and stamp pads, stickers, adhesive gems, etc.)

Preparation

On the wrong side of the cardstock, photocopy Party Favor Holder Patterns, making one for each child.

What Children Do

1. Cut out Party Favor Holder Patterns on all outside lines.
2. Score and fold the rectangle ¼ inch on the dashed lines.
3. Fold up the scored lines toward the center for form the box.
4. Glue or tape tabs to sides to secure the holder.
5. Glue or tape a pair of lips to each long side of the holder. Set aside to dry if you used glue.
6. Fill your container with small treats.

Optional: Use decorating materials to decorate Party Favor Holders.

Alternate Idea: Cut your own shape by cutting two of the same size shapes (3 by 2 inches).

Party Favor Holder Patterns

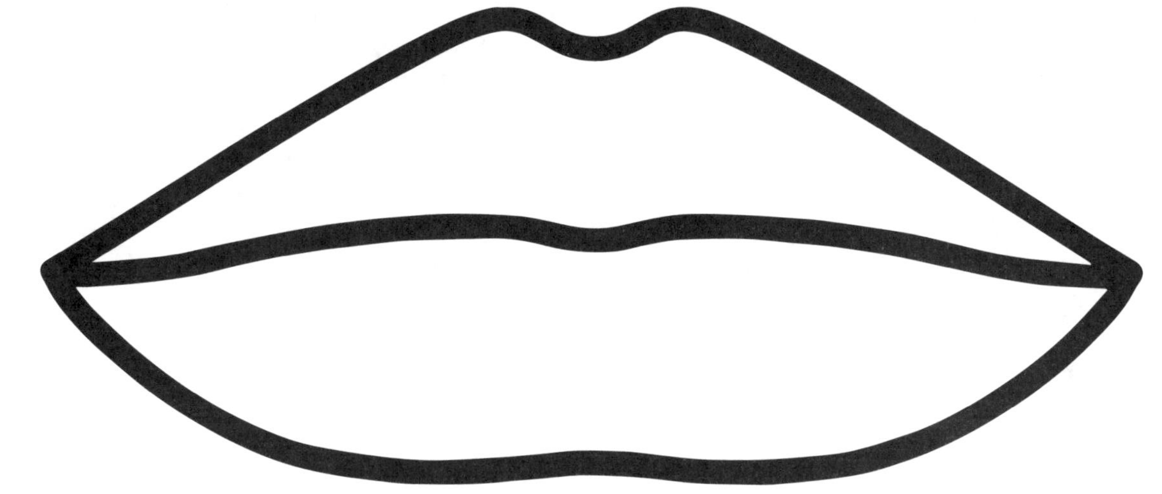

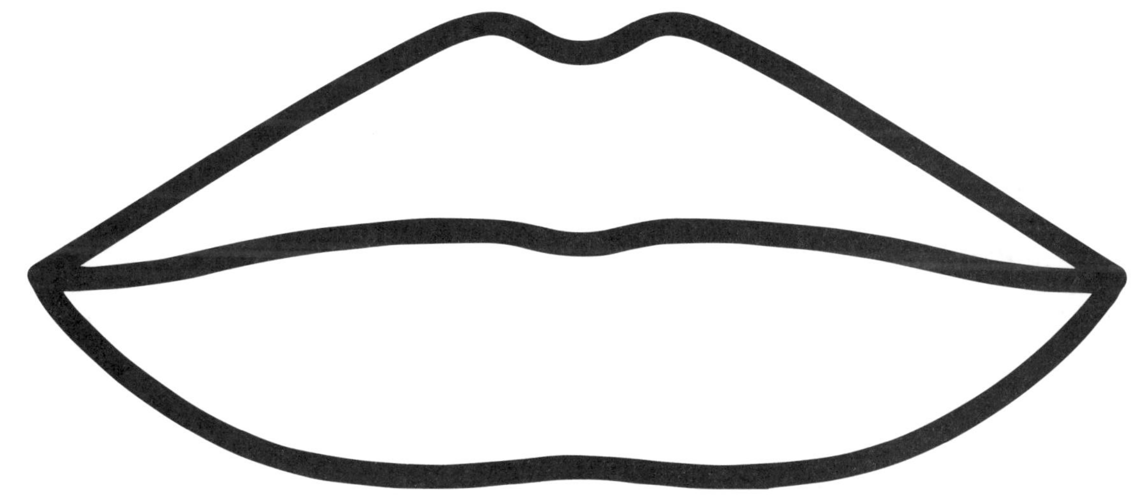

Party Banners

Age Level: ☆★

He escorts me to the banquet hall; it's obvious how much he loves me. SONG OF SOLOMON 2:4

What It's All About

The Lord invites us to his banquet table. Many times, one decoration you might see at banquets and other celebrations is a banner.

What You Need

- Party Banner Patterns (pp. 169–170)
- Coloring & Writing Instruments (see p. 8)
- Paper Cutting Tools (see p. 8)
- Scrap paper
- Cardstock
- String, yarn, ribbon, or other stringing material
- Hole punch
- Patterned paper
- Tape or push pins

Optional

- Decorating materials (buttons, beads, pearls, glitter, stamps and stamp pads, stickers, adhesive gems, etc.)

Preparation

Photocopy Party Banner Patterns, making one set for every three or four children to share.

What Children Do

1. Choose what you want the banner to say and write it out on a piece of scrap paper. You will make one shape for each letter on your banner plus one for each space between words, and one for any punctuation.
2. Choose shape or shapes you want to use for the pennants. We have included four shape patterns. You can use one, two, or even all four of the patterns to make your banner.
3. On cardstock, trace the correct number of pennants, and then cut the patterns out of cardstock.
4. Carefully print a letter on each pennant.
5. Punch a hole in the upper corners of each pennant.
6. Thread the string, yarn, ribbon, or other stringing material through the holes of each pennant. You can use one long piece of stringing material or tie small pieces between each pennant.
7. If you choose to have one lone piece of stringing material, first thread it through the hole in the front left corner of the first pennant. Run it behind the pennant, and then thread it back out the hole on the right side.
8. Continue in the same manner until you have treaded all of the pennants onto the stringing material in the correct order. Make sure to leave extra stringing material at the beginning and end so you can hang it up.
9. Tape or pin the banner across a wall to display.

Optional: Use decorating materials to decorate banners.

Alternate Ideas

- Instead of, or in addition to writing letters, children draw pictures on pennants.
- Print your letters on patterned cardstock, cut out, and glue to the pennants.

Party Banner Patterns

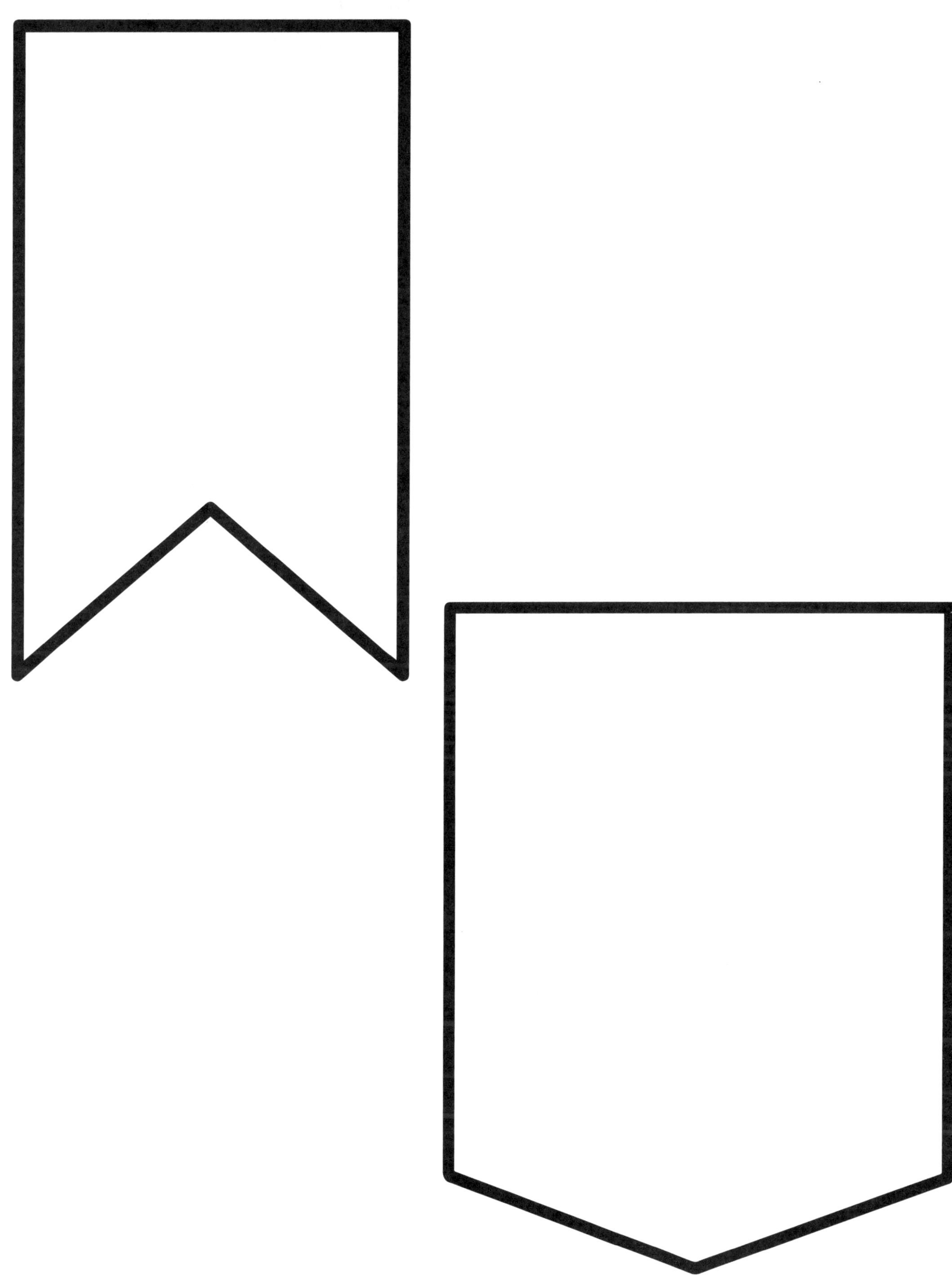

Party Banner Patterns, continued

Shaker Celebration Card

Age Level: ★

Let the sea and everything in it shout his praise! Let the fields and their crops burst out with joy! Let the trees of the forest sing for joy before the Lord, *for he is coming to judge the earth. Give thanks to the* Lord, *for he is good! His faithful love endures forever.* 1 CHRONICLES 16:32–34

What It's All About

This shaker card rustles and shakes to praise and celebrate. We are to praise God. Celebrating God and other people is kind as well as fun.

What You Need

- Paper Cutting Tools (see p. 8)
- Scoring materials (see p. 9)
- Coloring & Writing Instruments (see p. 8)
- Cardstock in a variety of colors and patterns
- Foam mounting tape
- Sequins or seed beads
- Acetate
- Craft glue

Preparation

Cut cardstock as listed below, making one of each for each child; or children choose cardstock and use scissors and cut for themselves:

- One 3x5-inch rectangle of cardstock
- Two 1x3-inch strips of cardstock
- Two 1x5-inch strips if cardstock
- One 3x5-inch rectangle of acetate
- One 6x8-inch rectangle of coordinating cardstock

What Children Do

Make the Shaker

1. Carefully apply foam tape all the way around the edges of the cardstock. Make sure that the tape fits snuggly against itself all the way around with no gaps. Keep the backing on the top of the tape until Step 3.
2. Put some sequins or seed beads inside the tape. Make sure there is some room so they can shake.
3. Pull off the backing on the top side of the foam tape.
4. Cut a piece of acetate 3 inches by 5 inches.
5. Carefully attach the acetate directly on top of the foam tape to seal the shaker.
6. Glue the 1x3-inch and 1x5-inch strips to the edges of the acetate to hide the foam tape.

Make the Card

7. Score and fold the paper in half to make a 4x6-inch card.
8. Glue the shaker to the center front of the card.
9. Put a message inside of the card celebrating the person to whom you will give the card.

Variations

- Put a message inside the shaker by writing it before you fill the shaker. Make sure the shaker isn't too full and the message can be seen.
- Make the shaker in other shapes. It just takes more cutting of the tape to make sure there are no gaps in the edges.
- Add glitter to the shaker. Make sure to rub the acetate with a cloth to keep static electricity from making it stick.

May Day Basket

Age Level: ✰★

Look, the winter is past, and the rains are over and gone. The flowers are springing up, the season of singing birds has come, and the cooing of turtledoves fills the air. SONG OF SOLOMON 2:11–12

What It's All About

In springtime, we see the renewal of the flowers and animals springing up. All this new life around us reminds us of God's love for us in giving us new life through Jesus.

What You Need

- Scoring materials (see p. 9)
- Paper Cutting Tools (see p. 8)
- Coloring & Writing Instruments (see p. 8)
- 12x12-inch sheets of cardstock, one for each child
- Narrow ribbon
- Hole punch

Optional

- Paper flowers

Preparation

Cut ribbon into 6- to 8-inch lengths, making two for each child.

What Children Do

1. If cardstock is not patterned, decorate it with drawings, shapes, etc.
2. Score the cardstock at 4-inch intervals both horizontally and vertically. Do this on what will be the inside of the basket (image a).
3. Fold along all of the score lines, toward the inside of the basket.
4. Open the paper back up and score each of the corner squares diagonally towards the center section (image b).
5. Fold the diagonal scores in the opposite direction from the way you folded the straight lines.

Assemble the Box

6. Fold up two parallel lines towards the center.
7. Fold the diagonal corners in to bring up the side of the basket.
8. Punch a hole through all of the layers.
9. Put one end of the ribbon through the holes and tie a knot (image c).
10. Repeat Steps 6–9 with the other side of the basket using the other end of the ribbon so it becomes your handle.

Optional

- Decorate the outside of the basket with flowers.
- Cut ribbon into 12- to 16-inch lengths, making one for each child. Tie each end of a ribbon to opposite sides of a basket to make a basket with a ribbon handle.

a.

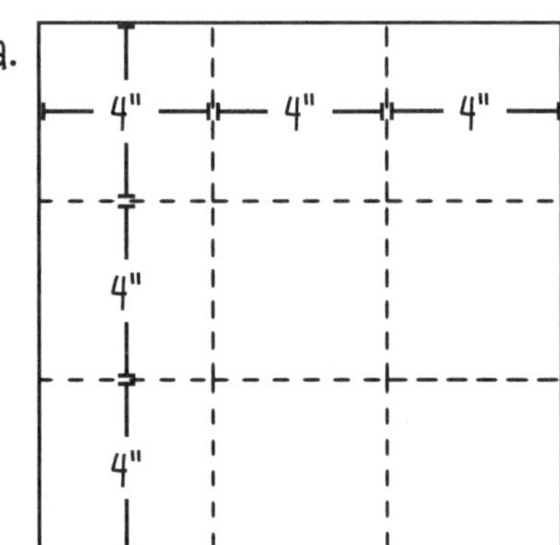

b.

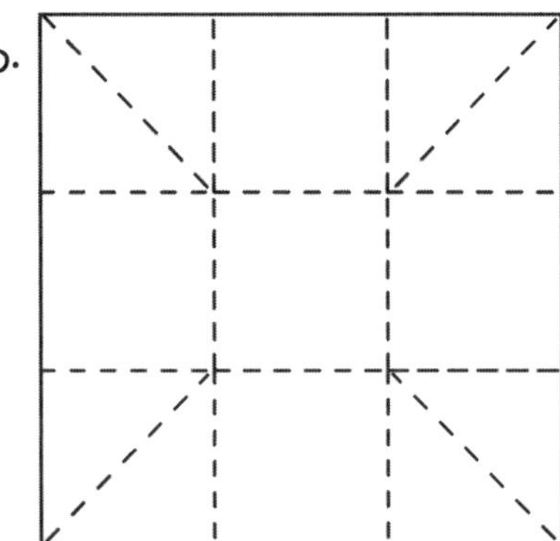

c.

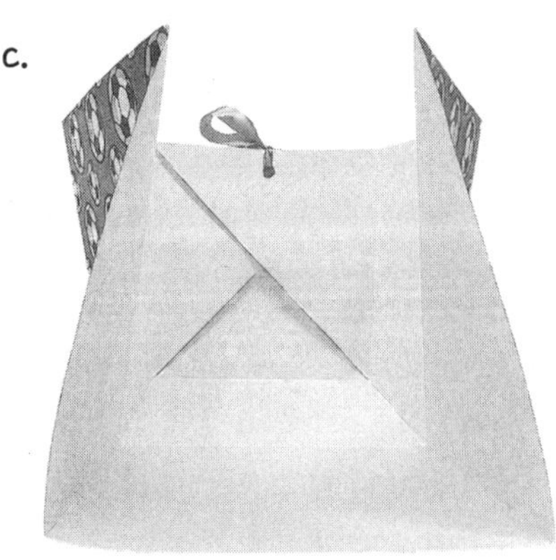

Accordion-Fold Tree Scene

Age Level: ★★

You will live in joy and peace. The mountains and hills will burst into song, and the trees of the field will clap their hands! Where once there were thorns, cypress trees will grow. Where nettles grew, myrtles will sprout up. These events will bring great honor to the Lord's name; they will be an everlasting sign of his power and love. ISAIAH 55:12–13

What It's All About

A forest is a great place to roam and play where trees of all kinds grow and live together. When the wind blows through the leaves it causes a rustling sound and the leaves sway and seem to clap. Let the sounds of the forest remind you to rejoice in all seasons. Depending on the colors you choose, you can make trees that reflect the Christmas season, autumn, spring, or summer!

What You Need

- Accordion-Folded Tree Scene Patterns (p. 174)
- Paper Cutting Tools (see p. 8)
- Coloring & Writing Instruments (see p. 8)
- White cardstock
- Hole punch with ¼-inch hole
- ¼-inch wooden skewers or dowels
- 4-inch or larger Styrofoam blocks, one for each child
- Glue

Preparation

On white cardstock, photocopy Accordion-Folded Tree Scene Patterns, making one for each child.

a.

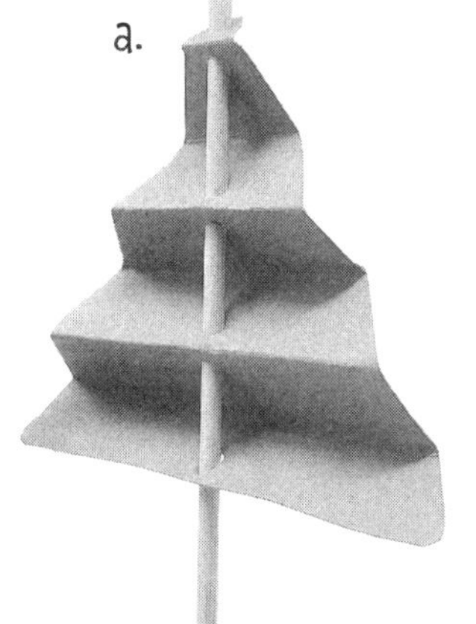

What Children Do

Make the Trees

1. Cut out pattern pieces and color.
2. Accordion (fan) fold each triangle.
3. Punch a hole through the folded layers.
4. Push a wooden skewers or dowels through the holes (image a).
5. If needed, use a drop of glue at the top hole to secure.
6. Repeat Step 4 (and Step 5 if needed) for other triangle pattern pieces.
7. For the deer, simply glue it to a skewer or dowel (image b).

b.

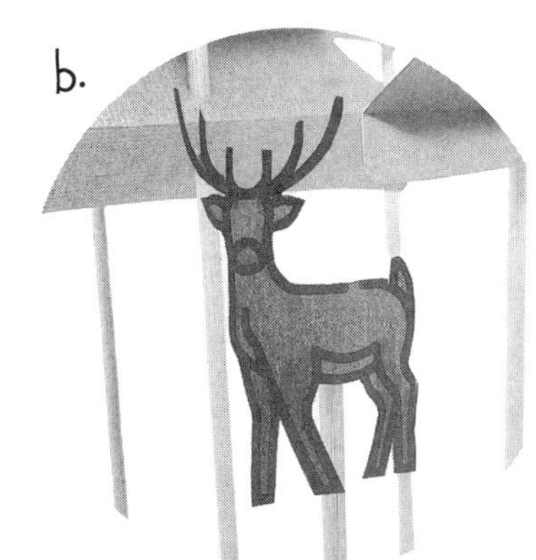

Assemble the Scene

8. Dip the other end of each skewer or dowel into glue and stick it into the Styrofoam to create a forest scene.

Enrichment Ideas

- Draw and then cut out little people, animals, trucks, or so on. Glue to a skewer and add them to the scene.
- Instead of coloring white cardstock patterns, trace the patterns onto cardstock, construction paper, gift wrap or other papers in colors or patterns that suggest tree leaves.
- Use pipe cleaners in addition to or instead of wooden skewers.

Accordion-Folded Tree Scene Patterns

Baby Card

Age Level: ★

You made all the delicate, inner parts of my body and knit me together in my mother's womb. Thank you for making me so wonderfully complex! Your workmanship is marvelous—how well I know it. PSALM 139:13–14

What It's All About

Babies are a gift from God. We welcome them to the world and celebrate a new life. Let's make a card we can give to celebrate a baby's birth.

What You Need

- Baby Card Patterns (pp. 176–177)
- Paper Cutting Tools (see p. 8)
- Coloring & Writing Instruments (see p. 8)
- White cardstock
- Glue

Preparation

On white cardstock, photocopy Baby Card Patterns, making one for each child.

What Children Do

Make the Buggy

1. Color and cut out the Baby Buggie Pattern.
2. The side of the buggy with the tabs is the back of the card. Lay it facedown on the table.
3. Fold the tabs in towards the card and put glue on them.
4. Fold the other side of the card over the tabs and glue them down.
5. On the outside of the card glue the baby carriage wheels to decorate them. Add a striped or polka dot design. You can draw or cut the design from cardstock scraps and glue on.

Add the Baby Items

6. Cut the template out of cardstock.
7. Have each person choose one of the baby items and write a small message on it.
8. Attach the items to the insert making sure to add them towards the top and so the messages can be seen.
9. Slide the insert into the card.
10. If you have a lot of people in the group, you can add more inserts or some items without attaching them to the insert.

Baby Buggy Pattern

Baby Items Patterns

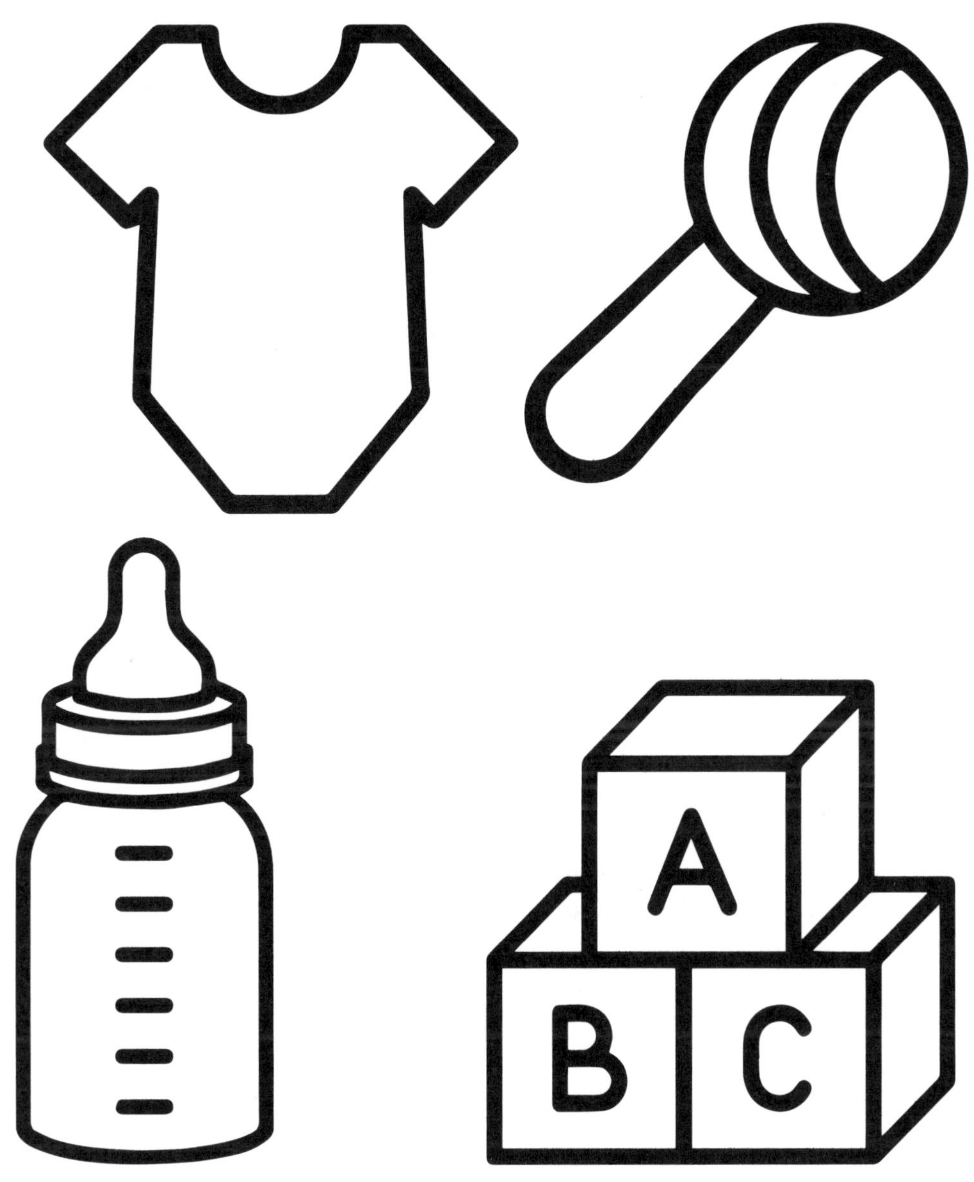

Watery Messages

Age Level: ✩★

Jesus came and told his disciples, "I have been given all authority in heaven and on earth. Therefore, go and make disciples of all the nations, baptizing them in the name of the Father and the Son and the Holy Spirit. Teach these new disciples to obey all the commands I have given you. And be sure of this: I am with you always, even to the end of the age." MATTHEW 28:18–20

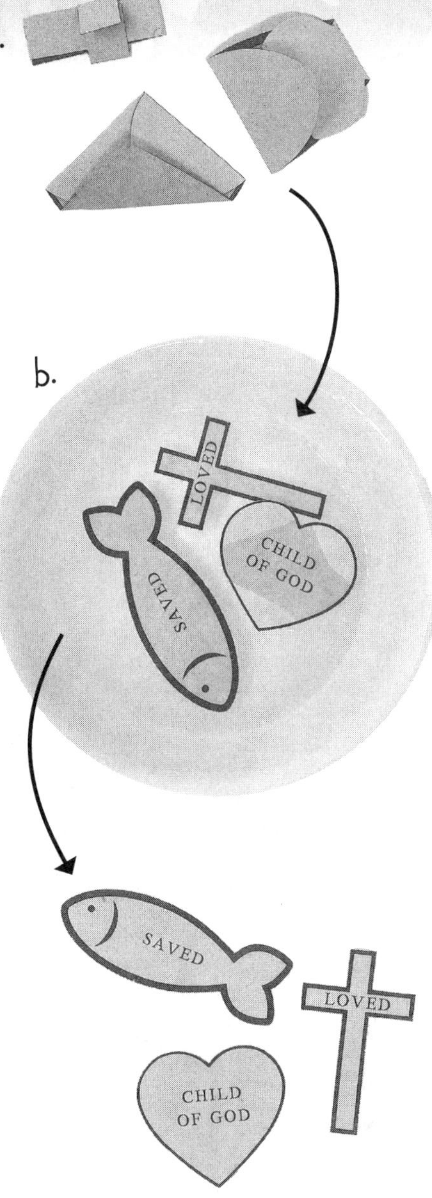

What It's All About

Jesus told his disciples to baptize people when they believed in him. The water represents the Holy Spirit and the living water Jesus promises to give us in John 4:10, when he spoke to a woman at Jacob's well. This fun way to give someone a hidden message reminds us of the power of water, and God's power to change us.

What You Need

- Watery Messages Patterns (below)
- Paper Cutting Tools (see p. 8)
- Construction paper
- Bowls of water

Preparation

Photocopy Watery Message Patterns, making one for each child.

What Children Do

1. Cut out pattern pieces. Optional: Cut out additional shapes. In the center of each write "Be saved," "Jesus loves you," "Be a fisher of men," etc.
2. Fold each paper from the edges to cover the words (image a).
3. Gently drop one paper onto top of water and watch it open up to reveal the hidden message (image b).

Why It Works

Paper is made from trees that drink water. The paper drinks (absorbs) the water, too. This is called *capillary action*. Capillary action causes the fibers in the paper to expand, flatten, and the paper to open up.

Watery Messages Patterns

Thankful Turkeys

Age Level: ★★

Enter his gates with thanksgiving; go into his courts with praise. Give thanks to him and praise his name. For the Lord is good. His unfailing love continues forever, and his faithfulness continues to each generation. PSALM 100:4–5

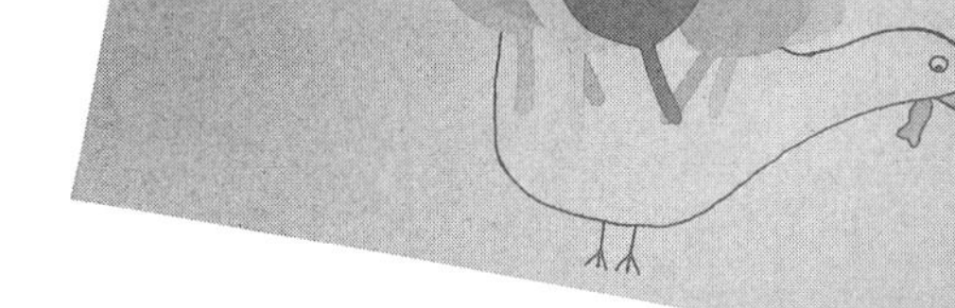

What It's All About

We are to be thankful to God. As you create this turkey remember to thank God for the little things and the big things in life. These turkeys can make great place decorations for a Thanksgiving meal.

What You Need

- Turkey Feather Pattern (below)
- Paper Cutting Tools (see p. 8)
- Coloring & Writing Instruments (see p. 8)
- Paper in fall colors (orange, yellow, red, etc.)
- Glue

Preparation

Photocopy Turkey Feather Pattern, making one for each child.

What Children Do

1. Take a full sheet of paper and trace around your hand with your thumb out to the side.
2. Decorate the thumb to be the face of the turkey.
3. Trace the feather pattern on paper and cut it out. Repeat, using different colors of paper, to make at least five feathers.
4. On each feather write something you are thankful for.
5. Glue the feathers over the four fingers on your handprint to make the turkey's tail.

Alternate Idea: Pinecone Turkey

On the small end of the pinecone glue wiggle eyes to make a turkey face. Prepare feathers as described above and glue the end of each feather onto the back of the pinecone. Use really large pinecones to make turkeys to use as a centerpiece for your Thanksgiving dinner table.

Turkey Feather Pattern

School Days

Much of the daily life of children revolves around school. These activities can help them and others to be organized, remember important facts and events, encourage others, and decorate their work.

For students, school is their biggest mission field. Many classmates won't be going to a church and sometimes these things can help them ask about Christ. When we give to others, we are saying that they are special and have value and so often today many children struggle with knowing they are unique and important to anyone.

Outreach Ideas

Here are a few outreach ideas for the crafts in this section:

- Make a School Memo Organizer (p. 182) for yourself and a friend so they can keep organized.
- Make a Flashcard Holder (p. 188) and fill it with cards that can help someone remember something they are struggling to learn. Offer to spend time with them quizzing them on the material so that they can learn what they need to know.
- Keep the Encouragement Cards (p. 192) with you. Leave a card on a desk for someone who is having a bad day or seems to be sad. Sometimes a little surprise can make a huge difference.
- Encourage teachers, coaches, and other adults with the All-Star Mentor Cards (p. 194). Keep one in your backpack to fill out when an adult does something that really helps or touches you.

School Memo Organizer

Age Level: ★

These are the proverbs of Solomon, David's son, king of Israel. Their purpose is to teach people wisdom and discipline, to help them understand the insights of the wise. Their purpose is to teach people to live disciplined and successful lives, to help them do what is right, just, and fair. These proverbs will give insight to the simple, knowledge and discernment to the young. PROVERBS 1:1–4

What It's All About

The purpose of school is to grow in wisdom and knowledge. Having a way to organize yourself is kind to both your parents and teachers as it helps them get you ready to learn.

To use this organizer keep information about each class or subject. Include information such as materials needed and larger projects. Use the tags to write down assignments and due dates, so you know what you need to be working on.

What You Need

- Memo Tag Patterns (p. 183)
- Paper Cutting Tools (see p. 8)
- Scoring materials (p. 9)
- Colored or patterned cardstock
- Coordinating colored or patterned double-sided cardstock
- Patterned paper in a coordinating colors
- Glue
- String, yarn, or thin ribbon
- Hole punch

Preparation

Photocopy Memo Tag Patterns, making one copy for every two children.

Cut colored or patterned cardstock into 3½x12-inch rectangles, making one of each for each child; or children choose cardstock, use scissors, and cut for themselves.

Cut the double-sided patterned cardstock as follows, making one set for each child, or children choose cardstock, use scissors, and cut for themselves:

- One 3¼x11¼-inch rectangle
- Two 3¼x3¾-inch rectangles

Cut a coordinating color of patterned paper as follows, making one set for each child, or children choose cardstock, use scissors, and cut for themselves:

- Four 3x3½-inch rectangles

What Children Do

Assemble the Organizer

1. Score the 3½x12-inch cardstock rectangle at 4-inch intervals (image a). Fold along the score lines towards the center.
2. Score the 3¼x11¼-inch rectangle at 3¾ inches and 7½ inches (image b). Fold along the score lines towards the center.

a.

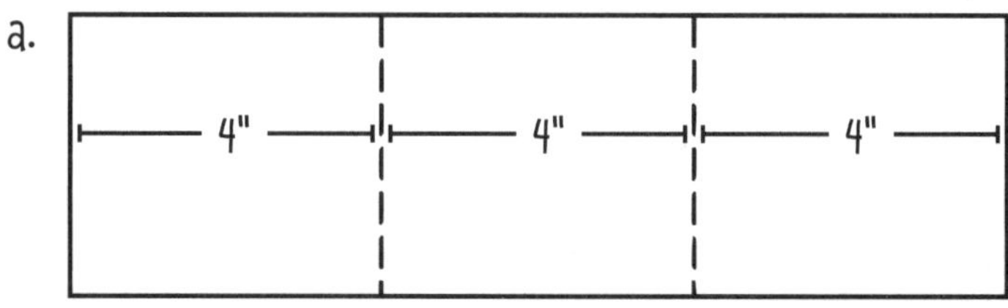

b.

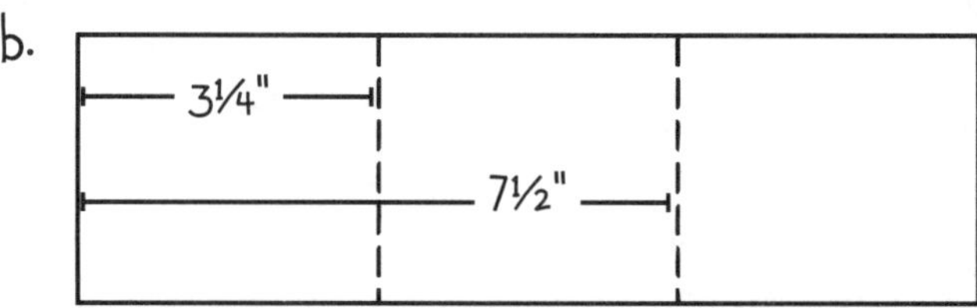

3. Put glue around the side and bottom edges of the back of the center panel of the patterned paper rectangle (image c) and glue it to the center of the cardstock. This will make a pocket in the center of the cardstock.

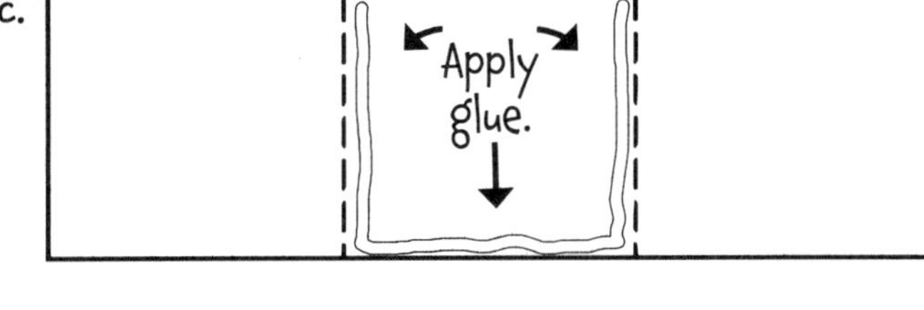

4. Glue the two 3¼x3¾-inch rectangles on the outer sections of cardstock, again gluing around the bottom and two sides of the papers to make pockets.
5. Glue the four 3x3½ rectangles of the second patterned paper onto the center of each side of the panels that are sticking out. Glue on the bottom and two sides to make pockets.

Create the Tags

6. Cut out Memo Tag Patterns.
7. Trace tag pattern onto pieces of cardstock or patterned paper. Make at least four tags.
8. Punch a hole in the top of each tag.
9. Cut a length of string, yarn, or thin ribbon, thread it through the hole of the tag, and tie to secure.
10. Stick the tags in pockets.

Tip: Make extra tags to replace the ones in the organizer as you fill them up.

Memo Tag Patterns

Reward Chart

Age Level: ★★

We who are strong must be considerate of those who are sensitive about things like this. We must not just please ourselves. We should help others do what is right and build them up in the Lord. For even Christ didn't live to please himself. ROMANS 15:1–3

What It's All About

We should encourage one another to do good things. Use this chart to encourage yourself to work on a behavior you wish to improve.

What You Need

- Reward Chart Pattern (p. 185)
- White or lightly colored paper
- Coloring & Writing Instruments (see p. 8)

Optional

- Small stickers
- Paper Cutting Tools (see p. 8)—If available, decorative-edged scissors
- Decorating materials (buttons, beads, pearls, glitter, stamps and stamp pads, stickers, adhesive gems, etc.)
- 12x12-inch cardstock
- Glue

Preparation

On white or lightly colored paper, photocopy Reward Chart Pattern, making one for each child. Cut off the header at the top and the page number at the bottom of each copy.

What Children Do

1. At the top of the chart, write a behavior you need to work on improving or doing more often.

a.

Optional

- Glue Reward Chart to a sheet of 12x12-inch cardstock. Use decorative-edged scissors to trim close to the chart, making an attractive border (image a).
- Use coloring and writing materials and decorating materials to decorate the chart with drawings or stickers.

How to Use

2. Take the Reward Chart home and post it in a prominent place.
3. Each time you make the choice to do that good thing, draw a mark in the chart. Optional: Place a small sticker in the chart.
4. Here are some ideas of things you might want to put on your chart:
   - Do chores without being told first.
   - Being kind to my siblings.
   - Sharing my games and toys.
   - Practice playing my instrument.
   - Doing homework right away.

Reward Chart Pattern

WHAT I AM WORKING ON:

Report Poster with Doors

Age Level: ★

John went from place to place on both sides of the Jordan River, preaching that people should be baptized to show that they had repented of their sins and turned to God to be forgiven. LUKE 3:3

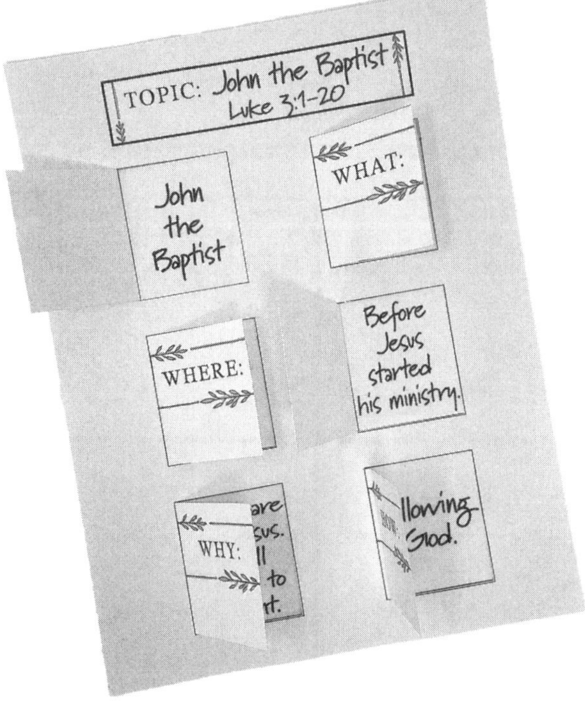

What It's All About

Sometimes having a unique format for things makes our work look better. This is an idea of how to make a report more interesting. In the example, we will be doing a report on John the Baptist, one of the most unique and interesting people in the New Testament.

What You Need

- Report Poster Pattern (p. 187)
- Paper Cutting Tools (see p. 8)
- White or lightly colored paper
- Glue
- Pen

Preparation

Photocopy Report Poster Pattern, making one for each child.

What Children Do

1. Cut slits on the three solid sides of each rectangle and fold on the dashed line to make doors. Warning: Do not cut the "Topic" rectangle at the top!
2. Glue the pattern onto a sheet of blank paper. Make sure get any glue on the doors.
3. Inside each door write a few words that answer the question on the outside of the door. For our example:
   - Who: John the Baptist
   - What: Preaches, Baptizes
   - Where: Wilderness
   - When: Before Jesus started his ministry
   - Why: To prepare for Jesus, to call people to repent
   - How: Following God
4. Use this paper as the cover of a report on any topic.

Alternate Idea: Create your own pattern for the cover. Try making the doors different shapes and sizes.

TOPIC:

WHO:

WHAT:

WHERE:

WHEN:

WHY:

HOW:

Flashcard Holder

Age Level: ☆★

Joyful are people of integrity, who follow the instructions of the Lord. Your laws are my treasure; they are my heart's delight. I am determined to keep your decrees to the very end. PSALM 119:1,111–112

What It's All About

One great way to memorize things is by using flashcards. Use this holder to make Bible verse flashcards to help you memorize Scripture or to give to a friend. You can also make these flashcards to help someone struggling in a subject at school.

What You Need

- Flashcard Holder Pattern (p. 189)
- Paper Cutting Tools (see p. 8)
- Scoring materials (see p. 9)
- Coloring & Writing Instruments (see p. 8)
- Cardstock
- Glue
- Index Cards

Optional

- Decorating materials (buttons, beads, wiggle eyes, glitter, stamps and stamp pads, stickers, adhesive gems, etc.)

Preparation

On the wrong side of the cardstock, photocopy Flashcard Holder Pattern, making one for each child.

What Children Do

1. Cut out the pattern from cardstock.
2. Score along the dotted lines.
3. Fold the score lines all in the same direction.
4. Put glue on the tabs.
5. Fold the holder closed, gluing the tabs securely.
6. Write Bible verses on the index cards and place in holder.

Optional: Use coloring and writing materials and decorating materials to decorate the flashcards and holder with drawings or stickers.

Tip: Make flash cards and holders for math, like multiplication tables, or history facts.

Flashcard Holder Pattern

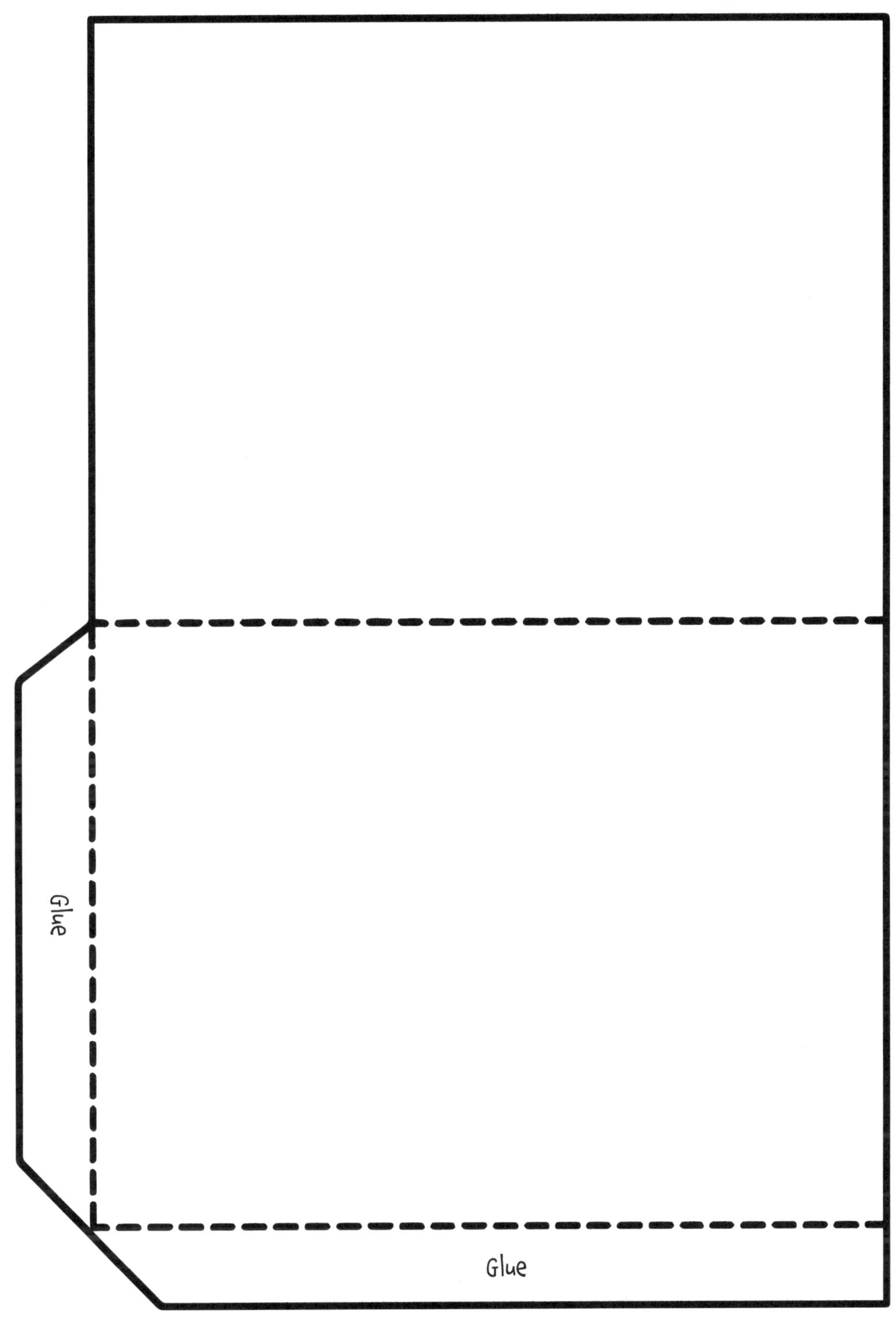

School Memory Album

Age Level: ★

Walk with the wise and become wise; associate with fools and get in trouble. PROVERBS 13:20

What It's All About

In Daniel 1:3–17, we learn that Daniel grew in knowledge and stature during school. "Growing in stature" means that you become someone others look up to. You can also grow in knowledge and stature. Use this album to preserve your memories from school for yourself, a friend, or both of you!

What You Need

- Scoring materials (see p. 9)
- Paper Cutting Tools (see p. 8)
- Cardstock
- Glue

Optional

- Coloring & Writing Instruments (see p. 8)
- Decorating materials (buttons, beads, wiggle eyes, glitter, stamps and stamp pads, stickers [especially clothing, hats, sunglasses, etc.], adhesive gems, etc.)

Preparation

Cut cardstock into the following, making one of each for each child; or children choose cardstock, use scissors, and cut for themselves. Use the same or different cardstock for each part of the album.

- One 4x12-inch rectangle for the spine
- Two 4x6-inch rectangles for the covers
- Five 4x6-inch rectangles for the pages

What Children Do

Make the Spine

1. Score the 4x12-inch rectangle on one side at 2-inch intervals beginning 2 inches from the edge (image a).

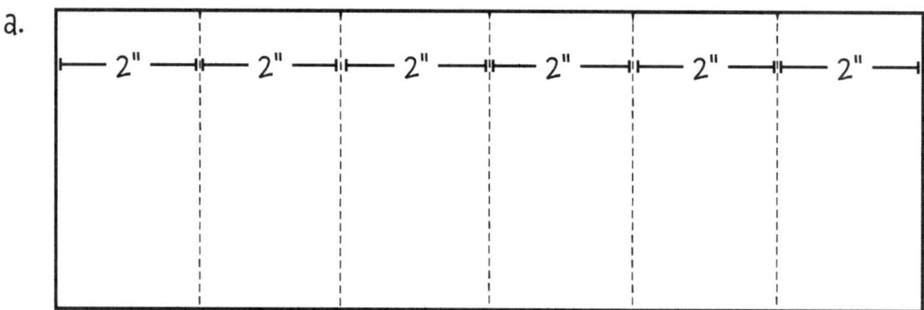

2. Turn the spine over and score it at 2-inch intervals beginning 1 inch from the edge (image b). In image b, the scored lines from Step 1 are shown as solid lines.

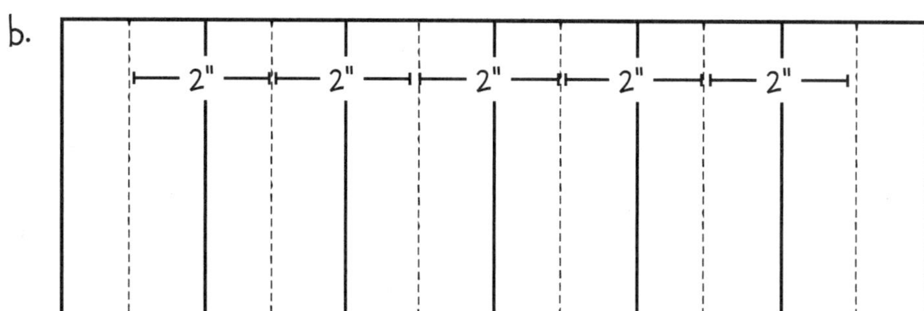

3. Accordion fold the spine at each score (image c).

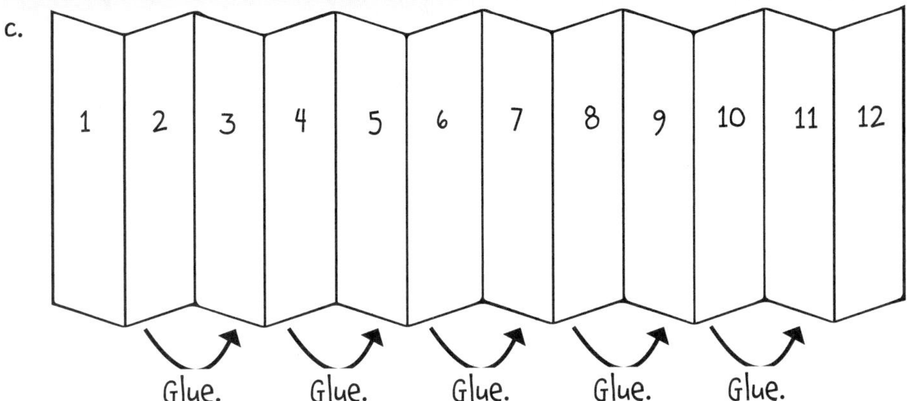

4. With a pencil, lightly label each panel from one to twelve as shown in image c.
5. Glue together as indicated in image c:
   - Panels 2 and 3
   - Panels 4 and 5
   - Panels 6 and 7
   - Panels 8 and 9
   - Panels 10 and 11

   Panels 1 and 12 remain unglued.

Make the Covers

6. Apply glue to Panel 1 and attach 4x6-inch cardstock cover so that the 4-inch edge of the cover lines up with the fold of Panel 1.
7. Repeat Step 6 to glue the other cover to the Panel 12 (image d).

Make the Pages

8. Open up the front cover of the book and put glue on panel 2. Attach 1 piece of cardstock to the panel.
9. Turn the page and put glue on the next spine panel and attach the next piece of cardstock. Continue doing this until all of the pages have been made (image e).
10. Now add pictures to the pages. You can add words or quotes too.

Optional: Use coloring and writing materials and decorating materials to decorate the memory album with drawings or stickers. You can also decorate people in the photos with stickers of clothing, hats, sunglasses, etc. See the crown and sunglasses stickers in image e.

Encouragement Cards

Age Level: ✯★

Worry weighs a person down; an encouraging word cheers a person up. PROVERBS 12:25

What It's All About

Encouraging others when you can see they are having a bad day is a great way to show kindness. Let's make a little kit that you can keep in a desk, bag, or locker. Having this kit will allow you to leave a little boost to those who are in need of some cheering up.

What You Need

- Encouragement Cards Patterns (p. 193)
- Paper Cutting Tools (see p. 8)
- Scoring materials (p. 9)
- Coloring & Writing Instruments (p. 8)
- Cardstock
- Glue

Preparation

Photocopy Encouragement Cards Patterns, making one set for each child.

Cut cardstock into the following, making one of each for each child; or children choose cardstock, use scissors, and cut for themselves:

- One 5½x8½-inch rectangle
- Two 4x4½-inch rectangles

What Children Do

1. Score and fold 5½x8½-inch rectangle in half so it's a 5½x4¼-inch folder (image a).
2. Score and fold 4x4½-inch rectangles at 2 inches on the longer side, creating a pocket that is 4 inches wide, 2½ inches high in the back, and 2 inches in the front (image b).
3. Finish the pocket by gluing each side edge together.
4. Glue one pocket at the top and one at the bottom of the folder you created. This will give you two pockets to hold cards.

a.

4¼"

Create Encouragement Cards

5. Cut out the card patterns.
6. Personalize cards by signing them and adding color or drawings.
7. Make more of your own cards. Cut cardstock into rectangles 3 inches wide and 2 to 2½ inches high.
8. Put the cards into the pockets in the folder and take them with you. Now you will have an encouragement card whenever someone needs a pick-me-up.

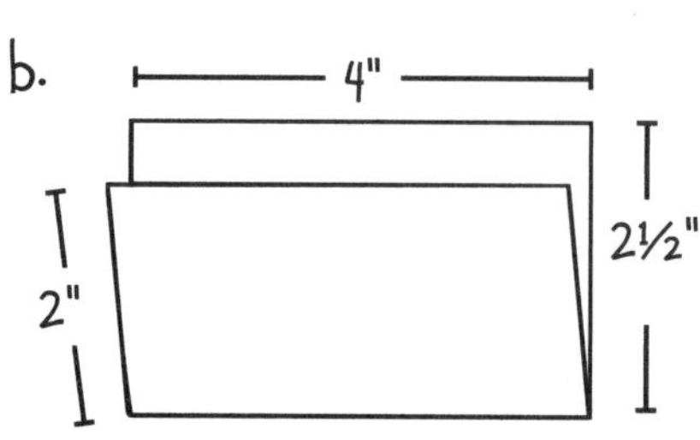

Encouragement Cards Patterns

YOU ARE SPECIAL!

YOU ARE ONE OF A KIND!

EVERY CLOUD HAS A RAINBOW. I HOPE YOU FIND YOURS SOON.

I AM PRAYING FOR YOU!

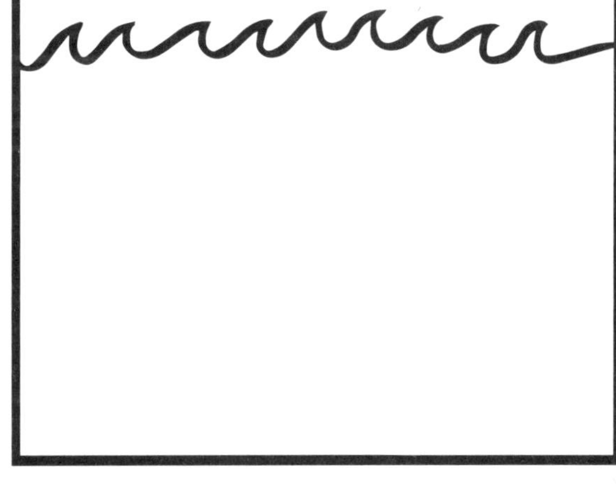

All-Star Mentor Cards

Age Level: ★

I urge you, first of all, to pray for all people. Ask God to help them; intercede on their behalf, and give thanks for them. Pray this way for kings and all who are in authority so that we can live peaceful and quiet lives marked by godliness and dignity. This is good and pleases God our Savior, who wants everyone to be saved and to understand the truth. 1 TIMOTHY 2:1–4

What It's All About

We are to pray for and respect those in authority over us. God has placed them over us, and it is kind to show them appreciation. Let's make some cards to tell them we think they are special.

What You Need

- All-Star Patterns (p. 195)
- Paper Cutting Tools (see p. 8)
- Scoring materials (see p. 9)
- Coloring & Writing Instruments (p. 8)
- Cardstock
- Patterned paper in two coordinating colors
- White paper
- Glue

- Decorating materials (buttons, beads, wiggle eyes, glitter, stamps and stamp pads, stickers, adhesive gems, etc.)

Preparation

Photocopy All-Star Patterns, making one set for each child.

Cut the following for each child; or children choose cardstock, use scissors, and cut for themselves:

- One 3x9-inch cardstock rectangle
- Three 2½-inch squares from one of the patterned papers
- One 2-inch square from white paper

What Children Do

Make the Base Card

1. Score the cardstock at 3 inches and 6 inches (image a).
2. Fold the cardstock in at both score lines.
3. Unfold the card and score the first and third panels diagonally from the top right corner down to the bottom left corner (image b).
4. Fold each panel along the scored diagonal to make them triangles.

a.

b.

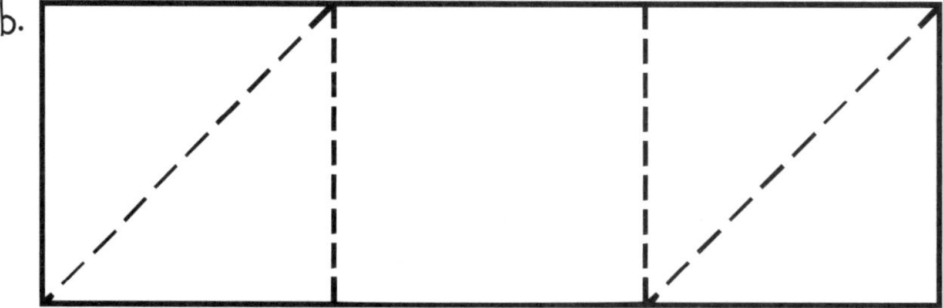

Prepare the Inside Center of the Card

5. Glue one of the 2½-inch squares onto the center panel of the inside of the card.
6. Glue the white 2-inch square onto the center of the patterned paper you just glued (image c). On the white paper, you can write a note or even just "Thank You!"

Finish the First and Third Panels

7. Cut the two remaining 2½-inch squares in half diagonally.
8. Glue the triangles onto the folded triangles on the card, one on both sides of the fold on the first and third panels (image c).
9. Fold up the card so that two triangles make up the front of the card—one from each end.

Add the Stars

10. Cut out the stars.
11. Trace each star onto a different color or patterned paper. Cut out stars.
12. Glue the small star to the center of the large star.
13. Glue the layered star onto the front triangle of the first panel (image c).

Optional

14. Use decorative materials to decorate cards.

c.

All-Star Patterns

Storytelling Crafts

Children love stories that capture their imagination. The power of a story is that we remember and learn from the characters, actions, and lessons contained within the tale. Equip children to tell stories and retell them, so that they can share their faith, give their testimony, and impact lives.

Encourage children to use crafts as tools for telling stories. Let them use their imagination to add their own designs and uses for the crafts.

Storytelling taps into a child's imagination and develops critical thinking skills. It brings faith, history, or any topic alive. Using their own artwork as a storytelling aid equips them and gives them courage to speak up and tell stories.

Outreach with Storytelling

- With Fish Tale with Moving Parts (p. 198), a favorite story helps a child connect a Bible story's lesson and how it can help them put love into action. It also gives them reasons to share great and timeless Bible stories.
- Let My Testimony Book (p. 202) become a tool for a child to identify their own testimony and then share it. It equips them at young ages to witness and share their faith.
- Use Hide & Seek Book (p. 206) to introduce children to making booklets where they create hidden windows to tell stories. The surprise of what's inside engages them and their audience.
- A Story Wheel (p. 208) helps a child recall a story and the order of the action, so they can retell it.

Fish Tale with Moving Parts

Age Level: ☆★

Dear children, let's not merely say that we love each other; let us show the truth by our actions. 1 JOHN 3:18

What It's All About

In our verse, John speaks about putting love into action. One way to do that is by spending time together. Fishing is a fun way to spend time with someone. Jesus did that with his disciples (John 21:1–8)**. You may enjoy fishing, boating, or other fun activities with family and friends. Make this moving story picture of fishing. Or instead, you could design your own story. A slit and some sticks help the pictured objects move.**

What You Need

- Fish Tale Patterns (p. 199)
- Paper Cutting Tools (see p. 8)
- Coloring & Writing Instruments (see p. 8)
- Assorted colors of cardstock: white, dark blue, medium blue, brown, yellow, gold, etc.
- Glue or double-sided tape
- Transparent tape
- Craft sticks

Preparation

On white cardstock, photocopy Fish Tale Patterns, making one set for each child.

Cut the following for each child; or children choose cardstock, use scissors, and cut for themselves:

- One ½x11-inch strip of medium blue paper
- One 2½x11-inch strip of medium blue paper

What Children Do

Make the Slits

1. Fold an 8½x11-inch sheet of dark blue paper in half, making it 5½x8½.
2. Beginning at the fold, cut a slit horizontally across the paper, 1½ inches from the bottom. Stop 1 inch from the other side (image a).
3. Cut a second slit 3 ½ inches from the bottom, again beginning at the fold and stopping 1 inch from the side (image a).
4. Open and smooth the paper, laying it flat on the table.

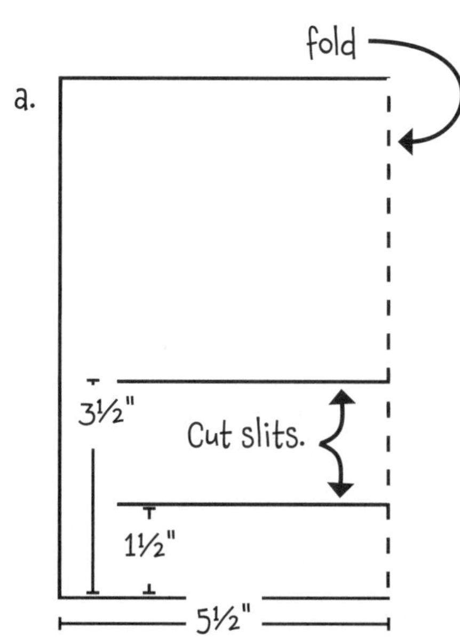

Make the Scene

5. On one side of both strips of medium blue paper, cut waves. You can make large or small waves.
6. Glue the straight bottom of the narrower blue strip just below the bottom slit, letting the waves sit above the slit.
7. Repeat for the wider strip and upper slit.
8. Cut a yellow circle or a sliver of the moon and place it in the top area of the picture.

Add the Moving Parts

9. Color the boat and oar, fish, people, and net of fish patterns. Add faces to the people patterns.
10. Cut out pattern pieces.
11. Glue or tape the people to the back of the boat so that it looks like they are riding in the boat.
12. Tape a craft stick to the back of the boat, the back of the net full of fish, and the back of the fish.
13. Slide the boat, net into the slits so that the pattern pieces are on the front and the craft sticks are on the back (image b).

b.

Fish Tale Patterns

Favorite Bible Stories Album

Age Level: ★

Until I get there, focus on reading the Scriptures to the church, encouraging the believers, and teaching them. 1 TIMOTHY 4:13

What It's All About

The Bible is full of amazing, wonderful stories that help us get to know Jesus and God. From the stories in the Bible, we can find out everything we need to know to live the very best life—the life God has planned for us. Make this album to record all your favorite Bible stories. It also makes a great gift for someone who is a new member of God's family.

Note

This kind of a book—where you use the pages to spell out a word—is called a *word book*. You can make others of your own design. Start with choosing a word. Then, draw 3- to 4-inch block letters for each letter in your chosen word. Figure out how long you want each page and cut them out accordingly. Set it up so that each letter's page is a little longer than the page of the letter before.

What You Need

- Favorite Bible Stories Album Patterns (p. 201)
- Paper Cutting Tools (see p. 8)
- Coloring & Writing Instruments (see p. 8)
- Cardstock in two contrasting colors
- Glue
- Hole punch
- Yarn, string, or thin ribbon

Preparation

Enlarge 200 percent as you photocopy Favorite Bible Stories Album Patterns, making one set of patterns for each child.

What Children Do

1. Cut out the patterns from cardstock.
2. On one color of cardstock, trace and cut out the two *B*s and the *E*.
3. On the second color of cardstock, trace and cut out the *I* and *L*.
4. Also on the second color of cardstock, trace and cut out the two semicircles. Trace and cut each semicircle twice. You will need two small semicircles (for the top of the *B*s) and two larger semicircles (for the bottom of the *B*s).
5. Glue semicircles to the center of the *B*s (image a).
6. Stack all the pages to spell the word *Bible*, putting the shortest *B* page on top.
7. Punch two holes on the flat side of the stack of pages, near the top edge. Punch two more holes near the bottom.
8. Bind the book together by threading a length of string, yarn, or ribbon through each pair of holes and tying a knot to secure. Trim any long ends (image b).

b.

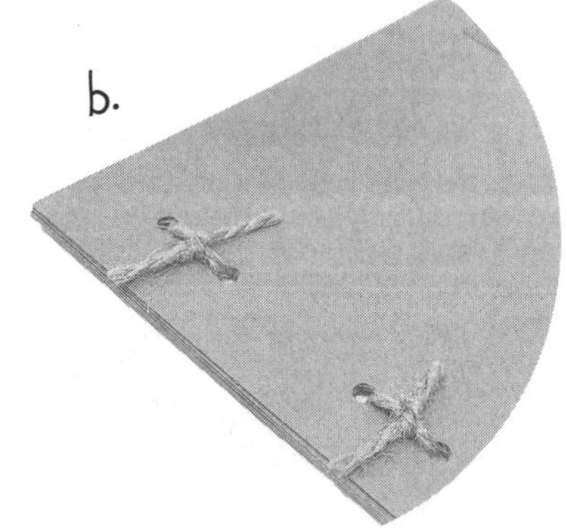

9. Write or draw a picture of a Bible story on each of the other pages. Here are some ideas:

- Noah's Ark
- Creation
- Jonah
- Tower of Babel
- Daniel and the Lion's Den
- Good Samaritan

Alternate Idea

Instead of punching holes and threading string, yarn, or ribbon through the holes to bind the book, staple the edges together. Cover the staples with a strip of washi tape on both the front and back of the book.

Favorite Bible Stories Album Patterns

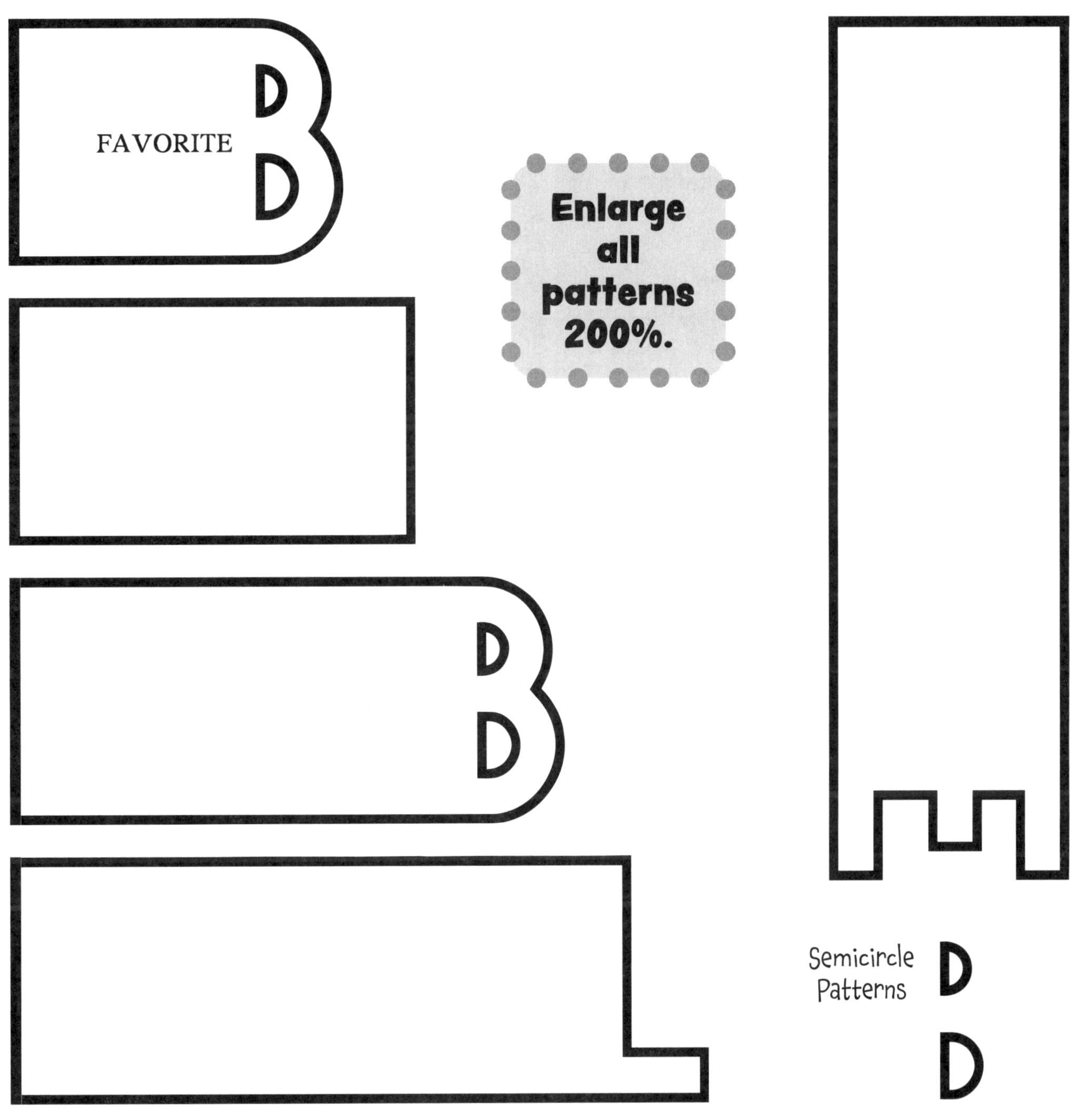

My Testimony Book

Age Level: ★★

Give thanks to the Lord and proclaim his greatness. Let the whole world know what he has done. 1 CHRONICLES 16:8

What It's All About

Sharing stories about Jesus and our faith in Jesus is the most loving thing we can do for someone. This book helps you tell your faith story.

What You Need

- My Testimony Patterns (p. 203)
- Paper Cutting Tools (see p. 8)
- Scoring materials (see p. 9)
- Cardstock
- Glue

Optional

- Decorating materials (buttons, beads, wiggle eyes, glitter, stamps and stamp pads, stickers, adhesive gems, etc.)

Preparation

Enlarge 200 percent as you photocopy My Testimony Patterns, making one set of patterns for each child.

From cardstock, cut two 4x12-inch rectangles for each child; or children choose cardstock, use scissors, and cut for themselves.

What Children Do

Make the Book's Base

1. Score the cardstock rectangles at 4-inch intervals horizontally (image a).
2. Accordion-fold along each of these lines to form your book panels.
3. Glue the bottom of the third panel of one rectangle to the front of the first panel of another rectangle. This will give you five panels on each side of the long rectangle.
4. Fold the panels back and forth to create the base of the book.

a.

4" 4" 4"

Complete the Pages

5. Cut out patterns.
6. Fill in the answers to the questions to help you develop your testimony.
7. Beginning with the Cover Pattern on the front of your book, glue each paper onto a panel of the book. Use both sides of the book base.

Optional

Use decorative materials to decorate your book.

My Testimony Patterns

Cover Pattern

MY
TESTIMONY
BOOK

PEOPLE WHO
TOLD ME
ABOUT JESUS:

Enlarge all patterns 200%.

FROM THEM
I LEARNED:

MY FIRST MEMORY OF DOING SOMETHING WRONG AND BEING FORGIVEN WAS:

WE ALL SIN, AND GOD FORGIVES US IF WE ASK.

ONE OF MY PRAYERS GOD ANSWERED IS:

WHEN I WAS HURT OR SICK, I LEARNED:

WHEN I WAS AFRAID, I DISCOVERED:

MY LIFE IS BETTER WITH JESUS, BECAUSE:

MY TESTIMONY OF JESUS:

YOUR LIFE CAN BE BETTER TOO JUST KNOW IT'S AS EASY AS ABC!

A ---- ADMIT YOU SIN (NO ONE IS PERFECT, EXCEPT JESUS)

B ---- BELIEVE JESUS DIED FOR YOU AND ROSE FROM THE DEAD

C ---- CONFESS YOUR SINS AND ASK JESUS TO FORGIVE YOU

Psalm 148 Rainbow Book

Age Level: ★★

Praise the Lord! Praise the Lord from the heavens! Praise him from the skies! PSALM 148:1

What It's All About

Our verse is from Psalm 148 which describes some of the many reasons we can praise God. (Read Psalm 148 aloud.) **Let's make a book with colors that reflect the images in the psalm. We'll then add our own drawings. It's an easy way to remember the psalm and reasons to praise God. Praising God is one way to be kind to God and to show others that we love him.**

What You Need

- Psalm 148 (p. 205)
- Paper Cutting Tools (see p. 8)
- Coloring & Writing Instruments (see p. 9)
- Lightweight paper in pink, blue, gold, red, brown, purple, gray, dark blue, green, aqua, yellow, white, and sky blue
- Stapler
- Washi tape

Optional

- 4-inch lid, bowl, cookie cutter or other circular object
- Decorating materials (buttons, beads, wiggle eyes, glitter, stamps and stamp pads, stickers, adhesive gems, etc.)

Preparation

From each color of paper, cut a 4x12-inch rectangle for each child; or children use scissors and cut for themselves.

What Children Do

1. Stack the colors in this order: pink, blue, gold, red, brown, purple, gray, dark blue, green, aqua blue, yellow, white, and sky blue.
2. Cut a curve at the top the stack of paper to form the arc of a rainbow. If it's too difficult to cut through the entire stack, cut paper three or four at a time, using a previously cut paper as a guide. Optional: Use a 4-inch lid, bowl, cookie cutter or other circular object as a guide for the arc.
3. Layer the papers to look like arcs of a rainbow by shifting each of the sheets down about ⅜ of an inch (image a). The pink will be on the bottom followed by the blue, etc.
4. Set aside the sky blue paper (on top) for Steps 5 and 6.
5. Turn over the stapled papers and cut across the stack at the bottom of the pink paper. Cut through all the layers of paper (Younger children may need an adult to do this cut, as it is thick).
6. Staple through the remaining layers a couple times. Ask an adult to help if you are having difficulty stapling through all the papers.
7. Place the sky blue paper on top again about ⅜ of an inch from the white sheet currently on top. Fold the remaining blue paper to the back of the stack. Staple a few more times (image b).

a.

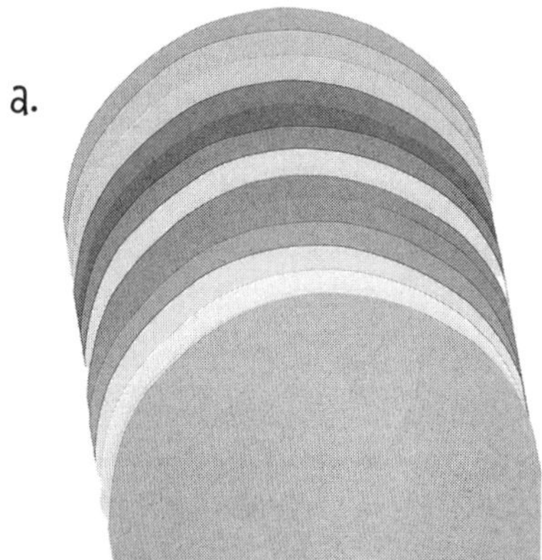

b.

c.

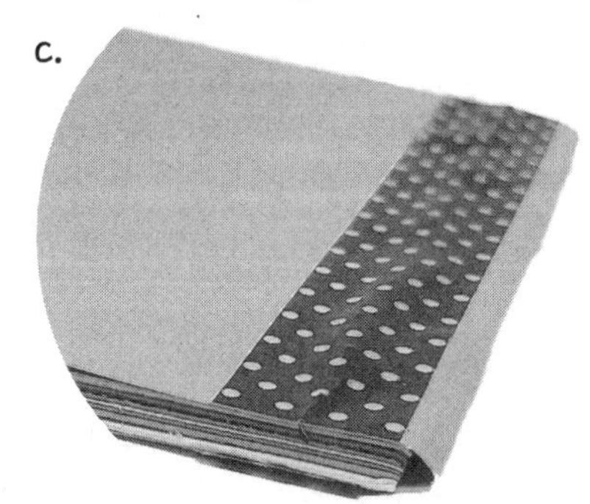

8. On both the front and back of the book, cover staples with washi tape (image c).
9. On the front of each colored arc you can draw something about the related verse and image. On the back of the paper, cut the verse and glue or tape it in place. (**Optional:** You can write the words on the paper). Add more staples if needed, on the left side edge.
10. Ideas for drawings:
    - **Sky Blue:** Hands apart towards heaven and the word *PRAISE*
    - **White:** Angel, snowman
    - **Yellow:** Sun, moon, and stars
    - **Aqua Blue:** Ocean waves and a cloudy sky
    - **Green:** Trees and flowers
    - **Dark Blue:** Sea creatures, whales, squid, etc.
    - **Gray:** Lightning bolt, clouds
    - **Purple:** Mountains, hills, trees, fruited plant
    - **Brown:** Paths with lion, cattle, birds, butterfly
    - **Red:** Many hearts, some with crowns for kings, some smaller for young people
    - **Gold:** Names of God (Jesus, Father, Holy Spirit) and musical notes
    - **Blue:** Cross with a large crown (Jesus is strong and has power of the cross)
    - **Pink:** Large heart with many hearts inside for we are close to God's heart

Optional

In addition to your drawings, use decorative materials to decorate your book.

Simplification Idea

Instead of asking children to cut an arc through the layers of paper, precut the sheets. Cut one end of each sheet into an arc, and then cut the length a bit shorter than the sheet before. Remember: Both the pink sheet and the sky blue sheets will remain a 4x12-inch rectangle. Children will then simply assemble the sheets in the correct order before stapling.

Psalm 148

1. Praise the LORD!

Praise the LORD from the heavens
Praise him from the skies!

2 *Praise him, all his angels!*
Praise him, all the armies of heaven!

3 *Praise him, sun and moon!*
Praise him, all you twinkling stars!

4 *Praise him, skies above!*
Praise him, vapors high above the clouds!

5 *Let every created thing give praise to the LORD,*
for he issued his command, and they came into being.

6 *He set them in place forever and ever.*
His decree will never be revoked.

7 *Praise the LORD from the earth,*
you creatures of the ocean depths,

8 *fire and hail, snow and clouds,*
wind and weather that obey him,

9 *mountains and all hills,*
fruit trees and all cedars,

10 *wild animals and all livestock,*
small scurrying animals and birds,

11 *kings of the earth and all people,*
rulers and judges of the earth,

12 *young men and young women,*
old men and children.

13 *Let them all praise the name of the LORD.*
For his name is very great;
his glory towers over the earth and heaven!

14 *He has made his people strong,*
honoring his faithful ones—
the people of Israel who are close to him.

Praise the Lord!

Hide & Seek Book

Age Level: ✩★

Then Jesus said, "What is the Kingdom of God like? How can I illustrate it? It is like a tiny mustard seed that a man planted in a garden; it grows and becomes a tree, and the birds make nests in its branches." LUKE 13:18–19

What It's All About

We can tell stories Jesus told, especially one about how prayer can do great things. This one is like the My Kindness Book on page 56, but different, too. You cut little windows to draw hidden pictures.

What You Need

- Hide and Seek Book Patterns (p. 207)
- Paper Cutting Tools (see p. 8)
- Coloring & Writing Instruments (see p. 8)

Preparation

Photocopy Hide and Seek Book Patterns, making one for each child.

What Children Do

Fold the Paper into a Booklet

a.

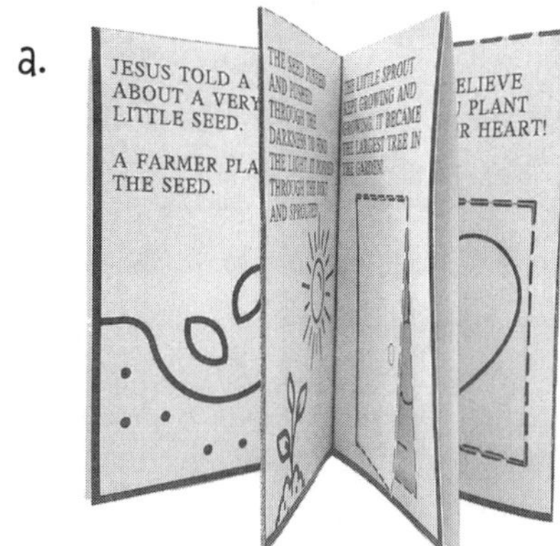

1. Cut out booklet by cutting along the solid outside lines.
2. Fold the paper along the dashed lines, one line at a time. Unfold.
3. Fold horizontally along the long center line, and then cut along the solid line.
4. With the pictures on the outside, hold the two ends of the folded paper and gently push them to meet at the center. This will form a booklet (image a).
5. Turn the pages so that the page that will have your name is the first page, the cover page.

Finish the Book

6. Color the pictures.
7. On the page with a door, cut the three solid lines. Fold the dashed line.
8. Draw a tree on the paper behind the open door. Color the tree.
9. On the page with a heart, cut the three solid lines around the heart. Fold the dashed line.
10. Draw a cross on the paper behind the open door (image b). Color the cross.

b.

THE MUSTARD SEED PRAYER
NAME
DATE
JESUS TOLD A STORY ABOUT A VERY TEENY LITTLE SEED. A FARMER PLANTED THE SEED.
THE LITTLE SEED THOUGHT, "I'M IN THE DARK EARTH. IT'S WARM AND MOIST BUT I WANT TO SEE THE SUN."
THE SEED PUSHED AND PUSHED THROUGH THE DARKNESS TO FIND THE LIGHT. IT POPPED THROUGH THE DIRT AND SPROUTED!
THE LITTLE SPROUT KEPT GROWING AND GROWING. IT BECAME THE LARGEST TREE IN THE GARDEN!
THE TREE GREW LARGE ENOUGH FOR BIRDS TO NEST IN ITS BRANCHES
WHEN YOU BELIEVE IN JESUS, YOU PLANT FAITH IN YOUR HEART!
JESUS SAID EVEN FAITH AS SMALL AS A MUSTARD SEED CAN MOVE MOUNTAINS

Story Wheel

Age Level: ★★

[Jesus] *said, "Anyone with ears to hear should listen and understand."* MARK 4:9

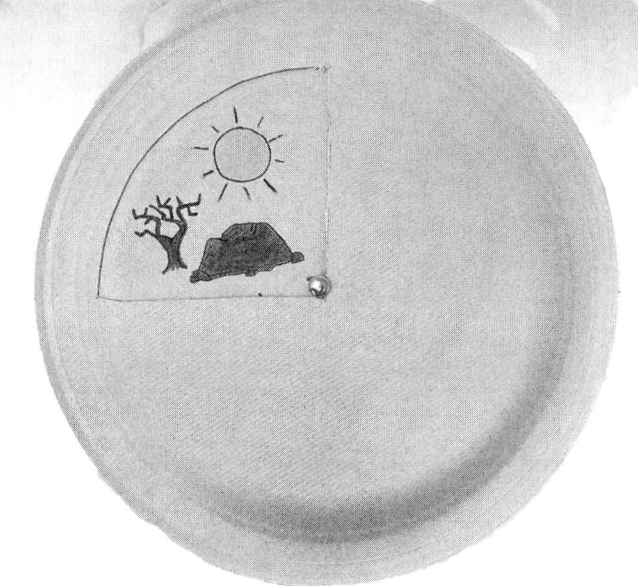

What It's All About

Today's verse is from one of Jesus' parables. It is found in Mark 4:1–20. A parable is a story that teaches a lesson about life. Today, we will make a Story Wheel that you can use to tell others Jesus' story.

You can make other story wheels to share all kinds of stories with others. Listening to one another as we share stories helps us understand each other.

What You Need

- Story Wheel Pattern (p. 209)
- Paper Cutting Tools (see p. 8)
- Coloring & Writing Instruments (see p. 8)
- Heavy-duty, 8-inch paper plates, two for each child
- Brads
- Glue

Optional

- Decorating materials (buttons, beads, wiggle eyes, glitter, stamps and stamp pads, stickers, adhesive gems, etc.)

Preparation

Photocopy Story Wheel Pattern, making one for each child.

What Children Do

1. Take two paper plates and line them up together on the back.
2. Use the point of the scissors to poke a hole in the middle of both plates.

Make the Top of Your Story Wheel

3. Choose the plate that will be the top of your story wheel. From the hole in the center, cut straight up to where the rim begins.
4. Starting from the center hole again, cut straight across the plate to the right edge.
5. Now cut around the rim to the first line you cut. You should have cut out a triangle with a rounded edge (image a).

a.

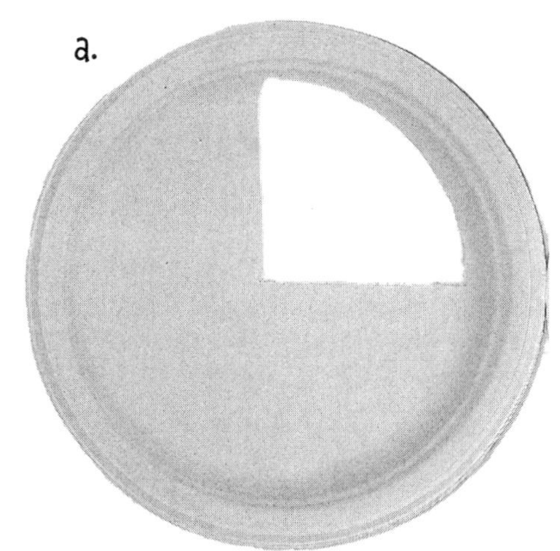

Make the Bottom of Your Story Wheel

6. Cut out the pattern piece.
7. Color each of the scenes.
8. Glue the pattern to the bottom plate (image b).

b.

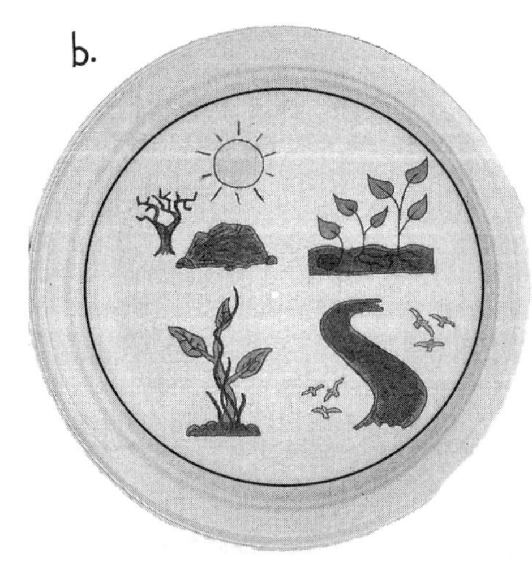

Attach the Plates Together

9. Once the bottom plate is completely dry, use a brad to attach the two plates together in the holes you made in Step 2.
10. On the front plate write the name of the story. In this case, write "The Parable of the Sower."

Optional

Use coloring and writing instruments to write or draw on the top plate. Use decorating materials to decorate the top of the plate.

Story Wheel Pattern

Circular Folding Diorama Story

Age Level: ☆★

I have placed my rainbow in the clouds. It is the sign of my covenant with you and with all the earth. GENESIS 9:13

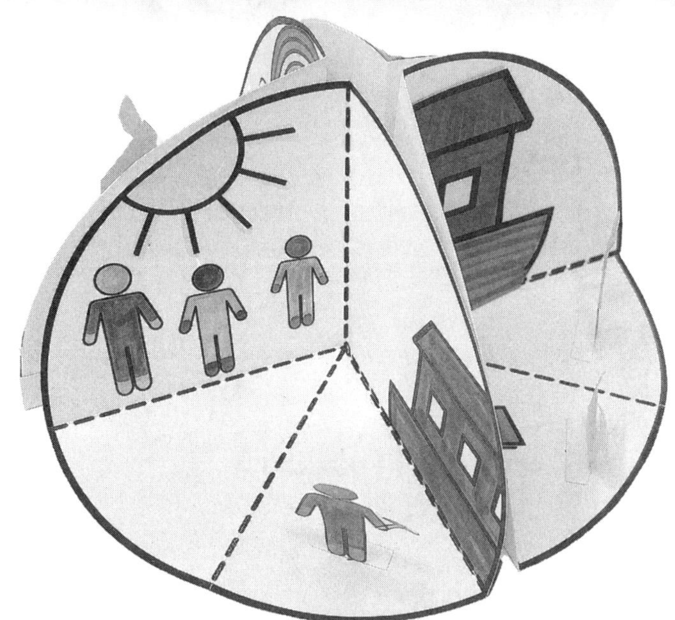

What It's All About

This Circular Folding Diorama Story tells the story of Noah and the Ark found in Genesis 6–9. Make other circular folding dioramas to tell other stories. Bible stories are the best stories because they are God's Word, they are true, and they tell us how to live the very best life.

What You Need

- Circular Folding Diorama Story Patterns (pp. 212–215)
- Paper Cutting Tools (see p. 8)
- Scoring materials (see p. 9)
- Coloring & Writing Instruments (see p. 8)
- White cardstock
- Craft glue

Preparation

On cardstock, photocopy Circular Folding Diorama Story Patterns, making one set for each child.

What Children Do

Prepare the Pattern Pieces

1. Cut out the patterns. There are four diorama semi-circles and stand-up figures, too.
2. Score each pattern on the dashed lines.
3. On one of the diorama semi-circles, fold the tab towards the back.
4. Fold the remaining dashed lines toward the center of the picture. Then unfold them.
5. Repeat Steps 3 and 4 for each of the four diorama semi-circles.
6. For each of the stand-up figures, on the scored lines, fold the tab toward the back of the figure so it can stand upright.
7. Color all of the pattern pieces.

Put the Pieces Together

8. Starting with Section 1, refold each section as described in Steps 3 and 4.
9. Put glue on the tab and glue it to the back of the large section along the open edge. This will form a quarter circle. The two small sections will fold up to make the section flat.
10. Repeat Step 8 and 9 for Sections 2, 3, and 4.
11. Put glue on the top part of Section 1 with the tab on it and glue it to the top part of Section 2 that does not have the tab on it.
12. Repeat gluing sections together in order from one to four (image a). Do not glue Section 4 to Section 1. This will allow you to fold the entire Circular Folding Diorama Story flat to carry. Later you can pop it back up to share the story.

a.

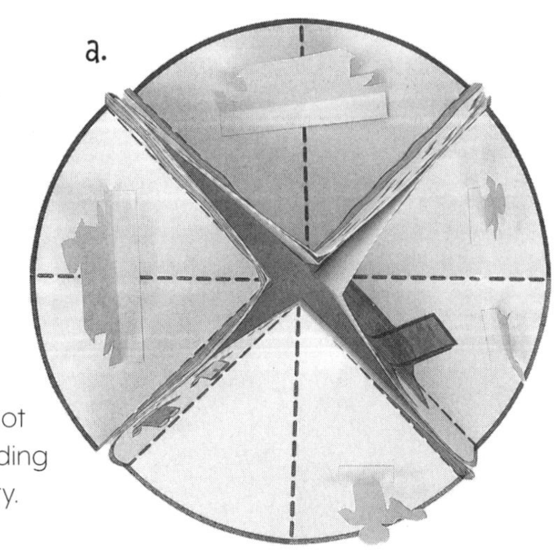

Attach the Stand-Up Figures

13. **Section 1:** Glue the Noah with a Hammer Stand-Up Figure on the X (image b).
14. **Section 2:** Glue the Noah Stand-Up Figure to one of the Xs and the Goats Stand-Up Figure to the other X (image c).
15. **Section 3:** Glue the Boat Stand-Up Figure to the X (image d).
16. **Section 4:** Glue the Boat with a Bird Stand-Up Figure to the X (image e).

Variation

Glue all four diorama semi-circles to a sheet of cardboard.

Optional

Use the blank template, Circular Diorama Pattern on page 216 to create your own circular folding diorama stories. Simple trace and cut the pattern four times. Then follow the steps above to create the diorama, using your own pictures. This is a great way to present a book report at school. Or make one of a friend's favorite story to give them as a gift.

Section 1 Patterns

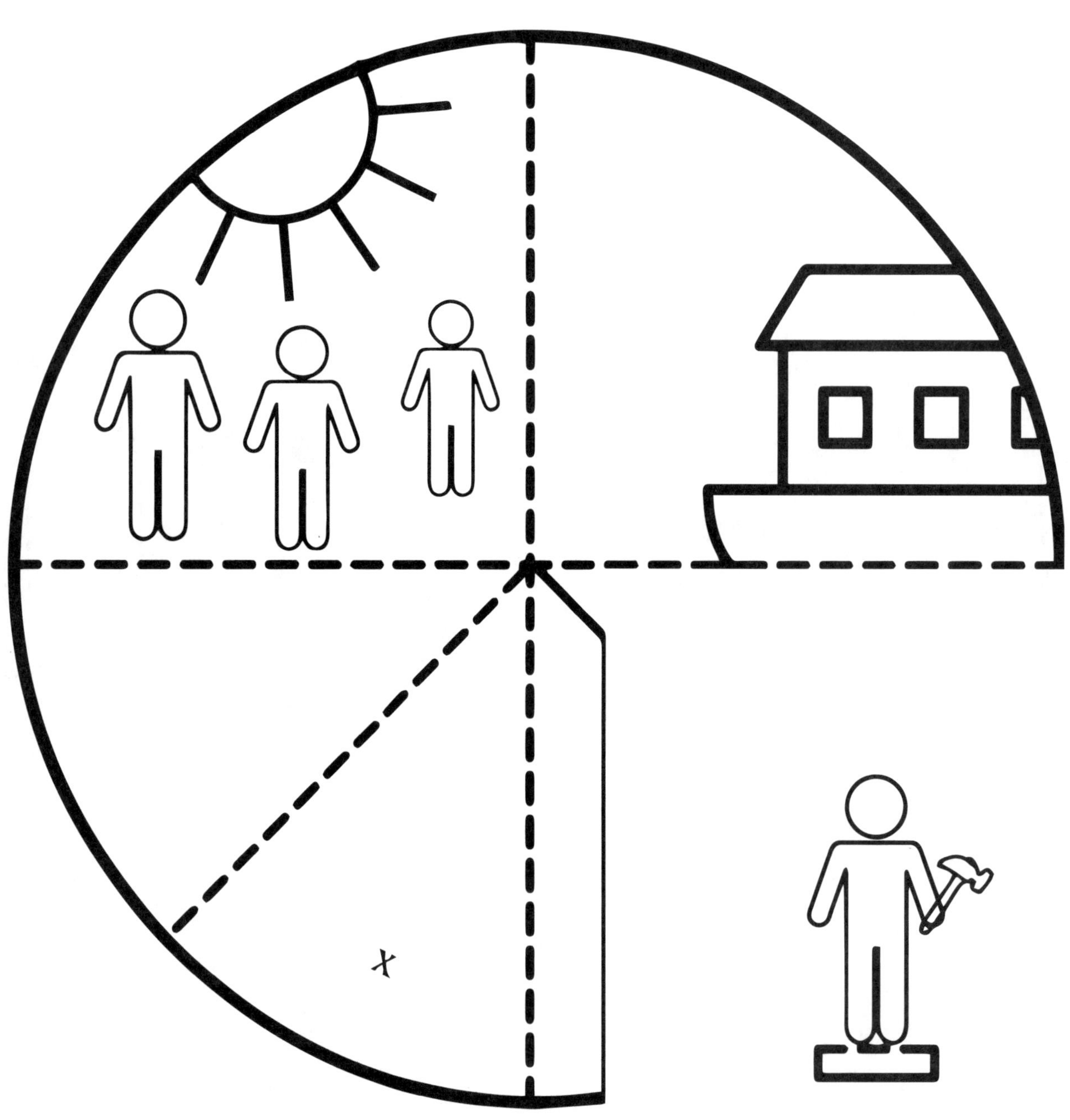

Section 2 Patterns

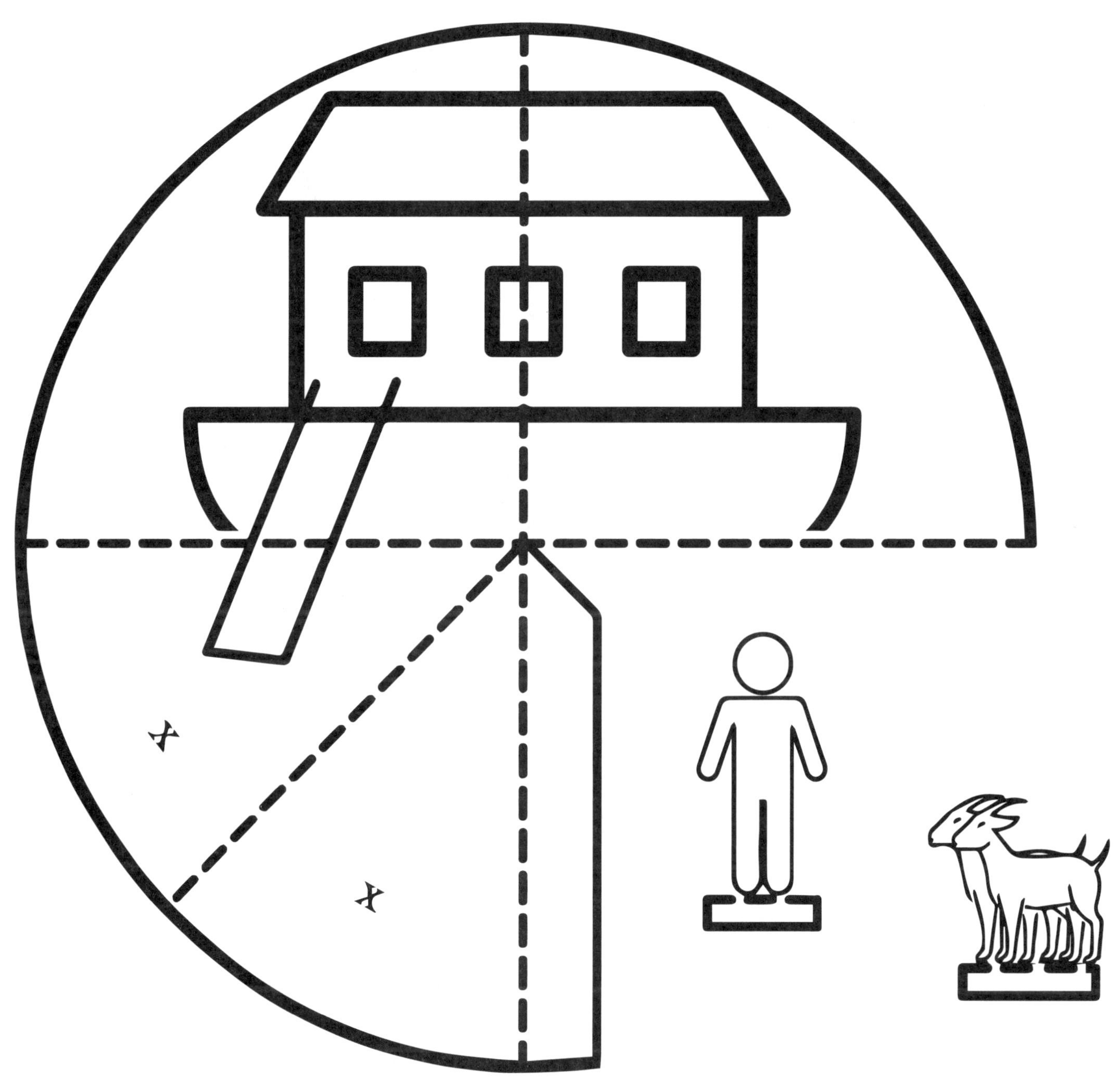

Section 3 Patterns

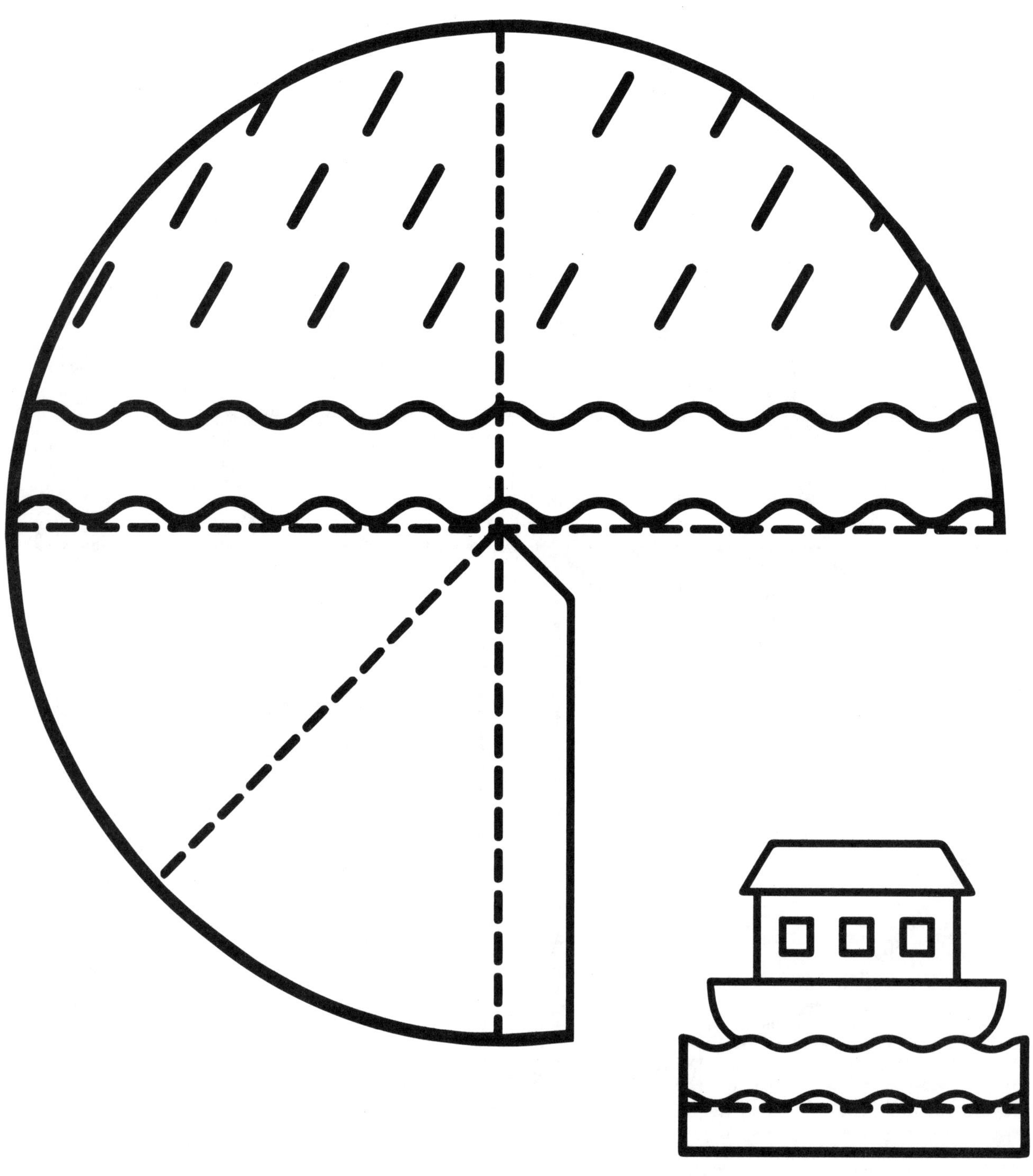

Section 4 Patterns

Circular Folding Diorama Story Patterns, continued

Circular Diorama Pattern

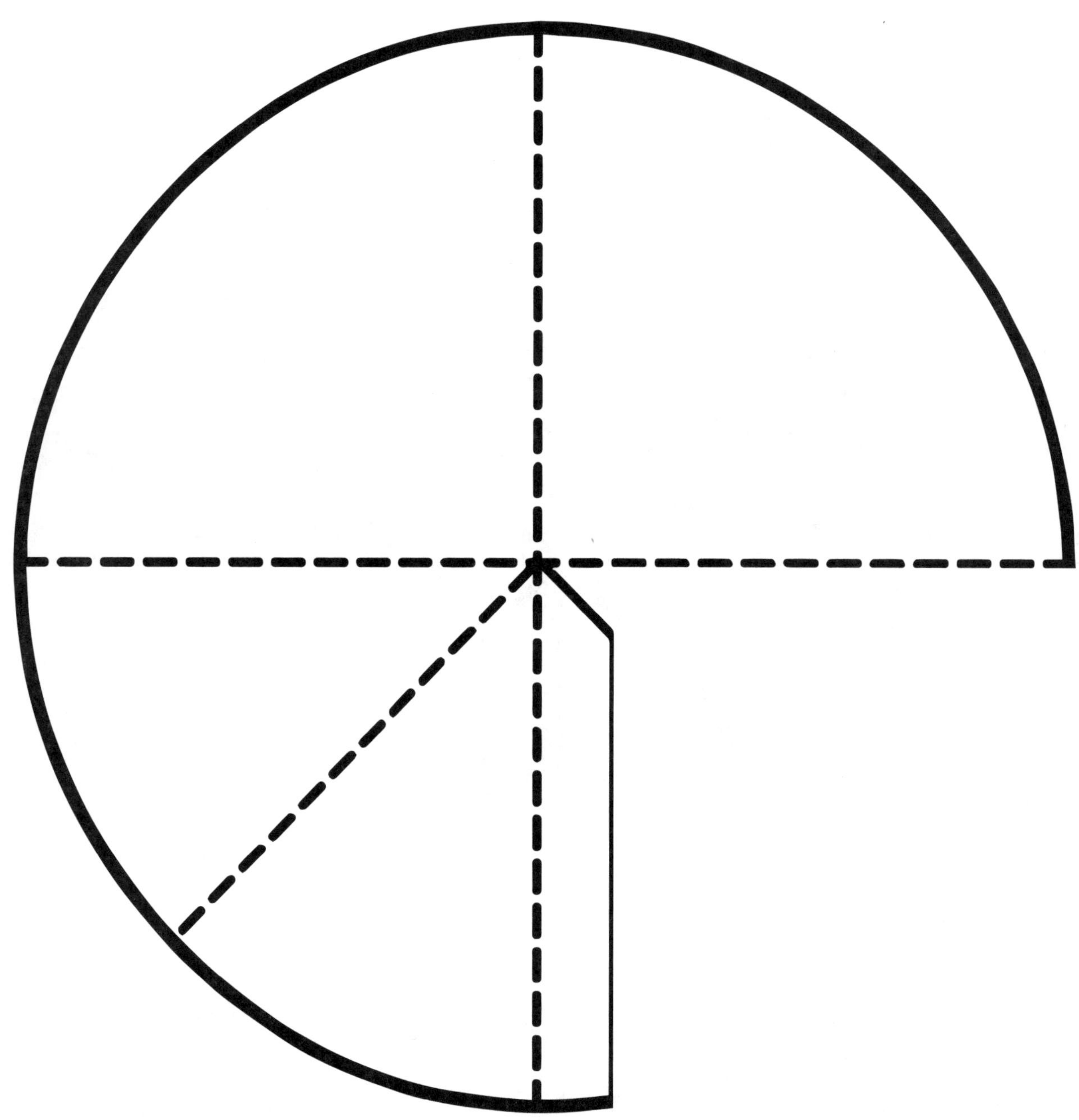

Appendix A

S.T.E.A.M. Lesson Extensions

Craft activities such as the ones in this book can open minds to exploring science, technology, engineering, art, and math (S.T.E.A.M.), plus develop language arts skills. It combines the fun of creativity with learning. Weave in vocabulary and conversation of S.T.E.A.M. concepts as you create with the kids in your class.

In addition, and most importantly, you can bring in biblical truths and Bible stories as they relate to the objects you're making.

Make the Most of Art Activities Through Conversations:

- Discuss measurements.
- Identify shapes.
- Share how bending, gluing, and putting pieces together creates new shapes and transforms flat paper into 2-D and 3-D objects.
- Try to visualize what shape each step will form.

Incorporate Science with Projects

- If making a flower or animal art project, chat about facts related to that flower or animal.
- Discuss how a process relates to science such as color blending when making wrapping paper or how rolling paper creates a new dimensional piece of jewelry.
- Simple tools such as rulers are part of understanding technology and engineering, measurement and distance, as well as proportion and dimension.

And There's More!

The following pages include ideas for ways to incorporate S.T.E.A.M. concepts to projects in this book. For those concepts that lend them to particular projects, these have been listed in a box titled Suggested Projects.

Symmetry

What It's All About

Many of the projects in this book use symmetry. Symmetry is when two parts are identical or a mirror image of one another. Anytime you are folding something in half and cutting out both sides the same you are using symmetry.

Suggested Projects

- Heart Tunnel Card, page 18
- Wreath Tunnel Card, page 20
- Twirling Turtle Card, page 23
- Snowflake Centerpiece, page 70

Explore Simple Symmetry

1. Take a piece of paper and fold it in half.
2. Cut something out along the fold.
3. Open the paper up. It is the same on both sides. That is symmetry!

Explore More Complex Symmetry

1. Fold a square piece of paper in half and then fold it in half again in the opposite direction.
2. Cut a shape leaving both fold lines (you could cut a curve).
3. Open the paper up all the way. You will have two lines of symmetry, both vertical and horizontal.

More Symmetry Ideas

1. Look for symmetry in decorating. Often, if someone puts a candlestick on one side of a mantle or table, they will add a second one on the other side to balance it out. This provides symmetry.
2. Draw something and then put a mirror on the edge of the paper. In the mirror you will see a drawing that provides symmetry to the one you drew.
3. Try this with a friend. Fold a paper in half and then unfold it. One of you draws something on their side of the paper. Then the other person tries to copy it on the other side of the paper completing the symmetry.

Clouds

What It's All About

What Is a Cloud?

A cloud is a visible mass of water droplets or ice suspended above the surface of a planet. Clouds are formed when water vapor in the air condenses into liquid or ice.

- Does a cloud float? They have a constant flow of warm air rising up to meet them, the warm air pushes up on them causing them to float.
- Clouds are part of the water cycle. Draw where clouds come into play as a part of the cycle.

Suggested Projects

- Layered Cloud Card, page31

Types of Clouds

Study and look for different types of clouds. Here are four of the most common ones:

- **Cirrus:** thin, wispy clouds that are high in the sky, they are made of ice crystals instead of water. The word means to curl. If more start forming it usually means the weather will change and a warm front may be coming.
- **Cumulus:** Puffy clouds scattered through the sky. They are formed when warm air with water vapor in it rises. The word means heap or pile. These are fair weather clouds as they are seen on pleasant days.
- **Stratus:** These clouds look like a huge thick blanket. They are a sign of rain or snow depending on the temperature. If they are near the ground, they are called fog. The word means spread out or layer. These clouds can make the sky look gloomy but generally it won't rain although it might drizzle a bit.
- **Cumulonimbus:** These are dark clouds that have rain or snow falling from them, they can form from a collection of either cumulus or stratus clouds. The word means high.

Try It Yourself!

- Draw all four types of clouds.
- Keep a cloud weather journal.
  - Record stratus and nimbus clouds and note the weather on those days.
  - Observe what clouds form on sunny days and record that, including days with no clouds.

Fish

Questions to Ask

Ask children the questions below.

1. **There are many kinds of fish and so many of them look very different. What are the scientific characteristics that make them a fish?** (All fish are cold-blooded. All fish live in water. Fish use gills to breath. Fish have a "swim bladder" that helps them stay buoyant and neither sink to the bottom or float to the surface. Fish use fins to move.)
2. **How do fish breathe?** (Through their gills.)
3. **The study of fish is called *ichthyology*. What is a person who studies fish called?** (An ichthyologist.)
4. **Fish are grouped into three different categories. What are they?** (Superclass Agnatha, or jawless fish; Cass Chondrichthyes, fish with a skeleton of cartilage; and Superclass Osteichthyes, fish with bones.)
5. **Pretend you are a fish in the ocean. What do you think you would do each day?**
6. **What would you eat if you were a fish?** (Answers will vary and may be creative. Some fish are meat eaters who eat marine animals, like worms, crustaceans, and even other fish. Some fish eat small organisms and plants. Some fish eat both meat and plants.)
7. **What are the different habitats fish live in?** (Oceans, rivers, lakes, etc.) **Which habitats are near where you live?**
8. **Why do fish have scales?** (Scales make fish sleek and slippery. This allows fish to swim through the water with very little resistance. Scales also make it difficult for other animals to grab hold of the fish.)

Suggested Project

- Fishing Game, page 44
- Fish Tale with Moving Parts, page 198

Try It Yourself!

- Choose one type of fish and find out what makes it special. Where does it live? What does it look like? Draw a picture of your fish. What does it eat? What animals try to eat or hunt it? How does it protect itself?
- Visit a waterway to explore it. Make a water scope to view things better. To make a water scope cut off both ends of a can. Attach a layer of plastic wrap to each side using a rubber band to attach it. Place one end into the water to view things more clearly and larger. The longer the can the deeper you can look.
- Participate in a waterway cleanup near you to make the water better for the marine creatures. If there's no community clean-up setup, clean it up yourself or if it is a really big job, invite others to clean it up with you. Be safe. Wear gloves.

Spatial Relationships

Suggested Projects

- Leaping, Twirling Robot, page 42
- Flextangle, page 45
- Heart Mobile, page 120
- Rolling with Joy, page 160

What It's All About

Spatial relationships are about

- How objects are in relation to one another
- How to move objects to fit into one another
- How to orient them mentally (visualize)

Learning to think spatially includes understanding **dimensions** (size and shape), **location** (above, beyond, etc.), and **interrelationships** (different, similar, how puzzle pieces fit).

Geometry is the higher-level study of spatial relationships. Understanding shapes helped a mathematician, Arthur H. Stone, to develop flextangles in 1939. Flextangles are made of six-sided shapes. Further work with this led to developing ways to describe subatomic particles. In a flextangle, the hexagon (six-sided, six-faced) shapes are bent into a type of mobius strip and the ends are fastened together.

Words Related to Spatial Skills

- Above below
- High, middle, low
- In front of, behind, in back of
- On top of, beneath
- Over, under
- Inside, outside
- Different, similar
- Two-dimensions, 3-D Shapes (circle, square, etc.)
- Before, during, after
- Together, apart
- Size: small, smaller, smallest

Ways to Develop Spatial Relationships (Basic Engineering Concepts)

- Fold a paper and cut shapes. Before opening the paper, try to visualize what the opened paper will look like.
- Play the game "Eye Spy" using clues relate to location (look above, below, beside, under).
- Jigsaw puzzles and tangrams reinforce the concepts of size and shape and how things fit together. They also help develop the skill of visualizing what a rotating a piece will look like.
- Jewelry making, sculpting with clay, and carpentry promote understanding size, interrelated parts, and dimension.
- Bike riding promotes navigation, direction, and space.
- Draw a map of a place after walking through it (park, house, etc.). This develops a sense of location, spacing, and comparison of sizes and distances.
- A number line helps children see the progression of numbers and understand size.
- Try putting three same-sized triangles together and using it for a pattern to cut and fold a pyramid. It is three sided shapes that form three faces.
- Identify different shapes, both two-dimensional shapes like the triangle and square, and the two-dimensional corollary shapes of the pyramid and cube.
- Discuss what 3-D objects look like inside. Discuss a variety of Styrofoam shapes, cupcakes, or fruits and then cut them open to see the shapes inside.
- Discuss shapes and size and how pieces fit together for many of the art projects in the book.
- Spatial relationships are used in architecture, landscaping, crafts, map making, and many other careers.

Search online or at the library to find out more about the benefits of spatial relationships and to find other fun activities:

Stars

What It's All About

Star gliders can help us think about stars and falling or shooting stars.

Suggested Projects

- Star Glider, page 47
- Night Sky Mobile, page 109

Star Facts

- There are 9,096 stars visible to the naked eye (no telescopes)
- Stars last billions of years
- Some stars are 100 times more massive that the sun in our solar system. Our sun is a star, and its name is Sol.
- All stars have the same chemical composition, meaning they have the same ingredients. The average star's consists mostly of hydrogen and helium, with all other elements making up about three percent.
- Stars change all the time in pressure and chemical makeup. They keep adjusting to balance outward and inward pressure.
- Stars do not twinkle. As the light passes through our atmosphere it deflects light to cause it to look like the star is twinkling.
- The earth orbits the sun.

Discover Your Own Star Facts

1. Sizes of stars and how far they are from Earth.
2. Read about star phases and list some facts.
3. Find out about red cool stars and blue hot stars.
4. Look up estimates for the number of stars in the universe.
5. Find out details of how stars are formed and how many are formed each day.

Try It Yourself!

- Look up what constellations you can see in the night sky in summer and in winter.
- Use Star Gliders (p. 47) or star shapes to lay out a constellation on the floor.
- On a clear night try to find specific constellations. Look for the north star, too.
- Look up the date of the next meteor shower and stay up to see it—with adult permission, of course.
- Use a telescope (borrow one if you don't have one), ask a parent or guardian to take you to a place with no electric lights, and see how stars and other objects in the sky look closer up. Write your observations.
- Visit a planetarium to learn more about stars and other things you see in the night sky.

Stress

What It's All About

Stress is your body's reaction to pressure from a situation or event. Good stress is called *eustress* and it inspires you to do something. For example, thirst is eustress that inspires you to drink something, especially water.

Distress is when we react negatively from stress such as becoming fearful when we hear sounds that we cannot identify. Stress gets worse if we dwell on it.

Suggested Projects

- Double Heart Pencil Holder, page 61
- Gift Box, page 101
- Diversity Circle Cutout, page 154
- Hand Puzzles, page 159

Stress Can Impact the Heart and General Health

Stress can cause you to breathe faster, your heart to beat faster, and can increase fear. Stress can also cause inflammation and increase blood pressure. Stress releases a burst of adrenaline (a hormone) that can increase breathing and heart rate.

Learn to Handle Stress

There are activities and responses you can choose to do that lowers stress. That's called managing stress. Try some. You can even check your heart rate before and after activities:

- Take a walk.
- Run
- Turn off the news if it upsets you
- Recite scriptures that calm you.
- Squeeze a stress ball.
- Let your mind focus on happy thoughts and good memories.
- Play a game that you enjoy.
- Jog.
- Unplug from electronics to let your mind rest.
- Read something that helps you relax or laugh.
- Pray
- Avoid what triggers your stress, like keeping peace at home to avoid the stress of fights.
- Reframe a problem causing stress to think of positive solutions. Set goals to solve the problem.

Try Drawing or Journaling When Stressed

1. Draw or journal your feelings.
2. Identify what happened that caused the stress.
3. When you stop, check and see how you feel. You may find this helps you de-stress.

Science Experiment on Stress

1. Design an age-appropriate but challenging math test or a timed obstacle course.
2. Before the test check heart rate, temperature, and ask how the person feels.
3. After the test, repeat Step Two.
4. Note the changes stress may have caused.

Technology and Stress

Science has linked technology use with stress and trouble resting or sleeping. Experiment with turning off all technology at various times to see how it impacts falling asleep and getting rest. Try to find the best time to finish using technology each day.

Snowflakes

What It's All About

A man named Wilson "Snowflake" Bentley became famous for his studies and early photographs of snowflakes. He loved snow and God. After he invented a way to photograph snowflakes and spent years studying them, he said,

> *Snowflakes were miracles of beauty; and it seemed a shame that this beauty should not be seen and appreciated by others. Every crystal was a masterpiece of design; and no one design was ever repeated. When a snowflake melted, that design was forever lost. Just that much beauty was gone, without leaving any record behind. I became possessed with a great desire to show people something of this wonderful loveliness, an ambition to become, in some measure, its preserver.*

Suggested Project

- Snowflake Centerpiece, page 70

Science of Snowflakes

If you live where snow falls, collect some snow. Or look online or in library books to find photographs of snowflakes. Examine the crystals with a magnifying glass or microscope. Each flake is a unique crystal with six stems.

Draw some snowflake crystals. Make them look like ones you found, or make up your own snowflake designs.

Wilson Bentley, Public domain, via Wikimedia Commons

Water Cycle

Snow is part of the water cycle in cold weather. Study the water cycle by doing the following:

- Draw the water cycle.
- Boil water and watch steam rise.
- Watch snow or ice melt.

Language Arts with Snowflakes and Snow

Find similes and quotes about snowflakes like "white as snow" or "as unique as a snowflake." You can make up your own simile.

Write a paragraph describing snow and snowflakes.

Technology

Do a search on Wilson "Snowflake" Bentley and find some of his actual photos to look at and study. Read about the methods he used to take the pictures. That kind of photography is early technology.

Faith and Snow to Discuss

- **The Bible compares being cleansed of sin to the whiteness of snow in Psalm 51:7 and Isaiah 1:18. How does it feel to know that Jesus' forgiveness makes you feel as clean as the whiteness of snow?**
- **Job 38:22 reads, "Have you visited the storehouses of the snow or seen the storehouses of hail?" What do you think this verse is talking about?** (God is the only one who can control the weather. We do not know nor are we as powerful as God is.)

Sports Science

What It's All About

Celebrate fitness and explore the science of muscles. Increase your physical ability with the right exercises. Regular exercise maintains fitness. Healthy eating also keeps us healthy. There are 650 skeletal muscles in your body. They are voluntary muscles, and you can control what they do.

Suggested Project

- Sports Centerpiece, page 72

Know the Terms

- Muscular strength is related to force and how much you can lift.
- Endurance is related to time and how long you can continue without resting.
- Flexibility is the ability to move joints freely through its normal range of motion.
- Look up other terms like cardiovascular, body composition, reaction time, and speed.

Exercises That Build Physical Ability

Strength Training

- Lift weights
- Do push-ups or wall push-ups
- Gardening, digging, shoveling
- Grip a tennis ball
- Exercise using a resistance band

Endurance: Aerobic exercises get your heart pumping and also helps your lungs:

- Walk fast or run
- Bike
- Climb stairs or hills
- Swim
- Dance or jump rope

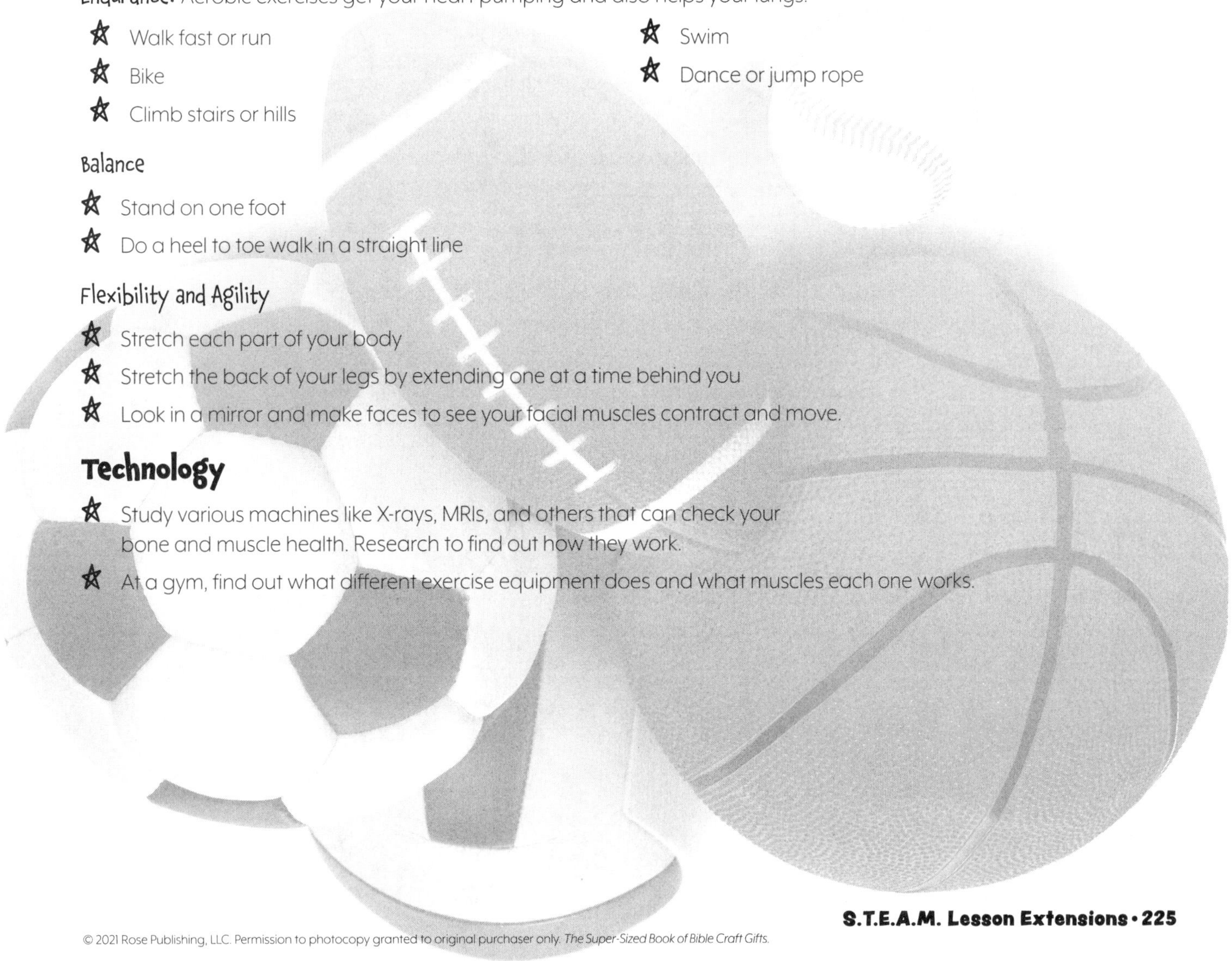

Balance

- Stand on one foot
- Do a heel to toe walk in a straight line

Flexibility and Agility

- Stretch each part of your body
- Stretch the back of your legs by extending one at a time behind you
- Look in a mirror and make faces to see your facial muscles contract and move.

Technology

- Study various machines like X-rays, MRIs, and others that can check your bone and muscle health. Research to find out how they work.
- At a gym, find out what different exercise equipment does and what muscles each one works.

Doves

Facts about White Dove

- Doves are symbols of peace, and also called love birds.
- Doves are in the pigeon family and are naturally peaceful and friendly.
- Doves pick up dropped seeds and store them in their esophagus to eat later.
- They adapt to the environment and live everywhere except harsh deserts and Antarctica.
- Doves mate for life and build their nest together.
- Both the female and the male turn the eggs over in the nest and sit on them. They both feed their newly hatched babies.
- Some varieties of doves are listed on the protected migratory bird list.
- Tame doves pictured in clay tablets date back more than 5,000 years.
- Doves are only about twelve inches in length from head to tail.
- Doves live an average of ten to fifteen years, with some living up to twenty-five years.

Suggested Project

- Twirling Centerpiece, page 79

Experiments

Find some bird feathers and try a few experiments.

Crystal Feathers

Make salt crystal feathers. As water evaporates in a mix of salt and water, the salt attaches to a feather in the water and forms crystals. The crystals can start forming in an hour and completely form in 24 hours. Here's how to do it:

1. Pour two cups of water in a saucepan and bring to a boil.
2. Add salt, a little at a time until a layer of crystallized salt forms over the top of the water. It looks like ice.
3. Pour the salty water into a mason jar.
4. Suspend a feather in the water. You can tape the end to the lip of the jar with a clothespin and sit the jar on a sunny windowsill.

Oil and Feathers

1. Coat a feather with oil. Observe how it gets heavy and how that might prevents birds from flying.
2. Try cleaning the oil off with water and different detergents. Record results, noting which cleansers worked best.

Feather Insulation

1. Place feathers against your arm and put an ice cube on top. What do you feel? What conclusions can you draw from that? (Feathers keep you warm.)
2. Time how long it takes for an ice cube to melt when on a feather on your arm.

Faith Lessons

Discuss how the dove is represented in the Bible:

- The dove is the first named bird in the Bible. A dove was used by Noah to find out if there was dry land after the flood. The dove carried an olive branch to Noah, another symbol of peace (Genesis 8).
- God named the dove as the bird to be used in sacrifices, or pigeons could be used. These served as sin offerings to cleanse people of sin (Leviticus 5:7,11).
- Psalm 55:6 speaks of a desire to fly away like a dove and be at rest.
- At the baptism of Jesus, the Holy Spirit descended on him like a dove (Matthew 3:16, Mark 1:10, Luke 3:22, John 1:32).

Nature

Facts about Leaves

- Leaves are the parts of plants that allow them to eat. Leaves do this by converting sunlight into sugar by a process called *photosynthesis*.
- Leaves have a variety of shapes including needles, broad leaves, sheaths (like grass blades), and fronds. Find plants in your area that show different shapes of leaves.
- Leaves are normally green, but some plants have other colors. One example is the Japanese Maple that has red leaves. Even if the plant's leaves are a different color, it has some chloroplast cells that are used in photosynthesis.
- Leaves change color in the fall as the plant absorbs the nutrients in the leaves into itself. This causes the leaves to change to yellow, red, brown, or other colors.

Try It Yourself!

You can watch how leaves get nutrients from water. Put some food coloring in a glass of water and place a piece of celery inside it. You will see the color move up the stem and into the leaves. You can also split the celery at the bottom and put each half in a different color of water to see how the colors mix at the top.

Facts about Rocks

- There are three different kinds of rocks: *sedimentary*, *igneous*, and *metamorphic*. The type of rock is determined by how the rock was formed. Online or in a book, find out about these different ways rocks are formed.
- Rocks are made up of minerals. The types of minerals in a rock make a difference in how heavy it is as well as its color.
- Rocks have been used for tools for most all of human history.
- Just like there is a water cycle, there is a rock cycle. Find out about the rock cycle and draw it.

Try It Yourself!

Limestone is one kind of rock. You can test and see if a rock has limestone in it by putting it in a glass or plastic bowl and pouring vinegar over it. If it has limestone in it then it will react with the vinegar within about a minute.

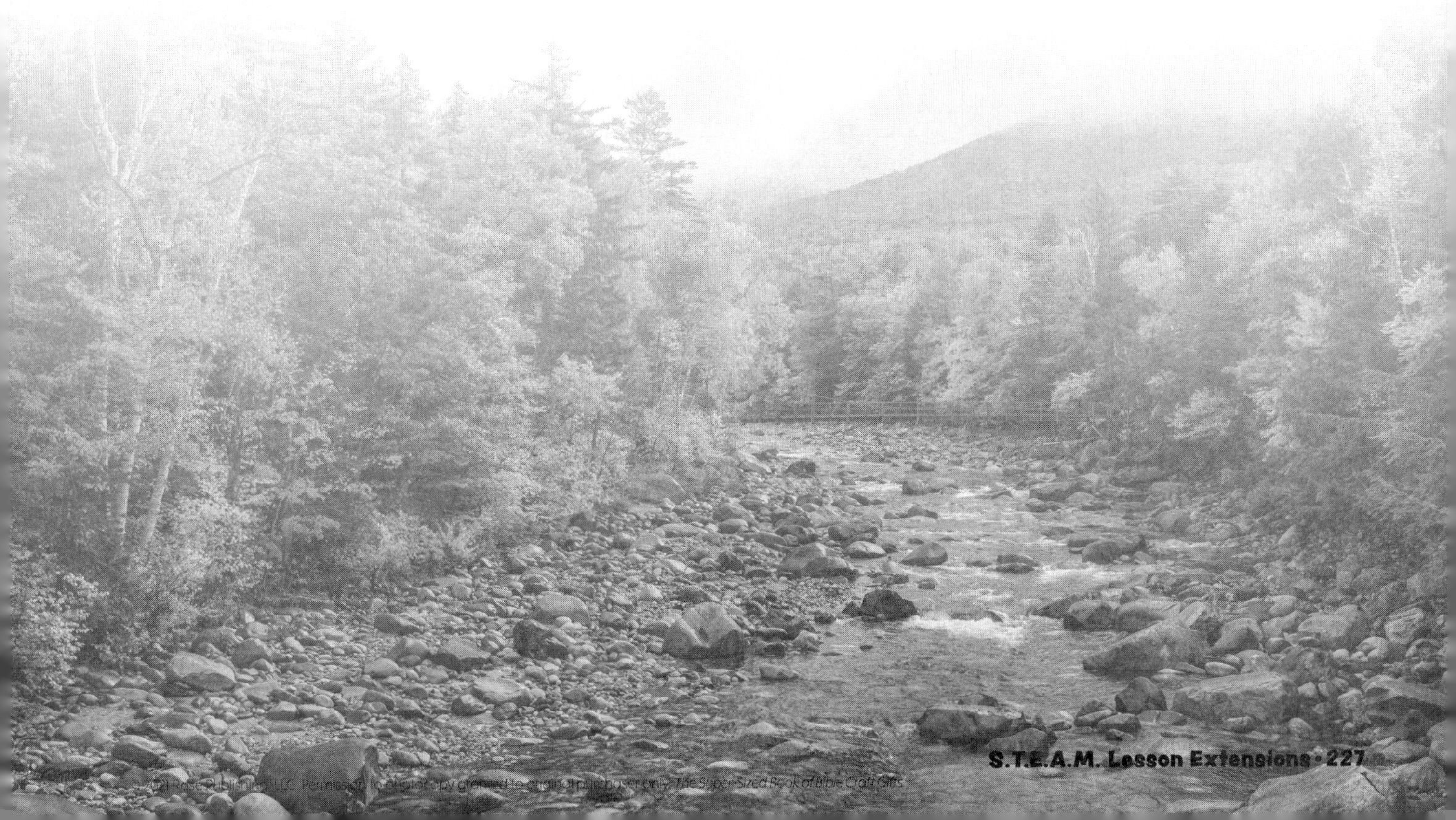

Colors

What It's All About

How do you choose colors when making a project and have them look nice together? You can use the color wheel and choose either supplementary or complimentary colors.

1. A very basic color wheel has six sections. Red, yellow, and blue are the *primary* colors. The *secondary* colors—orange, green, and violet—are made from the colors on each side of them.
2. A more advanced color wheel will have another six colors blending each of the main ones together. Try taking just primary colors and mixing them to get other colors you want to use.
3. The colors right next to another color on the wheel are *supplementary* or *analogous* colors. The shades can blend into each other and having them together helps things blend. These colors go together to make backgrounds. Use some paint and try choosing colors that are beside each other on the wheel to make your background on a paper. Fold up the paper once it is dry and use it as the background for a card.
4. Colors opposite each other on the wheel are called *complimentary* colors. These colors really stand out when they are used together. If you use one of them for the background and then use the other for your focal point it will really pop. Try putting complimentary colors of paper against each other and see what you think.
5. You can also decorate things using just one color in different shades, such as a light, dark, and medium shades of the same color. This can help calm the look. With paint, add some black or white to a color to make a variety of shades of that color. Try making a background for a picture or card by making strips of various shades of the same color as the background. Add a shape of a complimentary color onto it to see it pop up from the background.
6. Colors also invoke feelings. Talk about how you feel when you see certain colors. Do you feel happy, sad, or angry when you see them? Sometimes the shades of the colors add to these feelings.

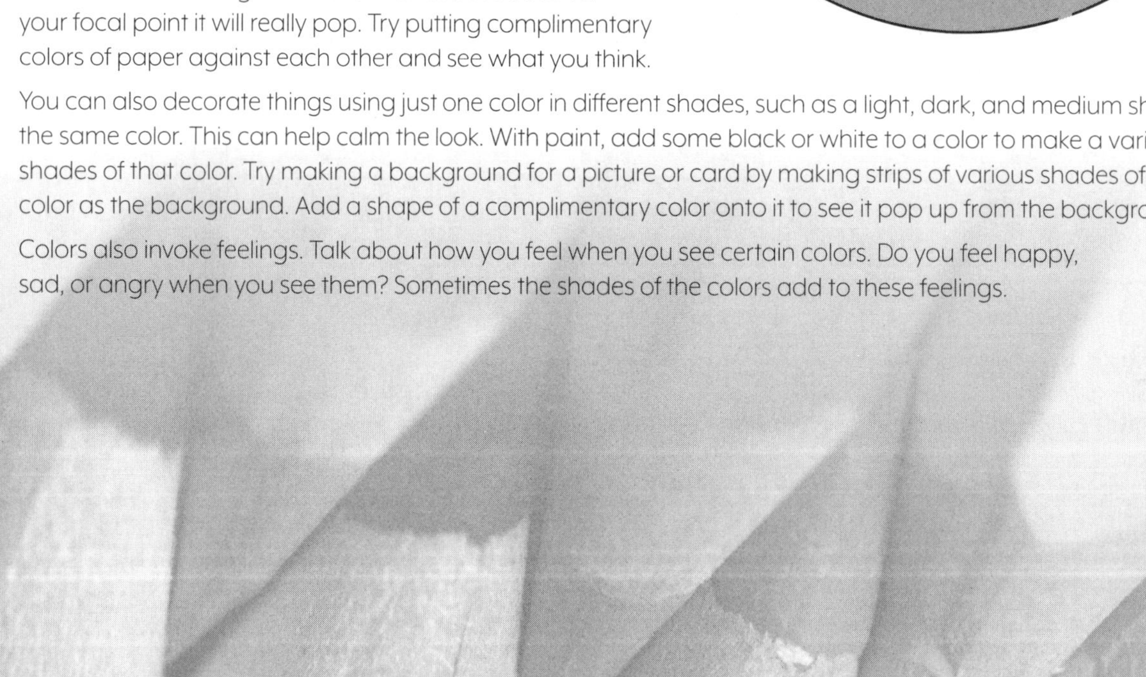

Gems

What It's All About

Gemstones are beautiful when they are polished and ready to be added to a piece of jewelry. However, getting them to that point takes time, effort, and uses a machine.

1. Gems are the result of minerals that have crystallized under high pressure. They are formed slowly over time. The color comes from the imperfections in the stones. How do the things that are not perfect about us make a difference in who we are?
2. Most gemstones are hard, but some are soft and valued for the shine they give off. How can you be like a rare gem and shine for Jesus?
3. Gems are valued based on the four Cs: color, cut, clarity, and carat weight. Search online to find out what each of those things mean.

Suggested Projects

- Paper Bead Jewelry, page 96

Grow Sugar Crystals to Eat

What You Need

- ½ cup boiling water for each child
- 2 cups of sugar for each child
- Clear container (drinking glass, mason jar, etc.)
- String

Optional

- Food coloring

What You Do

1. Boil one half cup of water.
2. Mix in 2 cups of sugar. If you want, add food coloring.
3. Pour the mixture into a clear container.
4. Hang a string down through the mixture (but don't let it touch the bottom of the container).
5. Leave it for a couple of weeks and your sugar crystal will grow. You can eat it once the crystals have formed. These sugar crystals are sometimes called *rock candy*.

Grow Borax Crystals

What You Need

- Hot water
- Bowl
- Borax
- Funnel
- Coffee filter
- Resealable container (such as an empty and clean jelly jar)
- Paper plate
- String

What You Do

- Start with really hot (but doesn't need to be boiling) water in a bowl
- Add in Borax, stirring as you add it until it no longer dissolves in the water (this means the water is saturated).
- Put the coffee filter into the funnel and pour the solution through it into the resealable container. This will separate the undissolved crystals.
- Pour a little of the solution onto a paper plate and let it sit overnight. This will grow small crystals. If you continue to leave the solution on the plate the crystals will keep forming but it will get easier and easier to break.
- To grow one larger crystal, tie a string around a small crystal and hang it in the jar with your solution in it. While the water evaporates the crystal will grow. If all of the water evaporates and you still want a larger crystal, repeat the process with more of the solution and put it in the airtight jar again.

Turtles

Suggested Projects

- Twirling Turtle Card, page 23

1. Find information about the following types of turtles:
   - ✯ Loggerhead
   - ✯ Green Turtle
   - ✯ Kemp's Riddley
   - ✯ Hawksbill
2. What does a turtle do for a day? Write a story about what you imagine a turtle might do. Then, look up information online or in a library book to find out.
3. Look up and list three facts about turtles.
   a.
   b.
   c.
4. Look up and list three facts about turtle habitats.
   a.
   b.
   c.
4. Look up and list three facts about turtle predators.
   a.
   b.
   c.
4. Find out which turtles are endangered.
5. Find and draw pictures of the food your turtle eats.
6. Write three math word problems about a turtle.

Calder & Balance

What It's All About

Alexander Calder was an engineer before he stared sculpting and creating mobiles. He worked with automobiles and hydraulics. Once he changed to art, Calder explored form, colors, and balance. Art and nature have many patterns that repeat, so it's not unusual for a mathematician or engineer to become interested in art or nature.

Calder wanted to bring new life to art and change it from flat, static designs to something that moved and became three-dimensional. His kinetic structures use balance and air to create art.

Suggested Projects

- Calder Sculpture, page 108
- Heart Mobile, page 120

Facts about Calder & Balance

- When a mobile has a number of levels, especially ones suspended with wire or using sticks and yarn, it needs balance. That is done by finding the *fulcrum,* the center of balance for the object.
- *Mobile* is a French word that means both movement and motive.
- When two sides weigh the same, the balance point is in the middle. When one object is heavier than the other, the balance point is closer to the heavier object.
- Mobiles like Calder's are built from the bottom up, balancing each new level as it is added. When more levels are added each lower level counts as one part when figuring out how to balance the next level.
- Balance is important in engineering, especially in constructing bridges and buildings so they stand and hold weight.

Try It Yourself

- An example of Calder's type of mobiles is done with coat hangers. An artist named Man Ray started with one hanger and attached others in a way that keeps them in balance. Try using coat hangers to create a balanced mobile.
- Look up some of Calder's mobiles made with wire. Try making your own.
- Try balancing on one foot. Then lean over as far as you can while staying balanced. Try leaning forward, backward, to the left, to the right, and so on.
- Get a friend and try a seesaw. Think about what it takes to balance it. Sometimes the lighter person needs to move toward the center.

Fruit

What It's All About

Fruit grows from blossoms. Once it turns ripe, it can rot when it is not picked or eaten in time. Fruits are a good source of different nutrients including antioxidants, potassium, folic acid, and vitamins. They also contain a lot of fiber and simple sugars.

Suggested Project

- Fruit of the Spirit Mobile, page 111

Fruit Facts

- Fruit can be dried (dehydrated) by removing the water. Once dehydrated, fruit will last much longer. Investigate different ways to dry fruits.
- Different colored fruits can be used to make dyes to change colors of fabrics.
- Online or in a library, look up how to test for glucose (sugar) in different fruits and give it a try!
- Discover how much fruit you should eat each day, by looking it up online or in a nutrition book.
- Look up the definition of fruit.
- Some fruits, like apples can grow almost anywhere and grow in all 50 states. Others need to grow in the right climate like oranges that need a hot climate with plenty of rain.
- Strawberries are actually part of the rose family. So are apples, raspberries, and pears.
- Pineapples are actually berries, even though they grow much larger than most berries, like blueberries.
- Apples last a long time. They can be a year old in the store when you buy them.
- Tomatoes are the most popular fruit in the world.

Try It Yourself!

- Every fruit contains different types of nutrients. Look up several fruits, including your favorites and make a chart of what they contain and the benefits of those nutrients.
- Cut open a fruit and leave a piece out for a while. See how long it takes to start to turn brown and rot.
- Drop fruit juices onto coffee filters and watch them color the paper. That shows what color of dyes can be made from those fruit.
- Chart the fruit you eat in a week and what nutrients they gave your body.
- Lemons contain lots of acid. Online or in a library book, look up how to make a lemon battery. Find out what makes it work.
- Fruits are actually magnetic. Look up experiments to check out the magnetic force in fruit. Grapes repel (move away) from magnets. See what other fruits react to magnets.

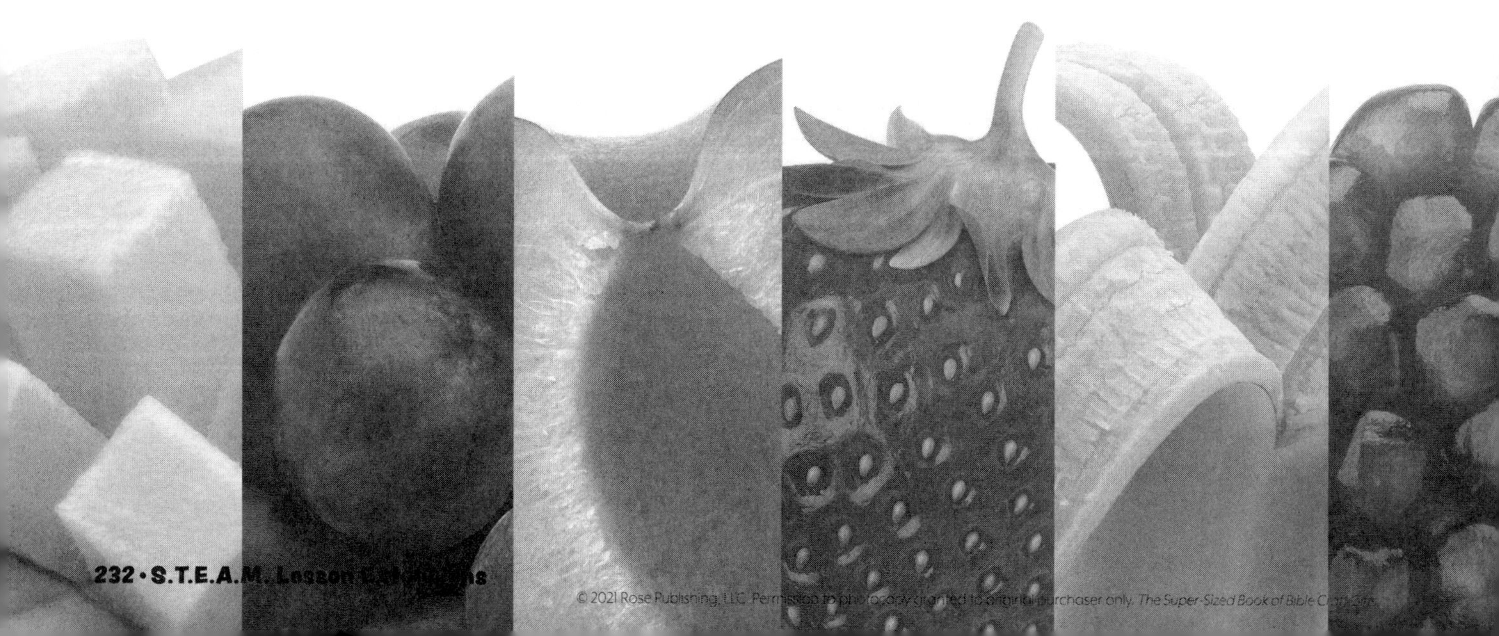

Animal Sounds

What It's All About

Animals make many different sounds and noises. They communicate with each other through these sounds. People do the same thing. We communicate with sounds we call *words*.

When we imitate animals by trying to make the sound they make—like saying "moo" for a cow's sound—those words are called *onomatopoeias* (ah-no-mah-toh-PAY-ahs).

Suggested Projects

- Bear Envelope, page 15
- Animal Mobile, page 113

All about Sound

- Sound waves carry sounds although we cannot see those waves in the air. There is technology that can map sound waves, however. You can watch sound waves on an *oscilloscope* to see them. You can find one online or at many children's museums.
- *Frequency* is how fast or slow the wave moves depending on how fast or slow the vibration.
- *Pitch* is related to frequency. Speak in a high and then low voice to note the difference in pitch.
- *Amplitude* is the size of the wave. A big sound wave creates a big noise.

Animal Sound Facts

- Prairie dogs have different sounds for distances, colors, enemies (predators), and even a sound for people.
- Chimps do not all speak the same. In different regions of the world, they use different dialects (like foreign languages), but can learn other dialects.
- The different sounds animals make are dependent on the animal's vocal cords or voice boxes. Vibrations of air create the sounds and depending on the shape and size of the animal's vocal cords or voice boxes, the sound will vary. It's like how different musical instruments make different sounds depending on the shape and how air moves through the instrument. Compare the sounds made by a tuba and a flute.
- People imitate animal sounds, and some animals, like parrots, can imitate people sounds. Lyrebirds in Australia are considered to be the best mimics of sounds.
- Some animals make sounds with their wings (birds) or by rubbing parts of their body together (crickets).
- Cats make eleven different kinds of sounds and not just purring, hissing, and meowing.

Try It Yourself!

- Sit outside in different places to listen to animals sounds. See what creatures you can identify by the sounds you hear.
- Try to describe each sound.
- Online, find and listen to the sounds of animals in the forest, amazon, or other locations. Try to mimic sounds.
- Look up and try some sound experiments to understand how vibrations work to make sounds.
- At the ocean, notice the size of waves and sounds made as the waves crash on the shore.

Rainbows

What It's All About

Rainbows can fill the sky with color. Rainbows are really full circles of light, but we only see part of it when we are on the ground. Light in water droplets in the sky bend to separate out the colors of light. The bending is caused by refraction and reflection.

Suggested Projects

- Heavenly Mobile, page 115
- Psalm 148 Rainbow Book, page 204

Facts about Rainbows

Some of the listed items are questions and some are fact. If you don't know the answer to any of the questions, look them up online or in a book about rainbows.

- What are the primary colors of rainbows? **Hint:** The acronym *Roy G Biv* is used as a way to remember these colors and the order in which they appear!
- A rainbow is light and not an object, so it cannot be touched.
- In what kind of weather can rainbows be seen?
- The seven primary colors of the rainbow are called the *visible spectrum*. White light is the combination of all these colors.
- When there are two or more rainbows together, their colors reverse. This is called a *double rainbow*. *Triple rainbows* are rare, but it's three rainbows above each other.
- Discover whether the sky inside (under the arc) or outside the rainbow is brighter. Look up why there is a difference.
- Find out what a *moonbow* is and why it looks white although all the colors are present.
- Look up *fogbows* to find out what they are and what faint colors can be seen.

Try It Yourself!

- Look through a prism towards light to see the spectrum of colors. As light passes through a prism, the light is split into the color spectrum.
- Hold a glass of water near a window above a white piece of paper. Watch as sunlight passes through the glass to form a rainbow on the paper.
- In a dark room, shine a flashlight onto a small mirror. A rainbow forms above the mirror.
- Try spraying a mist of water on grass on a sunny day and watch for a rainbow to appear.
- Blow bubbles in sunlight and look through the bubbles to see the rainbow colors.
- Fill a row of jars with water. Add a different food color to each in the order of rainbow colors. Place a stalk of celery in each jar and watch the tops form a leafy rainbow.

Photography

Photojournalism

Photojournalism tells a story through photos. Take photos to tell the story of how you are Board reaching out to others and sharing God's love.

Photography Vocabulary

Look up and write down the definition of these words as they apply to photography:

- Composition
- Crop
- Horizon lines
- Subject
- Viewfinder

Suggested Projects

- Easel Friendship Card, page 25
- Wall Photo Collage Board, page 84
- Wallet Album, page 91
- Photo Ornaments, page 139

Photography Tips to Try Yourself!

Use the Rule of Thirds.

If you're taking a landscape photo that means your composition will be divided with two lines horizontally, one-third land and two-thirds sky or the exact opposite. But now think of thirds the other way, vertically. If you notice on the diagram, there are four places where the four lines cross each other. Your photo will be more dramatic if you place your subject where those lines cross, instead of simply in the center of your viewfinder.

Use Lighting to Your Advantage.

Light can provide contrast in a picture. Generally, for outdoor shots keep the sun behind you, but avoid causing people to squint in the sun. Changing position by a few feet can help. Experiment with how the sun and your position change the light and shadow on a friend's face.

Keep an Eye on the Weather.

Clear blue skies with a few fluffy clouds make bright colors in your photos and create good pictures. Cloudy, overcast days dull the colors and make photos look fuzzy. So, on cloudy days keep the sky out of the frame and take close-ups. Late afternoon sun produces long shadows and a wonderful warm golden glow. Early morning casts a special pinkish light, turning to blue. Try taking pictures at different times of day.

A Great Composition Makes a Great Picture.

Be sure that you have as much of your subject in the picture as desired. You can always crop later, but if you've cut off the top of a head, you can't put it back on! Next, be aware of lines, whether they're horizon lines (keep those level) or tree branches, poles, or stripes on walls. Find some photos and look at the composition to see how items in the background and foreground make it better or worse.

Trees

How Old Is That Tree?

When you cut down a tree, it has rings through its trunk. Each ring shows a year. The larger the ring is, the more the tree grew that year. A thin ring shows the tree had trouble growing water that year. Look at stumps and see how many years some of the trees had lived before they were used for something else.

Suggested Projects

- Paper Cone Christmas Tree, page 133
- Christmas Tree Tunnel Card, page 145
- Accordion-Fold Tree Scene, page 173

Trees Breathe?

Trees take in carbon dioxide and give off oxygen. Trees that grow near highways tend to grow faster because of the carbon dioxide created by the traffic. You can hear a tree breathe if you listen to it with a stethoscope. Try placing the open mouth of a glass against the trunk and listen.

Tree Sap

Tree sap is like the lifeblood of a tree. Just like your blood, it carries water and nutrients through the tree. It can either come up through the tree from the roots or drip down from the surface of the leaves. Sap contains sugar. The most popular sap, from maple trees, is made into maple syrup.

Tree Resin

Tree resin is only produced in pine, fir, and cedar trees. It is formed between the inner and outer bark; it is a think substance and when you cut into a tree it oozes out. It acts like a scab on the tree protecting it while it heals from the cut. Resin is made up of lots of chemical compounds that are either created by the tree or deposited in the tree. Resin is used to make lots of products including varnish and jewelry.

Fibonacci Sequence

Many things in nature, including pinecones, have a special pattern in how they grow—it is called the *Fibonacci sequence*. This sequence is a number pattern created by adding the two numbers prior to the current number to make the sequence.

- The first numbers in it are: 1, 1, 2, 3, 5, 8, 13, and 21.
- If you look at flowers, the number of petals on each one is usually a number in the Fibonacci sequence.
- Spirals in nature also work with these numbers. Look at the bottom of a pinecone to see the spirals in this sequence. You find these spirals in flowers with lots of petals, the arrangement of sunflower seeds, and in a pineapple.

Trees That Shed and Trees That Don't

Some trees lose their leaves in the fall and others don't. Find out why. This fact is how trees are grouped by scientists.

Try It Yourself!

1. Go on a walk in nature. Use the shape of the leaves and type of bark to identify trees.
2. Plant a tree and nurture it.

Light

Facts about Light

- Light energy travels in waves.
- The human eye can only see some of the wavelengths.
- Different animals can see different wavelengths and therefore see light differently than we do.
- Plants turn light into food. This is called photosynthesis.
- Light travels at about 186,000 miles per second. It takes light from the sun about 8 and a half minutes to reach the Earth.

Suggested Projects

- Stained Glass Window Art, page 135
- Luminary, page 144

Wavelengths

Light travels in various wavelengths. It is made of different colors and each color has its own wavelength. Look up the wavelengths of each color and make a chart.

Create Your Own Wavelength

Want to see what a wavelength looks like? Take a friend and a rope and each of you hold one end of the rope. Leave a little slack between the two of you. One of you can hold the rope in place and the other can move it up and down. The rope will move like a wave. If you move it over a small distance it will look like a short wavelength and a large up and down distance simulates a larger wavelength.

Try It Yourself!

- Stand with half your body in the shade and half in the sun. You will soon feel that light has energy as the part of your body warms up faster in sunlight.
- Light reflects off of lots of objects. Gather mirrors and play with them to see how light reflects.

  To play a fun game with reflection, stand in a line while each person holds a mirror. Let the first child in line hold a flashlight and tell them to pass the light to each other by using their mirrors. They will have to move around a little bit but should be able to reflect the light from one mirror to the next all the way down the line.
- Light can bend when it goes into a substance such as water. This is called *refraction*. Use a jar to show how light refracts. Put a piece of paper with 2 lines in different colors behind a jar. Pour water in the jar and watch what happens. The lines will get bigger and look like they changed places. No matter what size clear container you use the lines will change but if the glass has a design to it or is a shape other than circular, what happens to the lines will be different.

Identity & Thumbprints

What It's All About

Fingerprints are unique. No two people have the same ones, not even identical twins. Scientists study the arrangement, shape, size, and number of ridges (or lines) in fingerprints to identify whose fingerprints they are.

Suggested Project

- Thumb-Body Special, page 161

Fingerprint Facts

- Fingerprints were not used to identify someone until the early 1900s.
- The FBI started the fingerprint division in 1924. They took and filed the fingerprints of prisoners in Leavenworth Prison.
- Many people use the fingerprint files including police, the FBI, and other law-enforcement agencies. The FBI has millions of fingerprints in its files.
- Some businesses use fingerprints to identify their employees (the people who work for them). Some have time clocks that use fingerprints to sign people in and out from work each day
- Fingerprints cannot be altered.
- Three basic forms of patterns are made by ridges of fingerprints (see images at right):
    1. Loops, found in seventy percent of fingerprints, start at one side of the finger, curve upward, and then exit the finger.
    2. Arches are found in five percent of people. The lines go up and then back down to make the outline of a little hill.
    3. Whorls, found in twenty-five percent of people, are circular or spiral patterns.

loops

arches

whorls

- Forensic science began because of fingerprints. Forensic science expanded to using DNA to help identify an individual. Either online or in a library book, look up what a forensic scientist does.
- A baby growing inside their mother's womb develops fingerprints by the third month.
- Koalas have similar fingerprints to people. But they also have two thumbs on each paw.

Investigate

- Find out which author first used fingerprints in a book.
- Discover in which court case, someone was first convicted of murder with fingerprint evidence.
- Search for *fuming*, a way to find and collect fingerprints. Find out how it is done. With adult supervision, you might even try it yourself!

Try It Yourself!

- Try different ways to collect and check fingerprints such as using play dough, powder on the fingers, bake clay, and ink pads. What ones are easier to see? What ones last longer?
- Use your favorite method for taking fingerprints to fingerprint everyone in your family. Examine the prints with a magnifying glass. See if you can identify the type of patterns of each fingerprint.
- Fingerprint friends at a party and then make up a crime that includes fingerprints. See who can identify the culprit with the fingerprints.

Seeds

What It's All About

Seeds are different for every type of plant. Each seed can only become the type of plant it came from. So, a mustard seed can only grow to be a mustard tree.

Suggested Projects

- Hide & Seek Book, page 206

Explore Seed Facts

- There are no standard sizes of seeds. The smallest seed is about one-quarter the size of a grain of salt. The largest seed weights about 40 pounds. Find out what the smallest and largest seeds are. Find out how long each takes to *germinate* (sprout).
- Seeds start to grow, or germinate, faster when the air around them is warmer. Find out what vegetable seeds are easy to germinate and plant some.
- What else do seeds need to germinate?
- Look up parts of a seed and draw the parts.
- Some of the easiest seeds to grow are marigold, carrots, and beans.
- Check out the depth different seeds need to be planted. It's not the same for every type of seed.
- Seeds come from the fruit of the plant. When you cut an apple crosswise you will see the seeds form a shape. How many seeds do you always find in an apple?
- One seed, like an apple, can produce lots of fruit, like all the apples on a tree for many years.
- Look up how seeds of various plants are spread in nature. The dandelion is a good one to check out online or in a library book.

Try It

- Cut open fruits and look at the seeds inside.
- Seeds can be soaked before you plant them. This helps them soak up all the water they need to start growing. Take seeds from a seed packet and soak some of the seeds and not others. Plant the seeds (be sure to label which were soaked and which were not!) and see which ones sprout first.
- Try sprouting seeds on a moist paper towel that is in a bowl with a little water. Drop a few seeds on the paper towel. Beans and lima beans are good seeds to try. Take a photo each day and record what happens.
- Try growing edible salad sprouts like alfalfa or bean sprouts. Look up directions online or in a library book.

Scriptural Index